Raising Caring, Capable Kids
with Habits of Mind

Lauren A. Carner, Ph.D.
Angela Iadavaia-Cox

THE INSTITUTE FOR
HABITS OF MIND
Educating for a more thoughtful world

To our children and
to all children, everywhere.

To our parents and to all parents,
who give so much of themselves
to raise the next generation.

Raising Caring, Capable Kids with Habits of Mind
Lauren A. Carner, Ph.D. and Angela Iadavaia-Cox

For accessing these and other resources including books, videos, teacher resource
materials, posters and both online and personal staff development opportunities
for the Habits of Mind, please visit our websites:
www.instituteforhabitsofmind.com and
www.instituteforhabitsofmind.ning.com

ISBN 978-0-615-61175-4

Raising Caring, Capable Kids
With Habits Of Mind

Table of Contents

Foreward ix
The Habits of Mind xii
Preface xiii

Section I
Family Connections: Improving Communication and Relationships with Habits of Mind

Off to a Good Start

Chapter
1   Mindful Communication: Metacogniton 3
2   Whoa: Managing Impulsivity.. 17
3   Fully Present: Managing Distractions 37

Taking Communication to the Next Level

Chapter
4   I Hear You: Listening with Empathy and Understanding 47
5   Say What You Mean and Mean What You Say: Thinking
     and Communicating with Clarity and Precision 69
6   I Believe in You: Questioning and Posing Problems 87

Section II
Children at Work: Achieving Meaning and Success with Habits of Mind

Off to a Good Start

Chapter
7   The Art and Science of Persistence.. 97
8   Slow Down: Managing Impulsivity 113
9   Thinking Like a Problem Solver: Metacognition 131

Taking Performance to the Next Level

Chapter

10 Life's Lessons: Applying Past Knowledge to New Situations 145

11 What's Your Hunch: Questioning and Posing Problems 153

12 Taking Responsible Risks: Go For It! (But Think About it First) 163

13 Out of the Box: Creating, Imagining, and Innovating 179

14 Open Up: Gathering Data Through all Senses 199

15 Love Affair with the World: Responding with
   Wonderment and Awe 209

16 Look at it Another Way: Thinking Flexibly 215

17 Lighten Up! Finding Humor 225

18 It's Not So Complicated: Thinking and Communicating with Clarity
   and Precision 231

19 Show Time: Striving for Accuracy and Precision 245

Section III
The Self-Directed Child, The-Self Directed Family

Chapter

20 Teamwork: Thinking Interdependently 257

21 Putting It All Together: Remaining Open to
   Continuous Learning 287

   References 299

Acknowledgements

We gratefully acknowledge Art Costa and Bena Kallick whose Habits of Mind have so profoundly influenced our work and relationships. We extend our appreciation to Nancy Modrak for the careful editing of this manuscript and for her thoughtful comments. Many thanks also to Karen Boyes and Carrie Neeson for shepherding our manuscript through the design and production process, and transforming our pages into a real book.

Our appreciation to Superintendent of Schools Dennis Lauro for recognizing the value of Habits of Mind and for inviting Art and Bena to the Pelham Schools to share their expertise.

There are many colleagues to recognize for each day making the Habits of Mind part of their work and for sharing their ideas, opinions and experiences with us. Richard P. Limato not only provided valuable insights but, through his leadership, creativity, and ability to think interdependently, made introducing the Habits of Mind at Prospect Hill School so much fun. We thank the Prospect Hill School Habits of Mind Team: Kate Alix, Eric Katz, Devon Fallon and Deborah Karson for their creative contributions as well as Kevin Clune, Linda Mancia, Maureen Morrissey, Alissa Schaps, Rebecca Schwarz and Gail Sider and all the teachers who embrace the Habits of Mind and enthusiastically put them into play in their classrooms.

Lauren's appreciation also goes to friends and colleagues who have read drafts of chapters and offered suggestions and encouragement: Stephanie Axinn, Kathryn Stenstrom Bisbee, Toby Glick, Lois Guberman, Judi Kemper, Gail Kotlus, Rosemary McGuire, and Janet McIntire. I would like to acknowledge the many hundreds, even thousands of children and adults I have encountered in my work as a school psychologist over the years. I am so grateful to have been able to learn from you and to have shared in part of your journey. Loving thanks go to my father, Richard L. Carner, whose thirst for learning and sense of adventure illuminated a path for me, and to my children Daniel and Anna who provided me with some great moments in mothering and who continue to challenge me to re-think everything I thought I knew! And finally, my deep appreciation to Kevin R. Whittaker for his wisdom and unwavering support.

Angela thanks her mother and sisters, Liz and Marie, for patiently enduring, "I can't... I have to work." and "What do you think about this?" And to her father and entire family for a treasure chest of childhood memories to draw from. To dear friends and wonderful writers Joanna Clapps Herman and Linda Tarrant Reid for advice and to Chris Latterner for encouragement and life insights that are expressed on many pages of this book. And always my love goes to my children Ariana and Paul – and now Bobby and Renata - who keep me honest, grounded, and grateful. Ariana, thank you for your perceptive editorial eye and Paul for your no nonsense curiosity as a reader.

Authors' Note

The vignettes and stories in this book are combinations of real life experiences and fictionalized illustrations of everyday situations. One of the great joys we experienced while writing these pages was discovering the limitless applications of the Habits of Mind. Our fervent hope is that you, the reader, will find yourself also turning to the Habits in the wide range of challenging situations you face as a parent. In the spirit of Remaining Open to Continuous Learning, *we look forward to hearing from you—what you found helpful and what was not—so that we may continue to learn.*

Lauren A. Carner, Ph.D.
Angela Iadavaia-Cox
caringcapablekids@gmail.com

March 2012

Foreword
by Bill Lucas

Take a moment to think of some of the parents you have known and how they look after their children.

It could be your own mom or dad. Or maybe it's a friend of yours or a parent of one of your own children's friends. Or just someone going about the craft of parenting in a supermarket that you noticed the other day when you were out shopping. What are they doing as you imagine them?

Here's what's happening in my mind's eye.

Making difficult parenting choices

I am seeing two different scenes. The first has a dad hovering over his son while his son is assembling a Lego fire engine. As the child looks for the next step, the father quickly tells him what he should do. It's a complicated assembly job and the boy's enthusiasm is waning. The father is increasingly impatient at the slow speed of his son who often gets stuck when faced with a difficult stage of construction. He is interested in getting the job done as soon as possible by any means so that the toy can be enjoyed. He alternates between doing it for his son and exhorting his son to stick with it. Eventually the job is complete and father and son look pleased. The boy starts pushing it round the kitchen floor making nee-naw-nee-naw fire engine noises.

The second scene is pretty similar. A mother is helping her daughter make a Lego fire-engine. The girl seems very engaged. She has sorted all the pieces into their different shapes and colors in piles on the floor and has laid out the instruction leaflet so that she can have a go at the first stage. From time to time she brings her model to show her mom who makes encouraging remarks and asks her how she is going to go about doing the next stage. Sometimes things don't go well and the child reluctantly but relatively cheerfully removes the last few pieces, ponders and then puts them back in the correct order. She and her mother chat about what she did wrong and how she will fix it. At one stage she stops and goes off to play with something else before returning refreshed to the task. Eventually the job is complete and mother and daughter look pleased. The girl starts pushing it round the kitchen floor making nee-naw-nee-naw fire engine noises.

Of course it might be a father and daughter or mother and son scenario; the point of these two vignettes is not about gender. I am conjuring them up because they illustrate two fundamentally different ways of going about parenting.

In the first example the emphasis is on completing the task. There is little discussion about how this might be done and getting stuck is seen as a sign of failure. The child is learning that success is about getting things right as quickly as possible. In the second the child is learning how to persist. She sees mistakes as an inevitable part of the process. She is using her parent to help but not to do it for her. Her parent, by contrast, is offering support but making sure that the child learns the process of building complex Lego models for herself.

Which of these two approaches will best equip a child to thrive in a complex and difficult world?

Acquiring helpful parenting habits

Raising Caring, Capable Kids with Habits of Mind is all about creating children like the one in the second example we have just read. Lauren Carner and Angela Iadavaia-Cox are as much interested in how we go about parenting as in what the immediate results of our labors are. They are playing the long game, ensuring that children leave home with the wider skills they will need to thrive throughout their lives.

The Habits of Mind movement created by Art Costa and Bena Kallick in the US, like the Building Learning Power approach developed by Guy Claxton and colleagues in the UK, is tried and tested in schools. But *Raising Caring, Capable Kids with Habits of Mind* breaks new ground by taking these methods out of the classroom into the kitchen and living room and gardens of children's homes.

Clearly explained theory and research is complemented by really practical and useful examples for parents to try out. What the authors offer in this book is not easy and it may take longer than more conventional approaches. But it is do-able!

The boy in our Lego example built the fire-engine in less time than the girl took; but who will be better equipped to build something the next time they are grappling with a construction toy?

I am certain that the long game of parenting is the one to focus on. By the same token I am confident that, if parents adopt the methods described in this book, their children will become better able to concentrate, good at managing distractions, confident in the face of difficulty, great at asking good questions, flexible in the way they go about solving problems and skilled at working with different people.

In short they will become powerful learners, well-equipped for the 21st century world in which we are bringing them up.

Parents are our first and most powerful educators. What they do matters. But how they do what they do matters even more. *Raising Caring, Capable Kids with Habits of Mind* offers wonderful support for parents across the world who want to help their children succeed and thrive.

Bill Lucas is Professor of Learning at the University of Winchester. He has written more than forty books about parenting and learning, including the best-selling Help Your Child To Succeed. *He is in demand internationally as a speaker and advisor.*

Habits of Mind

1. Persisting

Stick to it!
Persevering in task through to completion;
remaining focused. Looking for ways to
reach your goal when stuck.
Not giving up.

2. Managing Impulsivity

Take your Time!
Thinking before acting;
remaining calm,
thoughtful and deliberate.

3. Listening with understanding and empathy

Understand Others! Devoting mental
energy to another person's thoughts and
ideas; Make an effort to perceive
another's point of view and emotions.

4. Thinking flexibly

Look At It Another Way!
Being able to change perspectives,
generate alternatives,
consider options.

5. Thinking about your thinking
(Metacognition)

Know your knowing! Being aware of your
own thoughts, strategies, feelings and
actions and their effects on others.

6. Striving for accuracy

Check it again!
Always doing your best. Setting high
standards. Checking and finding ways
to improve constantly.

7. Questioning and problem posing

How do you know? Having a questioning
attitude; knowing what data are needed &
developing questioning strategies to produce those data. Finding problems to solve.

8. Applying past knowledge to new situations

Use what you Learn!
Accessing prior knowledge; transferring
knowledge beyond the situation in
which it was learned.

9. Thinking & communicating with clarity and precision

Be clear! Strive for accurate communication
in both written and oral form; avoiding
over-generalizations, distortions,
deletions and exaggerations.

10. Gather data through all senses

Use your natural pathways! Pay attention
to the world around you Gather data
through all the senses. taste, touch,
smell, hearing and sight.

11. Creating, imagining, and innovating

Try a different way!

Generating new and novel ideas,
fluency, originality

12. Responding with wonderment and awe:

Have fun figuring it out!
Finding the world awesome,
mysterious and being intrigued
with phenomena and beauty.

13. Taking responsible risks

Venture out!
Being adventuresome; living on the
edge of one's competence.
Try new things constantly.

14. Finding humor

Laugh a little!
Finding the whimsical, incongruous
and unexpected.
Being able to laugh at one's self.

15. Thinking interdependently

Work together!
Being able to work in and
learn from others in
reciprocal situations. Team work.

16. Remaining open to continuous learning

Learn from experiences!
Having humility and pride when admitting
we don't know; resisting complacency.

Preface

You are your child's first teacher. From the moment of birth, and even before, you have influenced your child's vocabulary, values, self-concept, personality, physical and mental health, relationships, attitudes toward learning and more.

That is why this book is so important. It provides numerous strategies for you to help your child develop the dispositions of a strong, motivated and successful learner—in school and throughout life.

Your child will be growing up during the 21st Century and possibly into the 22nd century. Parents around the world share these same questions—how can I make certain that my child will become a thoughtful and creative thinker equipped to face the complex problems of the future for which there are no easy answers? Children will need to know how to think critically, creatively and cooperatively. They will also need to develop a "can do" attitude that brings them confidence in the classroom, the school, and the community.

Much study and research over many years has shown that the 16 Habits of Mind described in this book are what make people successful in many walks of life. As your children grow throughout their elementary and secondary school years, if they choose to go on to college, as they decide on a career or job, as they become members of a community and as they raise a family of their own, these are the dispositions that will help to determine their satisfaction and success.

These Habits of Mind are not just for your kids. They are for the adults in the family as well. Being a parent is no easy job. You can draw upon the Habits of Mind when you face problems in which your feelings might get in the way of your intention to solve the problem. This book suggests ways of thinking that can help you plan for those difficult moments—whether it is discouragement in the face of a hard task, the quick anger that comes from a misunderstanding, or the frustration and anxiety we feel when our children don't seem to respond to our suggestions. The book offers concrete strategies to help you manage those feelings and behaviors that can be so frustrating. Instead of mutual misunderstandings and disharmony, family energy pours into solving problems effectively, and children feel understood, known, valued and secure.

This book is intended as a guide for parents to learn these Habits of Mind to enrich family life as well as to support their children's learning in school and in life. If you are fortunate enough to have your son or daughter in a school that has adopted the Habits of Mind, we encourage you to become a partner in the process. It is much more likely that your child will learn these habits if they are reinforced, discussed and modeled at home as well as at school. The authors of this book have collected a remarkable number of insights and strategies that will help you to do this work.

You, as well as educators in your child's school, may be interested in visiting this website for more resources and information about the Habits of Mind: www. instituteforhabitsofmind.com.

No one ever masters all of the Habits of Mind. It is the constant striving to get better at the Habits of Mind that describes the continuous learner.

We invite you to learn to employ them right along with your child. Tell your child which of the Habits of Mind you are working on. Invite your child to give you feedback when he or she observes you using any of the Habits or being alert to times when maybe you should have employed the Habits of Mind. (Don't be surprised if you hear your child saying something like, "Mom, you need to manage your impulsivity!") We grow alongside our children every day!

Children learn best through imitation. They "mirror" the behaviors of the significant adults around them. We hope that you will learn how to use the strategies provided in this book to make your home a thoughtful learning environment.

Arthur L. Costa, Ed. D.   Bena Kallick, Ph.D.
Granite Bay, California   Westport, Connecticut
Co-founders, The Institute for Habits of Mind

Family Connections:
Improving Communication and Relationships with Habits of Mind

The basic premise of Habits of Mind is that—with the right supports—children can come to wise conclusions through their own reflective thinking.

Chapter 1

Mindful Communication: Metacognition
(Or, Thinking About Thinking — and Feelings)

Dan is an assistant coach for his nine-year-old son Josh's Little League team. Before the season began, he put a lot of thought into how he would handle it if he had to discipline Josh. Josh was a good kid with a lot of energy and enthusiasm, but he also could be distractible and had a tendency to fool around. Dan had seen so many other coaches be especially hard on their own sons and didn't want to repeat that pattern with his boy. Time spent with his son was a precious commodity and he didn't want to turn his son against baseball or against him by publicly humiliating him. At the same time, he knew that part of his job would be to uphold expectations for effort and attitude.

Once the season began, Dan often noticed Josh fooling around during instruction and not always putting in his best effort. After Josh missed an easy play that they had practiced several times, Dan felt a surge of anger. He was tempted to bench him and make an example of him. But since Dan had actually thought about what he would do in a situation like this, he already knew how he would deal with it. He let a couple of minutes go by as he turned his attention to another boy on the team. When he felt calm, he walked over to where Josh sat alone in the dugout. Dan put his arm around Josh's shoulder and gave a little squeeze. "Hey, big guy.

Thinking about your thinking
(Metacognition)

Know your knowing!

Being aware of your own thoughts, strategies, feelings and actions and their effects on others.

3

What're you thinking about?" Josh kept his head down, but Dan thought he could see the glimmer of a tear in the corner of his eye. "I really blew it. I'm no good. You should just take me off the team," Josh whispered. Dan waited for a moment. "No way that's going to happen. You're an important part of this team. What's got you down?"

Dan was using Metacognition to anticipate the situation and to develop a scenario for handling it. This is what gave him mastery over his own emotional response. Because he was able to approach Josh in a supportive and respectful way, Josh was encouraged to learn an important lesson from the consequences of his behavior, something they discussed later. Dan's thoughtful handling of the situation allowed him to accomplish his most important goal: To spend time with Josh in a shared, beloved activity that would serve to deepen their relationship.

Metacognition **is the habit of mind that lays the foundation for better communication, better relationships and more effective living overall.** The term "metacognitive" usually refers to the ability to think about our own thinking, but in this Chapter we take a broader perspective to include thinking about our emotional responses as well. Why is it so important? Practicing Metacognition is like our mind doing a systems check as we go about performing all our normal activities. By intentionally engaging our thinking skills when we have tasks to accomplish or decisions to make, we work more efficiently and effectively. People who practice Metacognition see benefits *before, during* and *after* undertaking challenging tasks or difficult conversations. Here's how:

Before: Metacognition leads to better planning. You think ahead about what you will need to accomplish a task. You consider any obstacles that might arise and develop a plan for how you will deal with those obstacles. If you are anticipating a difficult conversation, you spend some time thinking about what you hope to accomplish by having the conversation, what you need to learn, what the likely reaction of the other person might be, and so on. You think about how you can convey your good intentions, how you might react if provoked, and how to stay calm and positive. When you think about your thinking ahead of time, you increase your chances of success.

During: As seen with Dan and Josh, anticipating and planning for problems ahead of time goes a long way in helping you to increase the control you have over your own negative emotions when a situation is unfolding. Still, when you are in the middle of a difficult task or conversation, you may need to ramp up the intensity of your metacognitive efforts. Now you are dealing with the real thing and there is likely to be an intensified emotional factor—whether from frustration at the part of the plan not working as expected or from the reactions of your partner in conversation. Consciously thinking about our thoughts and feelings gives us a moment to process them instead of just automatically reacting. When we acknowledge and label a feeling such as irritation, we can keep it from igniting into rage. If we can question a perception that we have—*Can I really be certain she was being sarcastic? Maybe I was being overly sensitive? She's not usually sarcastic*—we can often prevent misperceptions and the cascade of miscommunications that ensue.

In this chapter and in the next on Managing Impulsivity, we cover several strategies for summoning the quick thinking and emotional control that both habits foster, and that will help you navigate through those moments.

After: As you become more proficient in practicing Metacognition, you will automatically begin to process conversations and events after they occur. You will learn to assess what went well? Why? What didn't go so well, and why not? What could you do differently next time? If things didn't go so well, this is a time to ponder what you could do to repair the situation, to make it better. Many times we would prefer to just move on or put an uncomfortable situation behind us. It can be painful and embarrassing to do a post mortem on something gone wrong. But the processing of events through metacognition is what allows us to understand and store our experiences in memory. That metacognitive assessment is the very tool that empowers us to improve how we work, communicate, and get along with others in the future.

Many of us can easily recall instances when a little more thinking about our thinking would have helped a situation: Maybe your supervisor at work criticized your report a little too thoroughly and left you feeling slightly embarrassed and under-appreciated. Like most people, you might still be mulling over what your supervisor said, how you felt, what you said, and what you wish you had said as you walk through the front door at the end of the day. You certainly would not be in a frame of mind to give your children the kind of warm greeting that restores everyone's equilibrium after a day apart. As they rush to greet you and tell you the

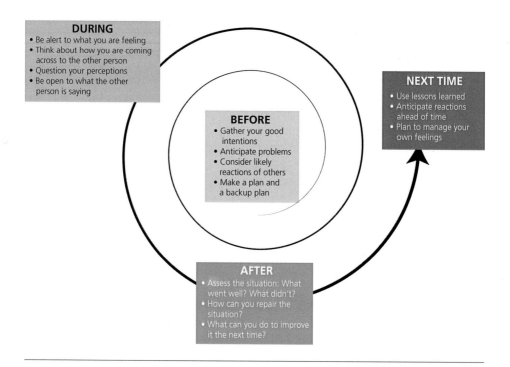

news of their day, you find it hard to respond in kind and instead snap at them to pick up the mess they made in the living room. Feeling rebuffed and rejected by your response (which, of course, they have no way of understanding), they find other, less positive ways of getting the attention they want and need from you. They immediately start a fight over who made the mess and who should have to pick it up. You can just imagine how the evening falls apart from there.

But let's push the rewind button and see how Metacognition could salvage the situation. Practicing Metacognition might have helped you to put your supervisor's criticism in perspective. No one likes criticism, but you can find a way to think about it that can turn it into a plus. You might remind yourself that you are still learning; that your supervisor is someone you respect and that she might have some good points. You could take some notes on the critique you got and promise yourself that you will go back and think about it later, when you are more up to it. You can use Metacognition to soothe your bruised ego and restore your own self-confidence. Think about all the positive comments your supervisor has made about your work, your excellent performance reviews and your own beliefs about what you have to offer. Try to see things with a little soothing balm of humor if possible. Then, use your metacognitive strategies to begin to make a plan to improve the situation. Think about what information you need to improve your report; think about whom you will discuss this with tomorrow and how you will go about repairing the situation. As your thoughts turn to home and the family and responsibilities that await, you are better prepared to walk in that door. You have already done much of the thinking, planning, and nurturing of yourself that allows you to temporarily put aside the worry and bad feelings from your workday, so that you can be more emotionally available to your loved ones.

Practicing Metacognition improves the quality of our efforts as well as the way in which we accomplish them. Unless we are laboring alone in a room somewhere, most of our undertakings require us to work and communicate with others.

No one likes criticism, but you can find a way to think about it that can turn it into a plus.

Kathryn is a warm and nurturing woman who loves to prepare wonderful dinners for her friends. But organization is not her strong suit. She usually selects a recipe at the last minute that looks great but is really complicated. Because she doesn't always read all the directions thoroughly, she discovers that she is lacking key ingredients as she is starting to cook. She tends not to involve her family in the initial planning, but then frantically enlists their help at the last minute. This often results in her barking orders at her children to help her clean the house, sending her husband, David, off to the store for forgotten ingredients, and ending up too exhausted to enjoy her company or her own wonderful cooking. After the last such episode, her family rebelled and all their frustration came tumbling out. The children complained that their whole Saturday got taken up by getting ready for Kathryn's party and it didn't feel fair. They also let her know that when Kathryn took her stress out on them, it made everyone feel miserable. David added that he was happy to help, that he would like to enjoy having friends over, but that the way it was being done took all the fun out of it.

Kathryn felt terrible. She took a walk around the neighborhood just to process what she had heard and realized that her family had some valid points. Later, she asked her children and husband for their ideas about what she could do differently. Together, the family helped her to think more realistically about the work that goes into having people over. David tactfully suggested that she

7

might think about preparing a simple, old favorite recipe instead of something so fancy. He offered to do the shopping for the party if she would sit down with him and agree on a list ahead of time. Together with the children, they came up with a list of the chores that could be done ahead of time. She also promised that she would think about the way she spoke to them when she was stressed. She thought that using a schedule and preparing simpler recipes would alleviate some of the stress, but that she would also monitor her words and tone of voice more carefully. Eventually, she achieved her real goal. "I have such happy memories of my mother and grandmother preparing wonderful feasts for family celebrations, and I guess I wanted my children to have something of that kind of experience too. But the way I was going about it was just turning them off to the whole idea. I needed to become more aware of how my behavior was affecting everybody else. I feel so much better now that we have a plan."

Metacognition can also be an important way to better understand and deal with many of the emotional upsets that occur between parents and children. Because we are often dealing with issues of such profound importance in child-rearing—issues of basic security, competence, and social and emotional adjustment—it is especially likely that old conflicts and upsets from our own childhood can get reactivated and played out as we try to help our children through their developmental milestones.

In their book, *Parenting from the Inside Out*, Daniel Siegel and Mary Hartzell (2003) explain that these "unresolved issues" may stem from events that occurred before we even had the language to understand them. Or perhaps we had the language, but we had no comforting and understanding adult available to help us process the upsetting event. Although the event itself is often forgotten, the *feelings* from these events stay within us until awakened by some uninvited reminder set off by our child's behavior. We then react as though the current situation was a replay of what happened long before. When this occurs, our feelings and behaviors are being hijacked by old "scripts" and do not necessarily reflect what is actually happening in the here and now with our own child. Almost as quickly as striking a match, we go automatically to those old feelings. The result can be rigid, predetermined responses to our child that do not give him the compassionate understanding he needs at that very moment. Without Metacognition, without the ability to take stock of our thinking, we may find ourselves stuck in the past tense without even knowing it.

Metacognition can also be an important way to better understand and deal with many of the emotional upsets that occur between parents and children.

Strategies we learn when we practice Metacognition can help us bring some of these automatic reactions into the bright light of knowing and back under our conscious control. As your approach to your children becomes more *intentional* and less subject to the tsunami waves of deeply buried history, good things start to happen: You become better able to meet your child's needs as you perceive him more clearly without the static from your own past. You are better able to empathize with and endure her emotional upset, and thus help her become more resilient and emotionally sturdy. Most importantly perhaps, when you break the old pattern, when you create a *different outcome* from what you yourself experienced long ago, you can actually realize some retroactive healing of your own.

One mother, Adrienne, found herself at the head of a long line at the paint counter of a warehouse store, trying frantically to get information by phone from her young daughter about the paint color needed to finish her daughter's room. As the line grew longer, Adrienne's heart began to pound. She imagined that everyone in the line behind her was getting really annoyed at how long she was taking. As her anxiety increased, she heard her own voice become more shrill and intense. She also heard the bewilderment in her daughter's voice at the other end of the connection. Suddenly Adrienne realized that the irritation and upset she was conveying to her daughter was threatening to spoil forever what had been a pleasant shared project of painting the room together. Adrienne took herself out of the line and then took stock of the situation. She promised to call her daughter right back and then thought about her own reaction. She asked herself, why am I getting so frantic about this? *She flashed back to her own mother's almost phobic fear of inconveniencing other adults and how she would anxiously and angrily rush her own children so as not to risk holding anyone else up. Adrienne recalled how helpless and worried she felt as a little girl in the face of her mother's pushing. Now, 30 years later, she was doing the exact same thing without even having been aware of it!*

Those few seconds of thought enabled Adrienne to bring to light a forgotten pattern of behavior she had grown up with. As she thought of her sweet daughter who was trying so earnestly to give her the information she needed, she felt flooded with warmth for her. She also experienced a sudden surge of empathy for the child she herself had been so many years ago. Adrienne resolved to handle things differently from then on. She would be more aware of when she felt that old anxiety and would take a couple of deep breaths when she started to feel that way so as not to react so automatically.

> **When you practice the habit of Metacognition, your thinking becomes more complex and deeper.**

When you practice the habit of Metacognition, your thinking becomes more complex and deeper. You are better able to consider a variety of explanations and causes for a situation and to recognize that there is usually more to it than what you first might have thought. You become more interested in hearing what the other person thinks than in telling them what you think you know. Taking a stance of "let's find out," instead of "let me tell you something," creates two beneficial side effects: First, you gain mastery over your own strong emotions. Many angry reactions come from misperceptions, misunderstandings, and faulty or incomplete information. When you approach someone in anger, it sets off a defensive or angry reaction in turn, and then it becomes even more difficult to get to the bottom of a story. You end up having to repair the damage from the angry words before you can even get to the underlying problem, and by then the original problem seems far, far away. When you practice Metacognition, however, and as you consider the likelihood that there are many sides to a story, you become calmer and less likely to fly off the handle. Metacognition helps to put the brakes on those automatic instantaneous reactions and allows you to create a new and more productive kind of response.

A second beneficial side effect of Metacognition is developing the ability to more clearly define what the actual problem is. We know that "problem definition" is key to coming up with good solutions. Practicing Metacognition helps you hone in on the real issues, which then enables you to come up with an effective resolution to the problem.

Putting Metacognition into Practice

Commit to Learn More

Create in your mind an intention to learn more about the situation. Before you say a word, you can be thinking to yourself: *I wonder what's going on? Let's see if we can figure this out. I wonder what her understanding of the situation is? How is he feeling about this?* These simple questions can remind you to slow down and not jump to conclusions. They encourage you to try to understand the whole situation, not just your own perspective. Thinking this way can pave the way to a more open and productive conversation.

Take a Few Seconds to Focus on Your Higher Intentions

When faced with a child's misbehavior or failure of responsibility, parents often just focus on correcting the specific behavior. You might instead approach it as a valuable opportunity to help your child learn an important lesson about your family values. By treating the incident as an opportunity to learn instead of a character flaw, you are demonstrating confidence in your child's inherent goodness and capacity to do better. You become a trusted guide on the long and tangled path to responsible adulthood.

Take a few seconds to reflect on the kind of person you hope your child will become and the faith you have in her good qualities. Think about how you can best help her to realize the hopes you have for her. Ask yourself: *How can I show her I have confidence in her? What does she most need from me at this moment? What is the larger lesson I hope to teach here?*

Align your good intentions with your facial expression, tone of voice, and choice of words. Your expression becomes softer and kinder. Your tone of voice is optimistic instead of accusatory, and your words reflect your belief in your child's ability to do better. Beginning a difficult conversation in this way allows your child to be able to think and express herself more clearly about the situation. This is possible because you are helping her to feel supported and understood. Feeling supported allows her to actually hear what you have to say when you are ready to suggest changes.

Think About Your Own Behavior in the Situation

It is a natural human tendency to notice other people's behavior but *not* be aware of how your own behavior may be triggering their reactions. If a videographer followed you around—imagine another variation of a reality show—what would the camera show? Many people are shocked when they see themselves on tape. They don't realize how a smile might look like a sneer or that what felt like a neutral but serious expression might actually appear to be angry and forbidding. Many people have developed a habit of sarcasm or disrespectful use of language and may be unaware of how hurtful that can be, especially to a young child.

As you practice the habit of Metacognition, you recognize that your own actions, tone of voice, choice of words, and attitude play a large role in how conversations turn out.

When Your Buttons Get Pushed

Often it feels like children know just how to push those buttons to bring out the worst in their parents. Practicing Metacognition can help you re-route those ingrained, automatic responses that, let's face it, *never* result in a good outcome. When you experience that familiar surge of irritation that indicates a button has been pushed, ask

TRY THIS

- Imagine yourself through your child's eyes when you are having a difficult conversation. Imagine what you look like to your child: Angry? Scornful? Scary? Kind? Loving?

- Now imagine what you sound like: Are your words clipped and dismissive or supportive and carefully chosen? Are you focused on the behavior or are your words critical and berating? Are you shouting?

- Next, put yourself in your child's place and imagine how he is feeling. Learning something new is almost impossible when you feel scared, criticized, embarrassed, or diminished. Remember that real learning takes place in an atmosphere of support and trust. If you are communicating to change a child's behavior, he or she has to feel that you are an ally and coach in helping them to learn what they need in order to make that change.

- Finally, using Metacognition to get a better handle on how your own behavior may be contributing to the situation, ask yourself: How am I coming across here? Does my child feel that I am here to help or is he feeling attacked? Am I giving him the support he needs to get his story out? How do I need to behave right now so that my good intentions toward my child can be realized?

yourself, *What's the big deal here? Why is this getting on my nerves so much? Would someone else in this situation react so strongly? Why, then, am I?*

You can run through this sequence in a nanosecond, but it can change the interaction profoundly. By taking a closer look at your own automatic response *as it is happening,* you take the first step in breaking an old habitual reaction and creating a new, more positive one.

Modeling and Teaching Metacognition

Put It on the Table

Make explicit your own efforts to practice Metacognition. Use the daily stuff of life to illustrate to your children the benefits of thinking about their thoughts and feelings. In the example given above about getting critical feedback about a report, you could say something like, "You know, my supervisor thought I should change some things in a report that I had worked very hard on. At first I felt kind of upset, but now I'm thinking about her comments, and I think she might have some good ideas. Has that ever happened to you? How did you feel when your teacher told you to rewrite part of your essay? How did you handle it?" That incident could open the door to a productive conversation about the value of considering feedback with an open mind.

In Kathryn's situation, the fact that she listened to her children's concerns and took active steps to address them was a powerful message affirming the value of respectful communication.

Think Out Loud

Let your child in on your thinking. Use lots of "thinking words" such as imagine, predict, wonder, analyze. Even young children can learn and delight in using words such as "hypothesis."

You can stimulate thinking by asking, "What do you think is going on in this situation? What's your hypothesis? Could there be another way to explain it?" Treat problems as interesting mysteries to be solved. Invite your child to share in the discovery of figuring things out.

Think about how you can use Metacognition *before, during,* and *after situations* and say it out loud. If you are getting ready to go on a family outing, engage the family in thinking ahead about what needs to be done to get ready. Put the children in charge of anticipating what they will need and encourage them to make lists. Young children feel very proud when they can use their emerging reading and writing skills in real life situations.

Make Connections

You can demonstrate the connection between metacognition and emotional regulation by telling stories of your own experiences: "Something interesting happened today. Jennifer, at work, said something to me, and I thought she was putting me down. At first I felt so angry that I almost said something sarcastic back to her. But then I *thought* for a second: 'Wait a minute, why would Jennifer say something mean to me? She's my friend and she's usually so nice, it doesn't make sense.' So instead of saying something mean to her, I said, 'I'm sorry Jennifer, I didn't get that. Could you say that again?' And do you know what? I had completely misunderstood what she said. She was actually giving me a compliment! I'm so glad I thought about it first!" You can introduce the idea that people tend to form impressions based on incomplete information or on misperceptions, but by asking questions of ourselves, or by asking others to clarify what they meant, we can understand situations more accurately.

Turn Lapses into Lessons

Mistakes are opportunities that help us grow. Use your own mistakes to illustrate how you can learn from them. By doing so, you demonstrate that there is no need to cover up or be ashamed when things don't go well. Instead, we can figure out what happened and make a plan to improve things in the future. Find some little sayings you can use such as, "That's why pencils have erasers!" or "We are problem-solvers. We can fix this!" Of course, if there is some emotional upset, you'll want to give it a little time before you go into the analysis, but the idea is to convey that there is no moral failure in making a mistake.

Acknowledge Your Child's Efforts in the Right Direction

Whenever your child makes some small step in the direction of Metacognition, show that you noticed it and that you appreciate it. Be specific in your acknowledgement: "I noticed that you seemed to think about a good way to respond to your little brother's teasing. It looked to me like you chose your words carefully. How did it seem to you?" It is not necessary and probably counterproductive to offer lavish or overly enthusiastic praise. We expect that children will experience the value of Metacognition in improved functioning and relationships. The rewards will be in the natural outcomes of using Metacognition. Things just go better when you think about your thinking! Your role is to make it explicit when your children use a metacognitive strategy so they know they are on the right track. You can then assess with them how well it worked. You can speculate with your child how the outcome might have been very different had they responded in the old habitual way.

Be Your Child's Partner in Developing this Habit of Mind

Let your child know that you are working on your metacognitive skills, too. Share that it is not always easy and that lots of times you forget. Still, when you do get it right, it feels so good, and seems to make a real difference in improving communication and relationships. Let the feedback go both ways. Encourage your child to notice when you are using metacognitive strategies and to let you know (respectfully) when you are not. Explain that you are both building a good new habit—one that will serve you well in every aspect of your lives.

Chapter 2

Whoa! Managing Impulsivity

Sixteen-month-old Jake approaches the stove for what must be the fifth time this morning. He has just been spoken to again for reaching up toward the burners. His parents stand close by watching to see what he will do. He takes another step toward the stove and looks back at his parents. His mother's brows are furrowed and her lips are pressed tightly together in a serious expression. The little boy points to the stove and then looks at his finger. "Hot," he says. "Hot," as if explaining the situation to them. "Yes, hot," his mother echoes. "Not safe!" Jake turns away from the stove and gets a warm hug from his mother and father. Our little friend has just taken his first step of what will be thousands over the course of his lifetime toward managing impulsivity.

Managing Impulsivity

Take your time!

Thinking before acting; remaining calm, thoughtful and deliberative.

Gaining control over one's impulses is an important part of a constellation of abilities that psychologists and researchers call "self-regulation." Self-regulation starts in infancy as the hungry newborn soothes herself by finding her thumb and placing it in her mouth until the breast or bottle magically arrives. Toddlers like Jake begin to be able to comply with very basic rules and expectations sometime after their first birthday. As children move into preschool and kindergarten, they become increasingly adept at figuring out social norms and following them. They learn to wait their turn, to not push ahead in line, to share, to play a game and not always win, and to clean up after play time. As children mature, the bar is raised at home and at school for appropriate social and academic behavior. Once children get out in the world a little bit, in play groups, nursery school, and especially elementary school, their understanding of what is expected expands as they observe their peers. They see other children behaving appropriately or not, and they note what happens in either case. When they are acknowledged for doing the right thing and experience consequences when they do not, children's ability for self-regulation becomes ever more sophisticated and nuanced. A six-year-old must learn that it is fine to run around and giggle with his friends at recess but not during reading instruction. A fifth grader will, on his own, quietly move his seat away from a temptingly talkative classmate so he can better concentrate.

We accept young children to be normally quite impulsive but to gradually become less so as they mature.

Academically, the ever-increasing complexity of the curriculum through the grades requires children to increase self-regulation in the cognitive realm. They must learn to push away competing thoughts when learning something new; to stay on topic when responding to a teacher's question; to remember when and how to apply strategies they've learned when they are working independently; and to gradually take increased responsibility for their own learning. These ever more demanding expectations require children to be able to manage internal distractions such as thinking about the compelling new video game acquired last weekend or the argument they had with a friend that morning. They must also find ways of lessening their responsiveness to all those external distractions that conspire to wrest their concentration away from the task at hand (*See Chapter 3*).

Impulsivity also affects children socially, particularly as they grow older. Although wonderful qualities of liveliness, spontaneity, enthusiasm, and creativity are often seen in impulsive children, there is also a tendency for such children to behave in unpredictable, erratic, or disruptive ways. They may be quicker to anger and blurt out hurtful words. Because they are so quickly on to the next thing, they are not as likely to reflect upon or learn from their experiences. Such children are often bewildered and saddened by the negative feedback they receive, and their self-esteem suffers.

We accept young children to be normally quite impulsive but to gradually become less so as they mature. Early on, children simply don't have the cognitive equipment or experience to successfully Manage Impulsivity on their own. With very young children like Jake, parents and caregivers need to be vigilant and stay close to ensure their child's safety. Even school-age children require responsible supervision, especially in less structured situations. It is important for adults to have a general understanding of what level of impulse control is more or less appropriate for any given age. Many behavior problems are a result of parents expecting either too little or too much from their child.

Allyssa, for example, is a bright, vivacious, strong-willed five-year-old. Her parents both work demanding jobs and treasure the time they have with her in the evening and on weekends. Because they get home rather late, they allow her to stay up until she falls asleep on their bed. They have few rules in the house and tend to give in to her demands because they are too tired to resist. They figure she will grow out of her tantrums in time. The nanny is uneasy setting limits because Allyssa's parents have made it clear they want their little girl to be happy. When Allyssa entered kindergarten, she expected things to go the same way at school as they had at home. When the class was seated on the rug for circle time, she interrupted the teacher incessantly. When the children were seated at their tables to do an activity, Allyssa wandered around the room, touching and not putting away any materials that caught her eye. If she wanted a red crayon and spotted her neighbor using one, she demanded to have it right then and there. Clearly, Allyssa has not yet learned the expectation that she must begin to subordinate her whims and impulses—not only to function within the group—but so she can learn and get along with others at an age appropriate level.

When expectations for impulse control are too high, we may see other outcomes.

Benjamin's parents believe that a strict upbringing is the best way to ensure a well-behaved and successful child. They often punish him with a reprimand, time-out, or removal of privileges when they feel he crosses the boundaries of acceptable behavior. The problem is that Benjamin doesn't have a way of knowing what those boundaries are. At home, if he asked too many questions, or spilled the milk while trying to help set the table, or was found looking through his father's beautiful coffee table book on astronomy, he was likely to be scolded or punished rather than taught. Benjamin's natural curiosity and initiative began to subside as his efforts to find out about his world were met with more disapproval than encouragement. When he got to school, Benjamin was well behaved and quiet, but showed little curiosity or initiative for school work. He did not behave impulsively, but nor did he show the spark or spontaneity that drives children to engage with their environment.

In this situation, Benjamin's parents' expectations for his ability to control himself are unrealistically high. They have a compliant child, but one whose initiative and curiosity have been dampened. In addition, we don't yet know how well Benjamin will regulate his own impulses when he is on his own and away from the watchful eyes of his parents and teachers.

We know that the ability to manage one's impulses tends to improve over time, with maturation. We also understand that the kinds of experiences and feedback a child receives from her parents and teachers have a profound influence on the development of this important habit.

In addition, there appear to be innate, temperamental differences on the continuum of impulsive to reflective behavior. Many years of research on ADHD (Attention Deficit Hyperactivity Disorder) suggests that there is indeed an inherited component to the tendency to be impulsive and distractible. If you have more than one child, chances are you notice differences between them on many different aspects of temperament, including impulsivity. You may also have noticed that these differences showed up very early on, even from infancy. One child may be more active, need less sleep, and be more difficult to soothe when upset. One child may rush toward new experiences while another may stay on the sidelines watching until he is quite sure it is safe. It is hard to account for those differences based on the way you have raised them. Parents are often surprised at how clearly and how early these temperamental differences show up.

One behavior that really stands out in impulsive children (or adults) is difficulty in *waiting*. Impulsivity feels like an internal agitation, an itchiness, an urge to get going and to move on to the next thing. Impulsive children have difficulty waiting in line, waiting for dinner, waiting for the candles to be blown out so they can open their presents. A sense of time is not yet developed in young children anyway, and for those on the impulsive end of the continuum, five minutes can seem an eternity. This can present real problems at home when we don't want our child to fill up on snacks before dinner, or we have things that must get done before we can sit down and play with them. Children tend to want what they want *right now!*

It takes maturation and many experiences over time to realize that, yes, they really will get dessert after dinner, or mom and dad really will take them to the park after the house is tidied up, and that they can lessen their clamoring for it to happen right this second. The ability to wait, to defer gratification, has long been recognized as an important component of success in life. We give up evenings of partying with our friends in order to study or to finish a report; we forgo appealing little luxuries as we save our money instead for a down payment or college tuition. Those acts of giving up something that would feel so good in the service of a far away goal are difficult to do, but necessary to accomplish what we want in the long run.

One study of children's ability to delay gratification that began in the 1960s continues to get attention today as follow up studies of the original investigation have yielded some remarkable findings (Lehrer, 2009). In the late 1960s Walter Mischel of Stanford University set up a situation in which four-year-olds were placed in front of a plate with a marshmallow on it. They were told that the experimenter had to leave the room for a few minutes, but if they waited until he returned they could have, not just one, but *two* marshmallows. If they couldn't wait, they could only have that one. Only about 30 percent of the children were able to resist the temptation of having that delicious treat immediately in order to be rewarded with a greater treat (*two* marshmallows) later. Those "patient" children, or "high-delayers" as they were described in the study, came up with a number of strategies to help them get through the 15 minutes or so of waiting. (They would talk to themselves, sing songs, play with their hands and feet, try to rest, close their eyes so as not to see those tempting sweets.) Among the more than two-thirds of the children studied who were not able to wait, some grabbed the marshmallow within a few seconds of the experimenter leaving the room; on average, they were only able to resist for less than three minutes .

Now this may not seem so momentous, but wait: Years later, a follow-up study of those same children revealed that those who had been able to wait for their reward were shown to have better social skills, better academic behaviors, and significantly higher SAT scores than those who could not wait to have the marshmallow. Mischel concluded that those children were successful because they were able to *direct their attention* to something *other* than the tempting treat. They were able to come up with metacognitive strategies that allowed them to endure what must have seemed to them to be the longest 15 minutes in their short lives! More important, that ability to wait for the extra treat grew into a *habit* of being able to put aside a short-term pleasure in order to accomplish a larger goal.

This same study was also described by Daniel Goleman (1995) in his book, *Emotional Intelligence*. As Goleman explains, "What shows up in a small way early in life blossoms into a wide range of social and emotional competences as life goes on. The capacity to impose a delay on impulse is at the root of a plethora of efforts, from staying on a diet to pursuing a medical degree." (p. 82.)

Inspired by those follow-up findings, Mischel and others have embarked on a new generation of research. In addition to using MRI data in an attempt to map specific areas of the brain that are implicated in self-control and the ability to regulate attention, they also hope to discover genetic influences on motivation and attention. They are observing and interviewing some of the original participants—now grown and with children of their own—to see if some of their own parenting practices may be contributing to the same ability to defer gratification in their children.

Mischel and his colleagues also worked with children directly to see if that quality of patience or ability to wait was something that could be taught. Consistent with the Habits of Mind approach, the researchers found that they could significantly increase a young child's ability to delay gratification by teaching him simple cognitive strategies, such as visualizing the marshmallow as a cloud, or as a picture within a frame. New studies are under way to pilot different programs and curricula that would be effective in teaching children some of the specific behaviors needed for self-control. The *New Yorker* article concludes with Mischel's observation that it is important that these cognitive skills become a *habit*. In order for that to happen, he says, years of practice are necessary. He cites the importance of parents in this process as he asks, "Have they established rituals that force you to delay on a daily basis? Do they encourage you to wait? And do they make the waiting worthwhile?" (p. 32).

By explicitly teaching children how to manage their impulses—at home and at school—our ultimate aim is to put them in the driver's seat. As with Jake, we start out by providing almost all the impulse control for the child. Over time, as children mature and learn, we expect them to gradually assume greater responsibility for their own impulse management.

Even kindergarten (perhaps younger) children can be taught what it means to be impulsive and how to bring their impulses under control. Young children especially, frequently find themselves in trouble for something they said or did that they didn't even realize they had done or understand might be a problem. Children are often relieved to learn that the ability to manage our impulses is something that grownups also have difficulty with sometimes. We teach them that it is something that we usually get better at as we get older, but there are strategies they can learn *right now* that can help. Children are learning that impulsivity is not "bad"—although the consequences of impulsive speech or action can have negative consequences—and that managing it is something we can practice and improve upon every day.

At one school, the children had been taught to not jump off a two-foot retaining wall dividing two sections of playground, but to use the steps instead. Nevertheless, children regularly went flying off the wall in full gallop, sometimes resulting in skinned knees. During recess, just after a class lesson on Managing Impulsivity, one lively five-year-old came hurtling toward the wall, but seeing the teacher, screeched to a dramatic stop at the edge, arms wind-milling. Looking up with an expression of great pride, he exclaimed, "I managed my impulsivity!" His teacher's warm and approving response guaranteed that he added to his growing self-concept one more facet: He is a boy with self-control, a boy who can manage his impulsivity!

Although some children may have an inherent tendency toward being more or less impulsive, the skills to Manage Impulsivity absolutely can and should be taught. It is a disservice to treat children who behave impulsively as though they have a character flaw. Just as we teach children who may be struggling to learn how to sound out words the specific skills they need to read better, so too should children receive the kind of instruction needed to manage their impulsivity. In this chapter we suggest many ways to help your children become less impulsive and more reflective in their words and actions. As the focus of this section is on communication and relationships, our attention is directed more to impulse management strategies that promote good listening and communication skills, which contribute to more fulfilling relationships.

How Impulsivity Impedes Communication and Affects Relationships

Taking a look at our own brushes with impulsivity may help us better understand and empathize with our children's efforts to gain mastery over their own. As with Metacognition, we offer a few pointers to help you gain increased awareness of and control over your own impulsive tendencies. (It is a life-long challenge!) We then suggest that you talk to your children about, and make explicit your own efforts to Manage Impulsivity. By explaining what it *looks like*, *sounds like*, and *feels like*, you establish a foundation for children to feel safe and motivated to practice managing impulsivity for themselves.

Impulsivity powers that hair-trigger response when our buttons are pushed. It is the *motion* in the word, *emotion*. Those responses are basically automatic shortcuts taken when you perceive a part of a situation and jump to conclusions based on just a little bit of information. Almost instantaneously, your emotional reaction registers on your face as a scowl, grimace, sneer, or gesture of dismissal. These manifestations of emotion often happen so fast and so automatically that you may not even know they are there. Those facial expressions can, however, pack a strong wallop for the conversational partner who may then react in turn with puzzlement, irritation, embarrassment, or hurt feelings. Unfortunately, the initial impulsive response may be based on an incomplete and inaccurate reading of the situation. As the misperceptions and emotional reactions begin to pile up, tensions escalate and it becomes increasingly difficult to untangle the original misunderstanding and to set things straight.

Impulsivity also interferes with the ability to listen in an open-minded and attentive way. Again, if you take a fragment of what your partner is saying and start to formulate your own counter-argument, you have stopped listening. You are no longer operating in the present moment but are focusing on defending yourself or "winning" the argument. In Chapter 4 (Listening with Understanding and Empathy) we offer several strategies to improve listening skills. For now, let us just suggest that it is important to try to catch yourself at the moment you stop listening. You can remind yourself that you will have time later to respond, but that it is important for you to hear and understand the whole story first.

> **The ability to wait, to defer gratification, has long been recognized as an important component of success in life.**

And of course, impulsivity is what leads to verbal gaffes, the uncensored jab, the "joke" at someone else's expense, that we may spend a lifetime regretting. In many cases, put-downs are veiled as "teasing" or "just joking," and the negative impact is often minimized or denied. In families where this is common, it is quite likely that parents experienced this kind of teasing from their own parents or from older siblings. Although they may not have liked it at the time, they may not have thought it through so as to intentionally choose not to do the same thing to their own child. At school, we often find that children who are quick to criticize or who engage in verbal put-downs of their peers experience the same thing at home. It is difficult to teach children the value of speaking respectfully to others at school when the norm at home is quite different. Many of these verbal behaviors are automatic and frequent, with little or no thought of their impact. Children are quite defenseless against teasing from adults, because their emotional experience of what is happening—"This doesn't feel good. It's hurting my feelings. This is embarrassing"—is denied by adults who claim that it's all in good fun. When children put down other children and claim to be joking, we always explain to them that unless both people find it funny, it is not a joke.

A particular danger with parent-child communications is the critical comment uttered in a moment of frustration or anger. Such comments can leave unseen scars that last a long time. Parents may later wish they had phrased their criticism more gently, but nevertheless may feel justified in telling the child a necessary truth. Children learn best when they feel understood and supported. A sharp critical comment about the child's character or personality presents a difficult dilemma for the child (as it would to any adult hearing something similar from a loved one): The child can either take it in as an unalterable truth about himself, in which case he is left to feel that he is inadequate and unworthy, or he can dismiss the parent's criticism as unwarranted and thus perceive the parent as an unhelpful teacher, one who cannot be counted on for help in growing up. Neither option provides much support to the child in developing the skills needed to understand himself and his world. In Chapter 6 (Questioning and Posing Problems) we take a closer look at how to frame comments to children so that they reflect "positive pre-suppositions." Positive pre-suppositions convey the message that you know the child to be good and capable and well intentioned. They permit the child to engage with you in a cooperative way to improve a problem situation, while keeping his dignity intact.

Strategies for Managing Impulsivity While Communicating

Start with Structure

Structure, routine, and predictability at home provide a foundation on which children can thrive. A child who can count on regular times for eating and sleeping is freed up to learn and explore her environment. If parents establish a few basic expectations and stick to them (for example: no hitting; use kind words; always brush teeth before bed; if you get a toy out, put it away when you're finished), there are fewer arguments and negotiations to endure. A child who is raised with an optimal amount of structure is less likely to continually test limits at home or school. When a child understands what the expectations are, is developmentally able to meet them, and is acknowledged for doing so, she derives a sense of satisfaction and mastery. That child feels secure in the structure of the family and where she fits in. She will be more cooperative and more motivated to continue to work towards mastery of her own impulses and of the challenges she faces in her environment.

It Helps to Have a Plan

Anticipate stressful times that are apt to result in thoughtless and impulsive communication. For some families, it's the witching hour of 5:00 to 7:00 p.m., when everyone is tired, hungry, cranky and in a rush to get activities out of the way and dinner on. For others, it's the morning rush. It is also common for many parents to become anxious and irritated when trying to help their child with homework. Whatever the trigger is for you, it helps to have a plan. When you anticipate that you may be entering a stress zone, you can approach it more intentionally. You might think to yourself, *"Okay, this is often a problem area for us. I tend to get annoyed, I get sarcastic, and then she shuts down. Instead of telling her what to do this time, I am going to ask her what would be most useful to her."*

> **The ability to Manage Impulsivity affects communication skills on every level—perceiving and reacting nonverbally, listening, and speaking.**

You might spend a little quiet time after the children are in bed, mapping out what tend to be the most difficult and stressful times during the day. Brainstorm some strategies for doing things a little differently to help those moments go more smoothly. In the spirit of Metacognition, you could tell your children that you've been thinking about how the family could be calmer and happier during those particularly stressful times. Ask them for their own ideas about how to make it better. Having a plan (and a backup plan) helps you feel more in control. You are then less likely to be overtaken by frustration, discouragement, or anger when stressful situations arise.

Don't Forget to Breathe

The ability to Manage Impulsivity affects communication skills on every level—perceiving and reacting nonverbally, listening, and speaking. As you become more practiced with using your metacognitive strategies—especially those that encourage you to question yourself about those automatic responses— you are simultaneously buying yourself time to lengthen the interval between *button pushed* and *impulsive reaction*. If you lengthen the interval enough, the impulsive reaction doesn't even have to happen.

One simple strategy is to simply *breathe* when you feel yourself tense up. Taking three deep breaths (in through the nose and out through the mouth) is a remarkably effective way to slow yourself down and begin to relax. Sometimes we feel stuck in a situation that feels like it is spiraling out of control. Michael

Popkin (1993), who developed the "Active Parenting" program, used the image of parents "taking their sails out of the child's wind" (p. 75). There's nothing wrong with taking yourself out of the situation briefly until you recover your composure. You can even say something to the effect of, "I'm feeling pretty annoyed and don't want to say something *impulsive* that I will regret, so I'm going to take a little break until I am calmer. You can do the same thing, too, and we'll talk about it in a little while." You don't have to stand there and let them push your buttons.

It's Only a Feeling

You can remind yourself, "*This is only a little feeling, I don't have to actually do anything with it.*" Often, when you simply name and accept the feeling you are having at that moment, it dissolves along with the pressure to do or say something. Impulsivity is an automatic response to something uncomfortable, like trying to shake off a fly that has landed on your arm. It is helpful to try to "sit with" those uncomfortable feelings of impatience or irritation that usually spur an impulsive response. If you can intentionally endure the discomfort of the feeling for a few seconds, you often find the moment passes and nothing bad happens. It is helpful to have a little saying or two in mind that you can call up when needed. When you are in a potential conflict situation you might think to yourself, "Just don't make it worse," or "That's just Tonya being Tonya." That little reminder can be enough to keep you from saying or doing something that would escalate the conflict. Each time you do this, you build up invisible "muscles" that increase your ability to manage your own impulsive responses.

Instead of Interrupting...

One very common manifestation of impulsivity is the habit of interrupting others. If you are used to interrupting, you may feel that you will just burst if you don't get out what you have to say *right* now. Interrupting can be generated by many different feelings. Anger, annoyance, defensiveness, competitiveness, and even a fear of forgetting your point can all spark an interruption. But interrupting is one of the communication blockers that derails a conversation, alienates the other person and makes it very difficult to solve a problem. If this is something you tend to do, you can acknowledge to yourself that it is so hard to wait until the other person is finished speaking. You can try to redirect your attention from what you want to say to what the other person is saying, and mentally commit to hearing the person out. As you practice this, try to remember to assess how you did afterward. Remind yourself that you don't have to be perfect; it's a difficult habit to break, but every time you intentionally refrain from interrupting, you are building up your capacity for managing your own impulsivity and becoming a better listener.

Modeling and Teaching How to Manage Impulsivity

Help Your Child Learn From Your "Mistakes"

As with Metacognition, we start with making our own efforts to master this habit explicit. Children as young as four or five can easily understand the idea of being impulsive, and there are many delightful children's books and stories that illustrate the concept. Even more meaningfully, you can offer up some of your own experiences with impulsivity. For some reason, the kitchen often provides opportunities to illuminate impulsivity: "Oops! I didn't read the recipe carefully. I was supposed to add the eggs *last*!" Or, "I was so impatient for the cake to be done, I opened the oven door and it collapsed!"

...if you take the approach that you are all working on these things together... your child will be more open to your efforts.

Any such mishap can be treated as an opportunity for you *both* to learn: "Next time I'm going to make sure I read the recipe all the way through, and I'll keep checking back to make sure I'm on track!" It is helpful to begin to use the word "impulsive" in context, so your child begins to get a clear sense of what it means. In the beginning, it is less threatening to "catch" yourself being impulsive, and then you can ask your child to help you think of a way to repair the situation. For example, we often interrupt when our children are speaking. That would be a good time to stop dramatically, and say something to the effect of: "You know, I realize that I just haven't been letting you finish what you want to say. I've been *interrupting* you. That must be frustrating for you. I'm really going to make an effort to stop myself from doing that and to really listen. I *want* to hear what you have to say." That certainly would put you on firmer ground, when you are then trying to teach your child to refrain from interrupting and be a better listener. *As your child begins to get the idea of what impulsivity looks like, sounds like, and feels like, he will begin to catch himself.* You want to be sure to acknowledge how wonderful it is that he is beginning to recognize when it happens. In a supportive way you could then explore together how a situation can be remedied, and what he could do next time to prevent it from happening again.

As with all the Habits of Mind, if you take the approach that you are all working on these things together, that perfection is not expected, just improvement, and if it is approached in a spirit of warm and optimistic support, your child will be more open to your efforts.

Practice "Wait Time"

Children often equate speed with intelligence and power. In school you may see these children with their hand waving in the air before the teacher finishes her question. Or you may see a beginning reader rushing through her words so quickly that she has no idea what she has just read. Wait time sets the stage to encourage thought and reflection before responding. So, at the dinner table, for example, you might preface a question with, "Now I want you to really think about this question I'm about to ask *before* you answer." Choose language that encourages reflection over speed. "I would love to hear your thoughts about that. I like the way you took your time and really thought about my question." Of course you can also model wait time when your child asks you a question: "That's such an interesting question! I want to think about it a bit before I give you an answer."

As you deal with daily situations, you can think out loud about how you will manage your impulsivity. If you are anticipating a difficult telephone conversation with a customer service representative, for example, you might comment about how it is difficult to be patient sometimes, but you are going to practice your breathing, listen carefully, think about your reply first, and remember that the other person is just trying to do their job. Dealing with these situations is a necessary skill. By talking aloud about the steps you take to help you manage your own impulsivity, you are passing on this skill to your children.

Rehearse Tricky Situations Ahead of Time

If you know that you'll be in a situation that can be over-stimulating and is likely to elicit impulsive behavior from your child (the mall, a carnival, the grocery store, a birthday party), try to review the situation ahead of time with your child. Speculate together on what the experience will be like. Ask your child to predict what parts of that experience might prove hard for her to handle. Establish limits ahead of time about what you will buy for her, if anything, how much she can spend, how much time you have, and so on. Together, try to identify strategies that will help her cope. Let her know you're there to help, but if you have to leave the setting because she is unable to manage it, you will both have to go. Work out something you can both say out loud to each other as a signal or a coping strategy. For example, when passing a display of stuffed animals at the fair, she could say to herself, "It's just a toy; I have nicer ones at home." You could (with a touch of humor) offer to hold your hand over her eyes as you pass a tempting display. Once you are in the situation, you can remind her of the conversation you both had before you left home and divert her attention to the fun you are having. As your child weathers the situation, empathize with how difficult it can be and compliment her on the effort she is making. Show interest in and appreciation for any strategies she seems to be coming up with on her own. Even if she doesn't do so well overall, try to point out one or two signs of progress and convey optimism that, little by little, she will manage that impulsivity.

Practice Waiting—But Find Ways to Enjoy the Time

Remember the successful marshmallow resisters? They found ways of diverting their attention away from the marshmallow and onto something else. If you find yourself waiting (at the doctor's office, for a table at a restaurant, for a bus or plane) or you are on a long car trip with no DVD player, have some ideas prepared ahead of time for things you can do to get the focus off the long wait. If you are outside you can listen for birdsongs and try to identify the kind of bird it is; you can speculate what it was like where you are now in the time of the dinosaurs or in Colonial times; you can play rhyming games or "I spy." For a car trip, you can ask your child to be on the lookout for particular milestones on the way to Grandma's house and mark them off as they occur.

Or you can just talk with each other. A column by Laura Munson in the *New York Times Magazine* described a long car trip taken by her and her teenage daughter. Normally the girl would have been texting her friends, but because they were crossing a mountain range, she was unable to send or receive messages. Munson imagined a long sullen silence as they made their way over the mountain, but instead a wonderful and interesting conversation took place. What could have been an arduous and boring trip instead became a magical opportunity for the mother and daughter to get to know and appreciate each other better. Car trips are opportunities for family conversations, but not if each family member is plugged in to his or her own entertainment device.

The point of *practicing waiting* is not just to pass time, or get through it somehow, but to savor the exact moment we are in, right now. If we use those moments with our children to share observations, tell stories, and talk, we are teaching them that life is not a set of stepping-stones from one exciting destination to the next, but rather to be enjoyed in its ordinary, in-between moments. When we practice waiting meaningfully, we give them the resources for a rich inner life: We teach them to think about and appreciate the world around them; to use their imagination; and to feel more comfortable in their own skin.

Use Visual and Action Cues

We sometimes forget how much children need to see and touch and interact with their environment in order to learn. Words alone seldom are enough for them to learn a new skill, let alone a challenging habit of mind. For younger children, it can be helpful to give them something to hold or to keep in their pocket as a reminder to stop and think. Sometimes a squishy ball to squeeze allows a child to discharge a little of that energy that might otherwise go to saying or doing something impulsive. A pocket-sized Stop sign, cut out of heavy paper and colored by your child gives a visual reminder that he can carry with him. As you are driving through a traffic signal, you can explain the purpose of the yellow light; how it tells us to slow down, be careful, look around, be ready to stop. You can use the image of the yellow light when your child needs to slow down. If your child tends to impulsively say not-so-nice things to brothers and sisters, you can get her to make a card to put on her dresser reminding her to speak nicely. Have her include in the card some specific compliments she *can* say.

If children are having a hard time waiting for a holiday or special occasion to arrive, use a calendar, and schedule some interim steps such as baking cookies or making cards, to break up the wait. If you have family rules such as speak nicely to one another, clean up after yourself, etc., put them on a poster the children design and decorate. If a rule is about to be broken, all you have to do is point to the poster. (Almost every elementary school classroom has a prominently posted list of rules and expectations that children help develop.)

If a child has behaved impulsively, by say, hitting a sibling, wrenching a toy out of the baby's hand, or saying something mean, it is important to stop the action right then and give him an opportunity to understand what has happened and to set things right. You never want a child to practice inappropriate behaviors, for eventually, those behaviors can become habitual. In a calm and neutral way, ask your child to explain what happened. If he needs a moment to calm down, allow him to do so. Don't get into a protracted discussion of who started it. Just focus on the behavior. Ask him to explain to you why that behavior is against the family rules (it hurts, it is unkind.) He may protest that he couldn't help it because he was just so mad and frustrated. You can empathize with him about those feelings, but try to get him to identify some strategies he could have used to prevent things from getting out of hand. The strategies we recommend in school are simple but surprisingly effective:

- Take a little break.
- Count to 10.
- Take 3 deep breaths.
- Talk it out.
- Get help from an adult.

Ask him to tell you which strategy he thinks might work for him next time he gets upset. Then help him to think of a way to repair the situation, and stay with him until he does. If he is able to do all this, make sure you acknowledge his effort and convey your warm confidence that next time he will *think* of how to manage his impulsivity.

Empathize and Acknowledge

Let your child know that you understand how hard it is to manage one's impulsivity and that you appreciate the efforts he is making toward that end. Convey your confidence that she is getting better and better at it. Be specific: If you see your child refuse to take the bait when teased, make sure you let her know you appreciate how hard that must have been and how proud you are of the self-restraint she showed. Point out the benefits of each incident you observe: "You could have gotten into a nasty fight, but you didn't. I'm so proud of you. If you said what you were thinking at that moment, you might have really hurt your friend's feelings. Aren't you glad you stopped yourself and waited?"

And why not acknowledge effort with an occasional, spontaneous treat? "You were so patient waiting all through your little brother's recital. I know it wasn't easy for you. Let's celebrate your being such a patient big brother with some ice cream."

Developmental Expectations for Managing Impulsivity

It's sometimes difficult to know exactly what we should expect from youngsters in terms of their ability to self-regulate. There is a wide range of what is considered "normal," especially with younger children. In addition, no one—not even an adult—behaves with absolute consistency. We all experience occasional lapses in our impulse control, whether it is due to fatigue, stress, or for no particular reason at all. When we see a child behaving impulsively, our response depends in part on how age appropriate we perceive that behavior to be. Generally, the younger the child, the more tolerant we are. But, in addition to chronological age, there are other developmental factors that influence a child's capacity to manage impulsivity. These include increased capacity for memory which permits, for example, a child to recall his mother's admonishment to stay away from that mud puddle in the back yard, and to also remember what consequences might ensue should he give in to the temptation of splashing through it. Preschool age children, of course, are famous for living in the moment, and cannot be expected to consistently remember rules and expectations for behavior without adult support, coaching and consequences when appropriate. That is why adult supervision is so necessary at this age. Even a well-coached four year old may dash into the street without looking if she sees her best friend waiting on the other side. A second factor that contributes to impulse control is the capacity for internalized or private speech (Bronson, 2000). A child who can think to himself, *I better not take that candy, even though it looks so good. Mom would be so upset with me*, is in a much better position to withstand the temptation than one who does not have the words that help him to put the brakes on. And thirdly, an increasing understanding of the concept of time, and a growing appreciation that our behavior in the present moment has implications into the future, contribute to our capacity to delay gratification in service of a greater goal (see Barkley, 1997).

Obviously all these capacities grow continuously throughout childhood, along with the child's physical and cognitive abilities. When lapses do occur, it may be helpful to try to identify the factors that may have contributed—memory, internal speech, or an imperfect ability to consider future consequences. Having a clearer picture of where the breakdown occurred may allow parents to identify some specific metacognitive strategies to help the child manage her impulsivity better next time.

In their book *Smart but Scattered*, Peg Dawson and Richard Guare (2009) provide some specific examples of the kinds of impulse control children at different grade levels should be expected to display. It is helpful to have a general sense of what is typical and what is not.

If you find that your children more or less can Manage Impulsivity as expected for their ages, they are likely to benefit from the strategies and suggestions in this chapter. If they are consistently unable to do so, you are probably already well aware of it. These recommendations should still lead to improvement and should help you better manage your reactions to your child's impulsivity. There may be a point, however, when it would be appropriate to seek additional guidance. Your child's teacher is the perfect person to ask for an opinion on how well your child is able to handle age-level expectations for managing impulsivity. If it is a problem, ask how *pervasive* it is. Does it happen throughout the day, in every different class or activity? Or does it just show up when the work is difficult or in less-structured situations? How *intense* is the problem behavior? Is it just fleeting and minor, or is it really disruptive? Finally, you need to know the extent to which the impulsive behaviors interfere with your child's academic progress and social relationships. If impulsivity, and the distractibility that usually accompanies it, are getting in your child's way, it is in her best interest to seek additional guidance on how to proceed. Your school psychologist can provide further information, and there are excellent books and resources on ADHD available for parents.

Chapter 3

Fully Present: Managing Distractions

An important part of Managing Impulsivity is developing strategies to take control of all the various things that conspire to distract us from all we have to do. Benedict Carey in the *New York Times* (May 22, 2010) described a study coming out of the University of California, Los Angeles, in which 32 diverse, middle class families agreed to be videotaped for nearly every waking moment while they were at home. All of the families had more than one child, and in each, both parents worked. The researchers were astounded by the complexity and busyness of such typical households. The author of the article summarized the thousands of hours of videotapes as depicting a "firestorm of stress, multitasking, and mutual nitpicking."

Twenty-first century families face unprecedented demands on their time, attention, and energy as they struggle with work, school, and extracurricular activities, and all the chores necessary to keep a family fed, clothed, and healthy. The idea of "quality time" with the family—once thought of as a poor substitute for real time, now may, in retrospect, seem to have been a pretty good thing after all. You may wonder how you can possibly implement some of the suggestions in this book when you hardly have time to have a thought to yourself. We fully recognize the strains that today's families are under. Some of those strains— financial hardship, dealing with the extraordinary needs of a child with a significant handicap, or supporting elderly and ill parents—are simply not amenable to quick fixes or easy answers. Those stressors require huge amounts of fortitude and endurance. However, we firmly believe that some of the stresses we feel—especially that sense of being under relentless assault by incoming stimuli—can be significantly reduced. In this section, we address some of the factors contributing to this type of stress and how we can take back control over our time and our attention.

Wired: Convenience or Distraction?

How often have you been at a restaurant or on a bus or train and observed parents busily immersed in their respective cell phones, texting away, while their children sit silently, waiting for the food to arrive or the ride to be over. Are those children feeling lonely in their own parents' presence? What about the missed opportunity for connection?

We are constantly interrupted by mostly unimportant data.

In the last few years there has been a tremendous cultural push toward constant connectedness in the form of email, social networking, and so on. As more people carry Internet-capable cell phones, patterns of communication have changed drastically. Letter writing is virtually obsolete, and even those long telephone conversations between teenage friends have been replaced by frequent short calls or text messages. Many people maintain large networks of acquaintances and business connections with whom they stay in touch by brief, coded, iconic messages. The very portability of our technology means that we are expected and expect others to be instantly available. We can summon information about almost anything from our cell phones within seconds (directions, addresses, who won the World Series in 1961).

One effect of all this convenience is that our perspective on time is also changing. In the early days of dial-up Internet connections, the very ability to connect to the web seemed so miraculous that the unreliable and "slow" dial-up process seemed a small price to pay. As technology has advanced, however, our expectations for speed and ease have also been raised, so that waiting more than a few seconds seems agonizing now. These technology-driven expectations may contribute to an increased sense of urgency and need for things to happen fast. Some of the subjective feelings of impatience and agitation that well up so quickly now would not have occurred a few years ago, when there were no expectations that you could instantly connect.

In addition, we may, as human beings, be hard-wired neurologically to focus and attend to any sound or sight in the environment that denotes change. Thus, the ring tones, beeps, and vibrations that indicate *incoming!* take on a compelling quality that is almost impossible to resist. If you get a beep that tells you a new email has landed in your inbox, it is hard not to look. Chances are it's an advertisement, but nevertheless the notice of its arrival prompts more attention from you than it probably deserves. This creates a situation in which we are constantly interrupted by mostly unimportant data. It is surely disruptive to the kind of sustained concentration that challenging work requires. It is also disruptive to conversations. What we may be losing is the patience to engage in an extended reciprocal conversation in which each partner listens, responds, and takes care to get the words just right.

Another casualty may be the ability to take delight in the moment, just being with one we love, and to offer the kind of warm, enveloping engagement our children need from us in order to feel secure, known, and loved. Good conversations with children are often filled with silences, silly asides, companionable comments about whatever activity you're doing together, and then—out of the blue—a child can say something profound or ask a perceptive question that takes your breath away. You can't schedule a moment like that. It can't be rushed, and it's not likely to happen unless the child feels relaxed and comfortable. Constantly checking or responding to communication devices does not put you "in the moment" with your child. Rather it conveys the message that your mind and attention are elsewhere.

As we become used to a nearly constant flow of incoming messages, we begin to feel uneasy without them. The *New York Times* published a series called "Your Brain on Computers" examining the impact of technology on our lives. In one article Matt Richtel (08/25/2010) noted an increased tendency to turn to our email, cell phones, and computer games and applications whenever we have a bit of time to fill. What mental processes do these diversions crowd out? Richtel quotes researchers who are beginning to take a look at the effects on our cognitive abilities of being so plugged in. The long-term effects will not be known for some years to come. What is known so far is that when you are learning something new, your brain needs a period of time to process that information, to consolidate it, and to store it in memory. In another piece (06/07/2010), Richtel looks at the mental costs of multitasking. Although multitaskers will argue with this, it is pretty well established that doing more than one thing at a time lessens the quality of each thing you're doing. Without that period of consolidation, you simply do not learn or remember as effectively. Taking a walk, doing a little gardening, or even going to sleep allows the thinking and learning to continue, to become deeper and richer. We encourage thinking time in this book. We ask you to think about your thinking, to come up with a plan to deal with stressful times, to problem solve, and more. This kind of thinking and planning will pay rich dividends for you and your family, but you have to make the time to do the thinking. It cannot be done while you are plugged in.

The Wall of Sound

The television is another major distraction to good communication. With large-screen television in high definition and the wall of sound provided by excellent stereo capability and huge speakers, it can be a real challenge to have a conversation. Many children cannot fall asleep now without the drone of the television to accompany them. Notwithstanding the often frightening content, bad language, and general "dumbing down" of interpersonal relationships as portrayed on television, the fact of its dominating presence in the home is indisputable. The net impact of these electronic devices is troubling. Their constant presence, their compelling demands for our attention, and the anxiety and distress we feel when we are deprived of them suggest they have much too important a place in our lives.

When children cannot sleep without the sound of a television going, it means they never learn the essential skill of being able to soothe and settle themselves. When they depend on television for entertainment, they lose the ability to imagine their own stories. Worse, the very content of what they see is often over-stimulating and even traumatizing for their developmental level. Children are often left anxious from having seen a horror movie or even a commercial for such a movie. They don't have the experience to understand that horrifying creatures don't really exist, and many live in fear of being the next victim. Even shows that are supposed to be comedies or meant for family viewing can portray mean, dishonest, disrespectful, or unethical behavior as normal or "funny." Many children assume that whatever they see a favorite character do on television must be okay. These influences make it more difficult for parents to stay "on message" about their own values and expectations for good behavior. The content of much programming complicates the already difficult job of parenting

> **When [children] depend on television for entertainment, they lose the ability to imagine their own stories.**

by creating an unrealistic view of the way people can and should interact. For parents to have to clarify and undo some of the expectations created by television is one more chore and distraction imposed on us by this onslaught of media.

Video games are another source of concern. They can provide something of a shared experience, but when video games are the only agenda item for a child's play date, it means the children are basically engaging in parallel play. Yes, those frisky children might be managed more easily as they sit before the game console, but what is lost? Children often get into conflicts when they get together for spontaneous unstructured play. Their judgment seldom matches their curiosity or energy level. Children learn to behave with attentive adults nearby to keep them safe, to set reasonable limits while encouraging creativity, and to communicate about behavioral expectations. Another concern is that, as technology improves and these games become ever more vivid and compelling, it may become more difficult to engage children with the simpler pleasures of books, board games, and just playing in the backyard. Board games may have lost some of their allure, as they cannot compete with the movement, dazzling special effects, and motor involvement of video games. Their value lies in what they teach: You have to take turns, no cheating or the game is ruined, it's not right to celebrate someone else's bad luck, sometimes you lose but it's not the end of the world. These strictures can be especially difficult for younger children, yet mastering them is an important milestone on the way to self-regulation. In the beginning (and maybe on into later childhood, as family game night) parents need to be there to model patience and sportsmanship and to keep it light. The opportunities then open up for really enjoyable moments together as a family.

Bringing Work Home

Almost anyone who works outside the home is faced with the challenge of meeting all of the end-of-day family demands and still finding a way to complete work that they have brought home. Knowing that you have to get something accomplished and yet trying to be patient and attentive can create tremendous stress and anxiety. Children seem to pick up on this and may then redouble their efforts to secure their parent's attention one way or another.

Children need "emotional refueling" when they get home from their day, and they need it from the people whom they expect and need to understand and to love them the most. Since so much of work brought home consists of communication through phone or email, once again the child is positioned to suspect that unknown people "out there" are more important than they are. It doesn't matter what you say otherwise to your child about how much you love him; he needs to experience your undistracted presence for some period of time every day in order to grow up secure.

In his book *The Secure Child*, psychiatrist Stanley Greenspan (2002) recounts a situation in which a young girl was experiencing a considerable amount of worry and anxiety as she went off to school each day. Although the child's mother was at home at 3:00, she was often absorbed in work from the office. Greenspan recommended that the mother put aside her work for the first half hour or so after her daughter's return and focus exclusively on her. At first the mother was reluctant to do this, thinking that her presence in the house ought to be enough. But she followed the suggestion, put her work away, and over a shared snack talked with her daughter about her day. The mother was amazed at how much color and detail her child used to describe her experiences, once she had her mother's full attention. As they talked, they were able to clarify a number of things that were worrying the child. Over time, the child's anxiety diminished significantly. She still enjoyed sharing her thoughts and feelings with her mother, but needed less of her undivided attention, as she grew secure in the knowledge that it was really there for her. Reading this account, we may surmise that something else important happened. We can be quite certain that the mother also came to treasure their own special time together. It is quite possible that she began to feel that those intimate conversations were as necessary to her as they were to her daughter. And that, as her relationship with her daughter deepened, her own sense of herself as a capable and loving mother also improved.

Obviously, there will be times when you are under a deadline or experience a crunch at work. If you are usually available for your child for a significant period of time at the end of the day, then she should be able to endure a brief withdrawal of your attention, especially if you explain the situation and make her feel that her cooperation is a big help to you. What is interesting is that, once she can count on being emotionally nourished by her time with you, she will become less needy and demanding of your attention.

Managing Electronic Distractions

The following suggestions are offered with one overarching idea: That we become more deliberate and intentional in our use of cell phones, the Internet, and entertainment devices. This technology all comes equipped with an on/off button.

Regulating the flow of incoming information and electronic demands for attention may be a significant way of reclaiming your time together as a family. Decide when you will use your devices and when you will turn them off. Think about intentionally slowing things down for yourself and your family.

Start by deciding to establish technology-free periods of time. Think about the limited amount of time you have together and how you can make the most of it. Many people carry their cell phones with them at all times and check constantly for messages. This can start to take on the characteristics of compulsive behavior (repetitive, ritualistic, and meant to alleviate anxiety). You can make a point of putting it away or turning it off. Let your child know that you would much rather be spending time with him than staring into a screen, and there isn't a call that could come in that would mean as much to you as that special time together.

Family dinners are ideal for everyone to reconnect, and it goes without saying that the television should be off. You might also think about not bringing cell phones to the table. Unless you are expecting an incredibly important call, there is no reason why the caller can't wait 30 or 40 minutes.

It is a good idea to establish some quieting rituals to help children wind-down before bedtime. Reading in bed, telling stories, listening to quiet music are all ways of transitioning to restful sleep. Often the "tucking in" rituals include a snuggle, a back rub, and a little conversation about the day. This is when children really open up about what's on their mind. If they have had a rough day or are worried about something, this is usually the time you have to help them sort it out and restore their equilibrium. It is important for a loving parent to be there at bedtime, to assure them of your love, and to help them feel safe and secure. This would also be one of those times to turn the cell phone off.

Turning on the television set should be an intentional choice, not an automatic gesture. Television programs should be carefully selected with some deliberation and discussion beforehand. It makes sense to limit television watching just because, after all the mandated activities are completed—sports, homework, chores, dinner, bath—there is little enough time left for meaningful leisure activities.

Use One-on-One Time as an Incentive

Parents often use the promise of television or video games as a reward for good behavior or completing homework. Unfortunately that may foster the illusion that watching television is a good thing to do with your time. If you are looking for an incentive, there is nothing more powerful to a child than the opportunity to spend a little one-on-one time with a beloved parent.

Children often find it hard to finish up a chore or homework assignment if they hear the television in the next room, or the excited laughter of younger siblings, blissfully free of responsibilities. Those distractions do make it difficult. You can empathize with the feeling your child has and offer up an incentive: "Come on. Just a little more to go. Then you and I can go out for a game of catch" (or a walk to the park, or whatever is feasible at the time).

Sometimes a more intensified involvement from a parent is required, especially if you are trying to wean a child away from a behavior or habit that is not benefiting him. One mother was advised that her 1st grade son seemed to be overly invested in video games to the exclusion of other interests or developing competencies. It was his main topic of conversation and seemed to be the only thing he felt he could do well. This mother immediately limited the video games, but took care to replace them with the shared activity of taking nice long bicycle rides together. The next day at school, the boy was overflowing with excitement about his new interest in biking. He described the journey they had taken to the park and proudly demonstrated some of the "moves" he was learning to make on his "big boy" bike. This mother was intentional in her effort to help wean her son off his dependence on the video games and followed through with a commitment to invest her own time and attention instead. The results were seen in his excitement about developing his prowess on the bike and spending time with his mom. As his intense interest in video games was modified by his real-life adventures with his mom, his focus and interest in school also improved.

Floor Time

Even more effective than using your time as an incentive or reward is the idea of having regularly scheduled time together.

Psychiatrist Stanley Greenspan developed the concept of "Floortime" as a way of ensuring that this quality time takes place. The idea is that parent and child spend about a half hour together with the telephone, computer, and video games turned off. You can chat over a snack, play cards or board games, take a walk, do whatever you both feel like doing together. It is important that the parent allow the child to set the agenda for the activity and the conversation. If you can allow the conversation to flow out of a pleasant shared activity, you will be surprised at what you learn. The warmth and good feelings that arise out of spending time together with the person you love most will build a stronger, more positive relationship. It will create the conditions in which your child will want to cooperate with you, because she will want to keep those good feelings going. The foundation you build with that time spent—relaxed, focused, and undistracted—will sustain you in your more challenging parental moments. For your child, that time spent with you is money in the bank for her sense of security.

Even 30 minutes a couple of times a week for some one-on-one time can present a logistical challenge. What do you do with the other children? What about all those things that need to get done? Many parents have had to get creative to make this happen: Parents can spell each other; siblings can be scheduled for play dates at a friend's house; a middle school or high school student can be employed for an hour or so during that busy afternoon period for crowd control; and bedtimes can be staggered so that each child gets his own special time. Chances are good that, once you start enjoying that time alone with your child, it will become a priority for you as well, and you will find a way to make it happen.

Make Multitasking Work for You

We often feel that mundane household tasks take us away from spending time with our children, but some of the best conversations can happen around a shared task: putting dishes in the dishwasher, folding laundry, or putting dinner together. Bringing children into the routine tasks needed to keep a household running can increase your time together as well as provide opportunities for those wonderful spontaneous conversations to arise. It may take longer to complete those chores, and they may not be done quite as well, but as long as you don't expect perfectly folded undershirts or expertly cut carrots, you can enjoy each other's companionship, and your child has the satisfaction of contributing to the family's well-being. Working together has the added benefit of teaching children competencies. There are many things even young children can safely do in the kitchen: They can be put in charge of the salad spinner or work off some of their energy mashing potatoes. Preschoolers can handle table setting and clearing of unbreakable pieces, and older children can clear their own plates when finished. Conversations can take place while you are doing evening chores together, such as making tomorrow's lunches or setting out the cereal bowls and spoons for breakfast.

By intentionally choosing to take control of our time and of the distractions that threaten to rob us of time, we can reduce stress and strengthen our family connections. When you think about how little time, really, we have to be together—18 years, maybe, and then they're off to college—can we really afford to waste so much of it?

Chapter 4

I Hear You: Listening with Understanding and Empathy

Nine-year-old Derek had not had a good day at school. He'd forgotten to bring in his spelling homework; a couple of boys had snickered in a mean way when he excitedly told them about his new pack of fantasy game cards; and at lunch recess, his one reliable friend quit the game they always played and ran off to join someone else. He lost his temper and ran after the boy, issuing threats, which created an unpleasant stir on the playground. His teacher made him apologize, and he spent most of the afternoon feeling miserable and alone. At the end of the day, while packing up, he was sure that Adam, who had snickered at him earlier, deliberately pushed into him as he squeezed by to get to his locker. Derek then punched Adam on the arm, and both boys ended up in the principal's office. Derek's mom, Karen, was already at school to pick him up so she was invited in to meet with the principal and her son. As she listened to the principal and Derek's teacher describe the sequence of events that led up to this, her heart sank. She felt embarrassed by his inappropriate behavior, yet she also felt hurt at how alone and isolated he seemed to

Listening with understanding and empathy!

Understand others!

Devoting mental energy to another person's thoughts and ideas; Make an effort to perceive another's point of view and emotions.

be. She was angry at the other boys, and thought it quite possible that they did provoke Derek, yet she also felt angry at her son for his behavior. The principal asked her to discuss the situation further with her son, and told her that the counselor would meet with both boys the next day.

When they arrived home, Derek put his backpack down with a huge sigh. Karen looked over at him, her heart aching for how difficult things seemed to be for him right now. "Come on into the kitchen, Derek. I'll get you something to eat." She microwaved a packet of popcorn and set out some carrot sticks and a glass of juice. After a few moments of silence, she said gently, "Sounds like you had one very rough day." "Yeah, the worst", Derek muttered. Another moment of silence, and she asked quietly, "So, what do you think happened?" Derek bit off a section of carrot, and then the words came tumbling out: "He's been mean to me since the start of the school year. I don't know why he doesn't like me, but he always looks like he's laughing at me. It makes me feel so dumb. I never know why they're laughing at me." Karen looked at him kindly and said softly, "It makes you feel dumb when it seems like someone's making fun of you and you don't know why." "Yeah! It's so embarrassing," Derek replied. His voice broke a little as he described his efforts to share his interest in fantasy cards, and how the other boys would roll their eyes and walk away. He explained that last year he and Adam often traded cards at recess and he thought they were friends. But this year, Adam seemed more interested in sports, and was hanging out with some of the more athletic kids. Karen leaned in toward him and looked into his eyes. "I can just hear in your voice how sad you are to feel like you've lost your friend. What do you usually do when they walk away like that?" Derek hesitated, and then admitted that he sometimes chased after them and called them names.

Karen could just picture the scene in her mind and was tempted to rebuke Derek for behaving in such an immature way. But she sensed that, on some level, he already knew that his behavior was inappropriate and that he was already embarrassed by it. She just said softly, "So...you called him names?" "I really liked him. I was looking forward to being in the same class with him again this year, and I wanted him back as a friend." After a few moments, Karen said, "Derek, it sounds like this is something that's been bothering you for a long time. It's been hard for you to move on from it, and you're having a hard time figuring out the best way to handle it, but can you help me understand just what happened today?" Derek's response was disorganized and meandering. Karen sensed that he was embarrassed at some of his own behaviors and was loathe to admit that he had made some mistakes. He stopped talking and looked down with an expression of guilt and regret. "You know, Derek, there isn't a person in the world who doesn't sometimes wish they could take back something they said or did. It's a bad feeling for sure. But we can use that bad feeling to help us grow and to learn better ways to behave. Do you want me to help you figure out some ways we can make this better?" Derek gave her a quick hug. "Okay, Mom," he replied, sounding relieved.

Listening with Understanding and Empathy is probably the most powerful of all the Habits of Mind for strengthening the parent-child relationship.

This conversation could have gone in so many different directions. Karen could have allowed her protective, motherly instincts to prevail, taken Derek's side about everything that happened, and demanded that the other boy be punished. Or, her embarrassment could have led her to scold Derek and ground him for a period of time. Neither of those responses, however, would have helped Derek come to a better understanding of his own emotions and his own behavior. Although the first option may have made him feel she was on his side, it would not have helped him to understand his own contribution to the problem. Without such an understanding (and without a game plan to change his own reactions) Derek's social difficulties would be likely to worsen and leave him even more isolated in relation to his peers. Neither would lecturing, scolding or punishing help Derek improve his situation. Punishment and harsh words tend to leave a seething resentment not at all conducive to reflection. Rather than being motivated to make things better, the punished child often fantasizes about revenge and feels misunderstood, bitter, and alone.

It is difficult for anyone—child or adult—to face head-on our own responsibility for an encounter gone awry. When parents can convey their unwavering belief in their child's inherent goodness and lovability, *even when the child has done something wrong*, they are making it possible for their child to acknowledge his responsibility and to do something about it. Karen's ability to listen *empathically* gave Derek the emotional support he needed to begin to understand the events of his day. The warm and gentle tone of voice she used made him feel loved and understood. When Karen assured Derek that *everyone* does or says something that they regret at one time or another, she lessened his sense of isolation and shame. By explaining to him that we can take those bad feelings and use them as a guide to learn more appropriate behavior, she gave him hope that things can be repaired.

Clearly, Karen and Derek had a lot more talking to do before he would be able to retrace his actions on that day and figure out some better alternatives. The counselor, in meeting with both boys, would help develop a plan for how they could interact more positively. Derek would also benefit from some "coaching" from his teacher on the playground, to help him respond more appropriately when he was upset. But it was his mother's ability to tune into his distress and confusion and to give him the emotional grounding he needed that enabled Derek to make good use of the supports he received at school. Her continued engagement in the effort to help Derek perceive situations more accurately and to behave more appropriately was crucial in the slow steady progress he made.

Listening with Understanding and Empathy is probably the most powerful of all the Habits of Mind for strengthening the parent-child relationship. When

you listen with empathy, you create a sense of *attunement* with your child. This sense of attunement, of being on the same wavelength, is what allows a person to feel truly known and loved for who she is. When you listen empathically, you convey this powerful message to your child: *We are in this together. I will not abandon you. I understand how you feel. Together we will figure this out. There is nothing so difficult that we cannot find a solution together.*

One challenge for parents in listening empathically is to temporarily hold in abeyance our natural tendency to comfort and soothe our distressed child. It takes some courage (and faith in the process) to be able to *listen* when your child tells you he feels ugly or stupid or that nobody likes him. It is so difficult to keep from rushing in with assurances: *You are so beautiful! You are very smart! People do too, like you!* When our child is in the throes of strongly negative feelings, it can threaten our parental self-esteem. We want our children to be happy and confident, and it is painful and anxiety producing for us to see them unhappy. However, just as you wouldn't try to distract or divert your child's attention away from a difficult math problem, nor should you when she is struggling with uncomfortable feelings. In order to learn how to regulate our feelings, we have to experience them, be able to identify and label what it is we are feeling, and somehow ride them out. When parents Listen with Understanding and Empathy, they are providing support and companionship for this difficult task.

The implications of this are profound. How many people have we seen who experience a "midlife crisis" or who behave in erratic or inexplicable ways, are just thrashing about heedlessly, at the mercy of powerful feelings they do not understand and cannot control? So much self-destructive behavior comes from running away from the discomfort of our feelings. Anxiety gets displaced as over-activity, or people self-medicate with drugs or alcohol. People who are feeling hurt or rejected may lash out in anger and then further alienate themselves. How many of us as children were told, "You shouldn't feel angry, you don't know how lucky you are," or "Don't feel sad; think of how much worse other children have it," or some other variation of that theme? Did those words help? Probably not. When children's feelings are met with criticism, dismissal, impatience, or bland assurances, the child is left to fend for himself, emotionally. Empathic listening establishes a different paradigm: It is possible to be calm and courageous and unafraid of exploring even your most uncomfortable feelings. Almost always, this results in the child feeling genuinely better afterward because, through your understanding and support, she has come to a deeper understanding of herself. She has also learned to identify, accept, and endure even very strong feelings, because you were there for her. Practice with this should give your child emotional strength and flexibility. As an adolescent or adult, she may then be less likely to be "hijacked" or panicked by strong feelings, which accompany some of the inevitable slings and arrows that life throws at us.

As with Metacognition and Managing Impulsivity, we start by suggesting some simple strategies to make your listening more intentional and empathic. As you practice these strategies, it will feel a little strange at first, because it may be quite different than what you usually do or say spontaneously. But keep trying.

These are time-honored ways of deepening communication and strengthening your relationship. As you practice your empathic listening, you are likely to see your child opening up and communicating more just because he is now encouraged by how good it feels to be *really* heard.

The feelings of strangeness you may have when first using these strategies diminish as you experience more satisfying and productive conversations. At that point, as with the other Habits of Mind, you can begin to make it explicit what you are doing; for example: "I want to be sure I understand just how you feel. You say you don't think you did anything wrong, and you are confused why your friend is mad at you?" Later, you can refer back to how you listened empathically to your child when she was distressed to begin to teach her how she can do the same.

Before You Begin...

Use your Metacognitive Strategies

Listening with Understanding and Empathy pulls from several other Habits of Mind, most notably Metacognition and Managing Impulsivity. You can remind yourself that your intention is to help you and your child come to a better understanding of herself and of the situation and to do so in a way that affirms your love and respect for her. If your own feelings are running high, take a few moments to reflect on what is going on within you, and what you need to do now in order to be most helpful to your child. If you are feeling distressed and anxious for your child, take a few deep breaths and remember that children don't automatically know the best ways to behave and react to others, and that your example is the best possible teacher. Try to remember (especially if your child has been treated unkindly) that we as parents often feel the pain more intensely than they do. It is helpful to focus on your child's feelings, which may be different from your own. If you are feeling angry or embarrassed by your child's behavior, take some time to cool down, and remind yourself that you don't yet know the whole story. If you have a little slogan or mantra that you use to help you regain control, repeat it to yourself a few times. For example, you could think to yourself, "Just don't make this situation worse."

Set aside distractions

As we discuss in Chapter 3 on Managing Distractions, it is helpful to turn off or put aside any distracting pieces of equipment such as cell phones, computers, and television. You may also find it helpful to remind yourself to put aside any internal distractions or worries that might get in the way of your ability to focus.

Stay focused on your child's perceptions and feelings

Keep in mind that you will be *modeling* for your child an effective approach to understanding and dealing with life's problems. Your ability to stay focused on your child's perceptions and feelings will encourage him to stay with it for as long as it takes to achieve better understanding. Obviously, the time and intensity vary with the age of your child. Short conversations are generally the rule for younger children. Your own feelings must temporarily take a back seat until your child's equilibrium is restored. An upset child is simply unable to absorb information, whether it is about your reactions or a reasonable explanation of why his behavior is unacceptable. *Later,* he may be able to hear some of that, but not while emotions are running high.

Your ability to stay calm and yet compassionately reflect back the feelings you are hearing from your son or daughter (*Oh, Jarred, you must have been so disappointed.*) will demonstrate that even very intense negative feelings such as shame, grief, and anger can be endured, understood, and mastered. When you listen empathically, you are temporarily sharing the burden of those heavy feelings for your child. By doing so, you are making sure she will one day to able to do it all by herself.

Empathic Listening is mostly nonverbal

After you have put some of your metacognitive strategies in gear so that you are mentally prepared to provide emotional support to your child, your warm and comforting presence will go a long way toward encouraging a good conversation. You'll want to monitor your body language, tone of voice, and eye contact. They too, should convey the message that the two of you are in-sync. Younger children, especially, benefit from a loving hug or hand-squeeze, but don't underestimate the healing value of touch for someone of any age. Your facial expressions are so important in an empathic conversation. If your child sees your warm interest reflected in your face, he will feel encouraged to continue. If your expressions are aligned with his (a little smile when he recounts a funny moment, a look of concern when he recalls something scary) he will feel that you are really getting it and that you are with him. You don't want your emotional reactions to take over. Just keep them low-key but in harmony with what he is saying. Don't worry so much about the words that you say. Often vocalizations such as "uh-huh" or a little groan of sympathy at the right time do a lot to keep the conversation going.

Give your child time

We often forget that even very bright children may struggle to organize their thoughts and feelings so that they are clearly expressed. Especially in an upsetting situation, it is hard for them to remember who said exactly what or the exact sequence of events (although in the first re-telling, the other person seems to "start it" an amazing 99% of the time!). Keep in mind that we are not conducting a criminal investigation or collecting evidence. As empathic listeners, we are simply trying to help our child gain a clearer understanding of the event, as well as to gain some emotional mastery over what happened. We want children to reflect on their experiences, and that means we have to give them time to do so. In our fast-paced adult world, we are accustomed to quick exchanges, but empathic listening requires us to slow things down. Very often children come up with amazing insights after a companionable silence. Allow little pauses and silences that permit thought.

Ask questions thoughtfully

Recall how Karen opened up her conversation with Derek. First, she acknowledged that the day had been a difficult one for him. Then, she asked, "So, what do you think *happened*?" The words she chose for her open-ended question conveyed her interest in learning more about Derek's thoughts, feelings, and perceptions. The phrase *"what happened"* is open ended and nonjudgmental. It allows the child to tell the story from his perspective, which is the necessary first step. Karen's tone of voice also carried a lot of meaning. It expressed her warmth and love for her *child*, but her inflections also indicated an acknowledgement that the situation was confusing and complex. That gave Derek a safe space from which to begin to look at his own behavior.

As empathic listeners, we are simply trying to help our child gain a clearer understanding [and] gain some emotional mastery.

When we are listening empathically, our questions should be carefully phrased and spoken so as to open up further communication. Open ended questions, such as the one Karen asked, are best for this purpose. If you ask questions that are answerable by a "yes" or "no," you may be imposing your own preconceived interpretations on the situation, thus making it more difficult to achieve a good understanding of your child's perspective. Avoid peppering your child with questions about details. They will come out eventually if they are important.

Another pitfall to avoid is asking rhetorical or loaded questions that contain within them a Taser-like zinger. If a child is asked, "What were you *thinking*?" in a tone that conveys harsh judgment, the child will feel shame and will not be able to learn from the situation. The same question, said in a tone of warm interest, conveys an entirely different meaning, and invites the child to reflect productively on her experiences. Your questions—both words and tone of voice— should convey your "positive presuppositions" (covered in Chapter 6) about your child.

Paraphrase

This is one of those key techniques universally taught in counseling programs, parenting classes, and conflict resolution/mediation training programs. Paraphrasing, for the uninitiated, can seem like a mindless parroting of the other person's words. But actually it is a way of staying focused on the speaker and eliciting a more comprehensive understanding of her thoughts and feelings. When you paraphrase, you are checking in with the speaker to see if you are getting it—not just the facts, but also the feelings underneath. When you paraphrase, you take some of your child's words, but you weave them into a slightly more expanded version, which you offer back in a tentative, somewhat questioning tone of voice. For example, six-year-old Ryan was telling his dad about an incident on the playground in which he felt insulted by another boy.

Ryan: *Allen makes me so mad I want to smash him!*

Ryan's dad, Brendan: *When he said that to you, it just made you furious.*

Ryan: *Yeah! I was furious! And everybody was watching, too.*

Brendan: *That must have been pretty embarrassing, especially with all those people there.*

Ryan: (starting to calm down now): *Well, mostly they were my friends. They were mad at him, too. Why did he have to say that to me?*

Notice that Brendan's empathic listening allowed Ryan to move from being "so mad" to being able to process other, more complex feelings. Once his anger was accepted by his dad and labeled (furious), Ryan began to think more reflectively about what happened (*Why did he have to say that to me?*). Brendan did not join in a condemnation of Allen. He kept his focus on Ryan's own perceptions and feelings. If Brendan is able to continue paraphrasing and encouraging Ryan with open-ended questions, Ryan may eventually surprise him with some very

Q&A

Common Concerns About Listening with Understanding and Empathy

Who has the time? *All right,* you might be thinking, *but who in the world has time for this sort of thing?* Aren't there times when you just have to say, "time for bed" or "please pass the salt" without worrying about how they really feel about it? You're right. Absolutely, there are many times when our typical mode of communication can and must prevail. But, that being said, empathic listening saves time in the long run. That is because it helps you get to the heart of what is really going on. More important, when your child feels that you care about his feelings and are making an effort to understand, he is more likely to cooperate than when he feels misunderstood and unfairly treated. And things just go more smoothly and quickly when children cooperate.

Isn't empathizing with my child just encouraging him to wallow in self-pity? No. When you empathize, you're not saying, "Oh you poor dear, that's terrible." You are seeking to understand and to help him understand just what it is that he is feeling. Sometimes children and adults take extreme emotional positions out of a conviction that they will not be paid attention to otherwise. This is a result of their legitimate feelings having been dismissed, criticized, or derided in the past. If a child is very upset and you listen empathically, he will not stay so upset. Secure in your understanding, he will be able to move forward much more quickly and be able to assess the situation more realistically.

mature insights about what may have motivated Allen, and how to handle similar situations in the future.

Paraphrasing allows children to refine their understanding of their own feelings. Hearing what they are saying "played back" to them in a slightly altered form allows for reconsideration of the original reaction. Very often, feelings of vulnerability, anxiety, embarrassment, or fear are masked behind expressions

But what if I don't agree with my child's perceptions of a situation?
In relationships as in politics, perception is everything. Empathic listening opens a window for you to really understand what is going on with your child. If her perceptions are distorted or her feelings are unjustified, chances are good that she will begin to come to that understanding on her own, once you have provided your emotional support. Once her upset is lessened, you may begin to suggest possible alternative explanations for what happened, which she may accept or reject. But at least she is in a position to begin to think about it. Parents sometimes ask, what if my child says that I am stupid or unfair? Do I have to agree with her? No, of course not. There is never a good reason to sacrifice your own dignity or the respect you are owed as a parent. In such a case, you could say something like, "It must seem that way to you now, and I can see how very angry you are about this. We can talk about it later when you are more calm, but we can't talk about it when you are speaking to me so disrespectfully."

What if my child is upset because of a rule or consequence that I have imposed? When you impose a consequence, be sure to do it in a way that makes clear that you take no pleasure at all in doing so. Even as you follow through on the consequence, you can empathize with your child's dismay. Even young children generally accept a consequence with the explanation, "that's the rule." Some parents keep basic family rules (no hitting, speak respectfully, clean up after yourself, etc.) and the consequences posted on the refrigerator so there is no ambiguity. Make it clear that, even though you are sad to impose the consequence, that is the family rule. You can express confidence in your child that he will remember the rule the next time. When you do this, you are making yourself an ally with your child in helping him to grow up to be a good citizen.

of anger. Paraphrasing can help get at the feelings that lie underneath the angry response. In Ryan's case, he had been embarrassed by something Allen had said to him in front of his friends.

In other cases, paraphrasing can reveal totally unexpected under-standings:

Meredith was driving her 12-year-old daughter, Nina, home after a long day at school. Nina attended school in the district where Meredith worked as a teacher, and it meant getting up extra early and getting home much later in the afternoon as they lived quite a distance away. Despite this tiring schedule, Nina kept up with her class work, participated in after-school activities, and had made wonderful friends. That afternoon, Meredith started telling her daughter about an upcoming holiday party for staff members that would be held at a fellow teacher's house next week after school. Meredith enthusiastically talked about how much fun it would be, how the teacher had children Nina's age, and how delicious the food would be. Her enthusiastic chatting was met by a stony silence, followed by a flat declaration from the back seat, "I don't want to go." Meredith's mind raced. She was really looking forward to this party as a way to unwind with colleagues after a difficult couple of months. There was no way she could attend if she had to drive Nina home first. Why couldn't she just come along for an hour or so? She was disappointed at her daughter's response, and then began to feel resentful. She's so selfish, Meredith thought. She doesn't care at all about my feelings or what I want. I stay late lots of times for her, why can't she do this one thing for me?

Fortunately, Meredith had just been teaching her 5th graders, who were being trained as peer mediators, about the technique of paraphrasing. She decided to give it a try. Glancing in the rearview mirror at her daughter in the back, Meredith said evenly, "You don't want to go?" A moment of silence, and Nina repeated emphatically, "I don't want to go." Meredith was tempted to try to talk her into it, but instead waited a moment more and said, "You really don't want to go." Another brief silence, and Meredith was sure the girl was about to make a sarcastic comment about there being a parrot in the car. Instead, she wailed in a voice filled with stress and fatigue, "It's too long a day!" Suddenly, Meredith understood. Nina endured the long commute without complaint, but to pile something extra on, felt just overwhelming to her. Meredith's heart swelled with appreciation for her daughter who was working so hard and doing all the right things. She felt ashamed that she had held such unfair thoughts about Nina's motives a moment ago. As she thought about how differently the conversation would have gone had she voiced her original resentment, she was so grateful that she had thought to try paraphrasing at that moment. After a pause, she said softly, "You do put in a very long day, honey, and you do a great job with it. Don't worry about it. We'll figure something out."

Paraphrasing typically feels awkward at first, because we are so used to a different pattern of communication. Someone says something, and we usually counter with our own opinion or our own feelings. With some kinds of conversations that is just fine. But when you are dealing with strong feelings or a problem that needs to be better understood before it is solved, paraphrasing is a valuable key that will unlock many levels of understanding.

When You Listen with Understanding and Empathy, What Are You <u>NOT</u> Doing?

Once you get the hang of it, Listening with Understanding and Empathy is actually simpler than the kind of communication most of us think we should be doing with our child. Most of us think we should be actively teaching our children, and we do this through lengthy verbal explanations and advice. Most children (adults, too) just can't process a lot of verbiage, and they start to tune out. Your good example is the most powerful way you have of teaching your child.

But there are some behaviors that can get in the way of Listening with Understanding and Empathy:

Giving advice
"If I were you, I'd…." It is so hard to refrain from sharing your hard-won wisdom with your child. But just think back to when you were younger. How well did you listen to and follow advice given by adults? It seems like a short cut at the time. If only they would listen, we could save them so much pain and futility.

According to Deborah Tannen (1990), there are probably inherent male-female differences in the tendency to give advice. Generally, women tend to like to just hash things out, think out loud, and vent their feelings. They are often frustrated and irritated when their spouse or significant other jumps in with advice. It feels to them that they are being hurried along and short-changed.

They feel perfectly capable of coming up with solutions; what they want is to be heard and understood. Husbands are often bewildered by this reaction as they intended only to be helpful. In general, men prefer to cut to the chase and get on with a solution.

When parents detect a pattern of problem behavior, it is difficult not to let our anxiety and irritation show.

The basic premise of Habits of Mind is that—with the right supports—children can come to wise conclusions through their own reflective thinking. This Habit of Mind is effective at stimulating a child's thinking. Once you have provided the emotional support, a question like, "What do you think are some things you could do now to make it better?" can lead to practical and creative ideas. The child then "owns" the suggestion and will be more motivated to make it work. With younger children, especially, you certainly can help jump start their thinking if they are truly stumped about where to begin. Whenever possible, however, it is desirable to let them take the lead on thinking up solutions.

Bringing up the past

When parents detect a pattern of problem behavior, it is difficult not to let our anxiety and irritation show. Somehow we expect children to pick up on the urgency we feel and use it to motivate them to do better. More often, though, when parents bring up past mistakes, it feels discouraging and dispiriting to the child, and does not lead to productive efforts to solve the problem. Instead of pointing out past mistakes, try using Listening with Understanding and Empathy to acknowledge what an uphill battle it must seem to continue to struggle with the same problem over and over. A comment such as, "Honey, you must get so tired of losing recess" can elicit a torrent of feelings. Once the child feels heard and understood, she is better situated to start working on the problem.

Interrupting

As mentioned in Chapter 2 on Managing Impulsivity, interrupting is a difficult habit to break. It is important to try to rein it in, however. Frequent interruptions convey a sense of impatience and lack of respect. Our larger goal, remember, is to use the Habits of Mind to improve our communication within a relationship. We want our children to learn to process and put into words their feelings and experiences. When we interrupt, we are short-circuiting their learning. It is as if we are saying, *I already know what you are going to say and I already have an argument for that.* We are denying them opportunities to develop as thinkers and communicators. We may also be creating conditions in which children feel discouraged and give up the effort of trying to express themselves verbally. If you notice that your children are frequent interrupters, try to monitor your own tendency to do the same, and make it explicit that you are working on it.

"Winning" a conversation

As an adult, your speed of thought and ability to summon just the words you need are so much better developed than your child's. It's just not fair to use these abilities to overpower a child in a conversation. If you think back, you can probably remember a time or two when, as a child, you were on the receiving end of an adult's greater verbal power. How did it feel? How did it make you feel about the adult? About yourself? Sadly, many adults have rarely experienced being listened to in an unhurried, empathic, and caring way, unless they have been in therapy. That is why it may take quite a bit of practice before this Habit of Mind feels natural. Listening with Empathy and Understanding posits a different purpose for conversations with your child. Rather than winning an argument, we are seeking to understand and to support our child in his development. We are working to help our child understand and regulate his own feelings and behavior. It is a different kind of winning we are talking about here—one that leads to a much more meaningful victory in the long run.

Teaching Your Child to Listen More Empathically

Work on basic listening skills first

Many schools teach "Whole Body Listening" in the earlier grades. The premise here is that you don't just listen with your ears alone, but you also need to keep your body still, your eyes on the speaker, and your brain engaged in order to truly understand what you are hearing. In addition to modeling these basic listening skills in conversation, you can make those expectations explicit. For example, you might remind your son, "I need your eyes on me, so I know you are really listening." Or you might say, "You seem distracted by that little toy in your hand. I'll hold it for you till we're done talking." To encourage your child to really think about what you are saying, you can cue her ahead of time: "I'm going to tell you about how I felt about what happened today. When I'm done talking, I want you to be able to describe what I said, and tell me how I felt, and why you think I felt that way. Now, listen closely."

With almost all children, you need to be close up and initiate eye contact yourself before you begin speaking. If you try to convey information from across the backyard or playground, or from another room within the house, you are following a recipe for miscommunication and frustration. They might "hear" you, but the likelihood that they actually processed what you said is very small. In order to teach children to be better listeners, it is important to not keep talking when they are clearly not paying attention. If you do that, you are inadvertently teaching them that it is okay to not listen. A brief, pointed silence from you may be enough to convey your expectation, but if not, you can remind them of what they need to do to listen better before you continue. If they still aren't listening, you can up the ante a little bit. You can suggest that she has a choice: She can listen to what you have to say now, or spend the next few minutes sitting quietly until she is ready to do so. Under no circumstances should a child who is refusing to listen be allowed to resume play until you have gotten her cooperation.

Be aware of developmental considerations

Empathic listening depends on the ability to take the perspective of another person. This is a cognitive skill that grows over time and experience. Babies and toddlers often show distress when they see another baby crying, and they may even try to offer some comfort, by offering their bottle or toy to their upset friend. These behaviors certainly foreshadow the development of empathy. It is thought, however, that the ability to really understand that other people have an internal life separate and apart from one's own only begins to develop in mid to late childhood.

A big part of the curriculum in kindergarten centers on helping children increase their awareness of and concern for other children. A good kindergarten teacher will probably utter these words several times a day: "How do you think that made your friend feel?" A five-year-old will usually answer that question after the fact, but may not always think about it ahead of time. With maturation and experience, children are increasingly able to expand their egocentric view of the world and take into account that others have their own thoughts and feelings. By the time children are around nine or ten years old (4th or 5th grade) they should, with prompting, be able to more fully consider the perspective, perceptions, and feelings of another person. Knowing this, you would of course tailor your expectations to your child's age and maturational level.

Understand that there are individual differences

Some people just seem to pick up social cues more easily than others. Just as some of us fall toward the more impulsive end of the reflective/impulsive continuum, so, too, are some individuals more tuned into and responsive to the feelings of others, while others seem nearly oblivious. Although we cannot change a person's innate temperament, we can teach him to become a better "reader" of the different signals others transmit. Children who are less sensitive to reading facial expressions can be encouraged to look at their friend's face or listen to their voice in order to better understand how they are feeling.

> **Some children have difficulty understanding that a good social conversation involves *reciprocity*.**

Some children may not seem to be especially concerned if they hurt someone else's feelings, but they might be motivated to become more aware of others if they understand they may lose a friend and the fun activities that go with play dates unless they become more tuned in. For these children, it may work better to teach them simple rules, such as the guest always gets first choice of an activity; if you have a disagreement, get help instead of fighting, etc. If your child does better at learning positive social behaviors by being given a few concrete rules to follow, that is fine. The goal is to establish a backlog of happy social experiences that lead to friendship and ease in those situations.

If your child tends to have difficulty sharing or getting along on a play date, you might rehearse a couple of scenarios ahead of time, such as "What would you do if Ronnie chooses a game that you don't want to play?" You could then act out the scene with your child until you both come up with some possible solutions.

Some children have difficulty understanding that a good social conversation involves *reciprocity*. For example, if your child's friend mentions that his parents are thinking about getting a new puppy, your child would do well to show interest by asking a few good questions, such as, *What kind of puppy? When do you think you'll get it? How do you feel about that?* This may seem obvious to you, but many children (and some adults) tend to turn the conversation right back to themselves without acknowledging their friend's overture. You can coach them by modeling a good reciprocal conversation, and also by role-playing different scenarios in which they have to follow up with a question or comment that is on-topic.

Practice empathic listening together

When we teach conflict resolution skills in the elementary school, we introduce empathic listening by performing a little improvisational skit for the students. The teacher approaches the psychologist with a "problem" she wants to discuss. As she tries to explain her dilemma, the psychologist acts out a series of horrible listening skills. She looks through her appointment book, mutters to herself about how busy she is, checks her cell phone, interrupts, changes the subject, and talks instead about herself and her own experiences. The "conversation" ends with the teacher walking away bewildered and disappointed.

The student audience is appropriately appalled by this behavior, and when asked, they expertly identify all the ways in which the psychologist failed to be a good listener. The psychologist then asks if they would give her a chance to do it all over again, if they could push the rewind button and let her try out some better listening skills instead. This time, they see the psychologist use empathic listening skills by making eye contact, asking open-ended questions, paraphrasing, and demonstrating emotional attunement with the teacher. This time, the teacher appears to have found genuine comfort and support in the conversation.

Dramatically depicting the contrast between poor listening skills and empathic listening makes a strong impression on the students. They are then paired up and given an opportunity to practice empathic listening with one another. We set the timer for two minutes. One person talks about a "problem" they have, while their partner practices her listening skills. At the end of two minutes they switch roles. Afterward, many children report that they have never been listened to like that before. It is a revelation to some of them that another person would listen in such a way as to show such interest in their thoughts and feelings.

Why not play such "listening games" with your children? You could explain that the goal is to become better at understanding each other's thoughts and feelings. Teach them the ground rules: no interrupting, stay on topic, no judgmental comments about what the other person is saying, and so on. If you keep it short and simple, with lots of laughter, it's a fun way to practice some very sophisticated listening skills.

When Siblings Squabble

Listening With Understanding and Empathy transforms an argument into an opportunity to improve and deepen a relationship. Most often, we are moved and grateful when we feel someone has "gotten" what we are trying to express. Siblings can be perfectly situated to provide that kind of understanding to each other. Who else would have the memories of what it was like to be raised by their particular parents?

Relationships between siblings, however, can also be marked by crosscurrents of rivalry, jealousy, striving for power and control that may bring out their worst Machiavellian impulses. There may also be a bit of a biological imperative here as well. Humans are, after all, mammals, and it does seem that all baby mammals love to wrestle and jockey for position with one another.

But just because fighting and arguing may come naturally doesn't mean we can't improve on things. The Habits of Mind approach is clear that, when children are taught *how*, they can greatly exceed our expectations. There is a wide range of opinion about the extent to which adults should get involved in children's conflicts, from the adult dictating terms of a truce and demanding apologies, to a "let them work it out themselves" approach. Neither extreme provides children with the tools they will need to eventually resolve conflicts effectively and peacefully. We recommend a middle way, which teaches listening and communication skills that will serve them well for life.

Here are some suggestions for handling children's conflicts:

- If things are heated or there has been physical aggression, send them off to their rooms or separate corners for a brief period in order to cool off.
- When things have calmed down, bring them together for a conversation. You might explain that you are interested in helping them find a solution to their problem, and that you are not interested in blaming or punishing anyone.

- Start by assessing if each person is willing to work on solving the problem. You can explain that it will be better for them if they do, because they will be better able to come up with solutions that work. If they are not willing to work on it, you can just assign consequences to everyone.

- Establish some ground rules. Insist that each person have a chance to tell what happened without being interrupted. Reassure each child that they will have a chance to explain their feelings and perceptions fully, but they each need to really listen to and try to understand the other. No put-downs, insults or accusations of "she's lying!" will be allowed. Ask each child to agree to the ground rules.

- Decide who will start and ask that child to tell you what happened. Expect interruptions or interjections by the other child. Remind them of the ground rules, and that they will soon have a chance. As Child #1 tells her story, use your empathic listening skills to paraphrase, clarify, and summarize what she is saying. Remember to paraphrase for feelings as well as events; for instance: "So, when Michael came into your room and took your game without asking, you felt frustrated and taken advantage of." Ask if there is anything she would like to add. If she feels satisfied that she has gotten the whole story out, feelings included, turn to Child #2 and ask him to first summarize what he heard his sister saying. Something like, "Michael, you've heard a lot here, and you will get your turn in just a second, but could you just tell me what you think you understand of what Cheryl just said? What was the thing that bothered her most?" Sometimes the conflict fizzles out right then and there. At other times, Child # 2 may have a different version and will need the same opportunity to express his thoughts and feelings. You may have to go back and forth a few times to establish a coherent account of what happened that both children can agree to. Remember that you are not looking to determine who started it or to assign blame. Your calm demeanor and tone of voice will make it clear that you are most interested in helping them find a way to solve the problem.

- When each child has had a chance to give full expression to their experience, you might then summarize what you have learned from them both. Try to find points of commonality, such as, "So you both wanted to play with the same video game, and you each felt the other was being unfair." Be sure to leave pauses so that the children can jump in to clarify a point.

Maintain the ground rules about interrupting and respectful language. What we hope to have happen here, is that each child begins to understand the other's perspective a little better, and that they will begin to soften their combative stances so as to work cooperatively toward a solution.

- Aim for a "Win-Win" solution. A child's version of this is to ask, "How can we solve this problem so that both people are happy?" You can then go right into the problem-solving process described in Chapter 9 with brainstorming solutions, agreeing on ones they will try, and so on. Ask them what they think might happen if a particular solution doesn't work. How could they deal with it? What would their back-up plan be?

- It is a good idea to have a written record of the agreement to refer back to. Ask each child how he feels about the agreement and the process you just went through. Let them know that you are confident they will work it out, but if they run into any problem, they don't have to fight. They can come back and work on it again until they find a solution that makes them both happy.

At first, you will need to take the lead as facilitator and mediator. Once you all achieve a successful resolution and you sense your children understand the process, however, you can begin to make explicit how they can do the same for themselves. You can point out how you asked questions, how you listened for feelings, and how important it was to hear what each child thought and how they felt. Ask them how they think they could do that for themselves next time they disagree. These are skills that require practice and coaching—even for adults— as they don't always come naturally. However, the feelings of satisfaction gained from working through what might have seemed like an intractable problem can be empowering. The pleasure of more peaceable interactions can be very motivating in continuing to work on perfecting those skills.

Chapter 5

Say What You Mean and Mean What You Say

We have surely come a long way from the days of "children should be seen and not heard." Not only do parents today generally encourage their children to express themselves freely, adults also tend to express their own thoughts and feelings more openly to their children than would have been common a generation or two ago. In fact, all of us are pretty much barraged by words from the moment we arise.

We are literally awash in language. Every moment of the day we are subjected to incoming messages from the television, car radio, loudspeaker announcements, overheard cell phone conversations, and the myriad verbal communications that must take place to do our jobs, complete our chores, and interact appropriately with others. And yet, it sometimes seems that the more talking there is, the less meaning is conveyed. If you tune in to some of the cable news shows, you may notice lots of strongly worded opinions,

Thinking & communicating with clarity and precision

Be clear!

Strive for accurate communication in both written and oral form; avoiding over-generalizations, distortions, deletions and exaggerations.

assertions, and generalizations, yet very little in the way of clear, precise, and specific ideas for actually solving the problems that are discussed.

In addition to the *amount* of language, it seems likely that the *speed* of the language to which children are exposed has also increased. Business communication tends to be rapid-fire and telegraphic. When that style is brought home, children may be left bewildered and uncomprehending. The late, great Mr. Rogers was sometimes criticized for his very slow rate of speech. He knew his audience, though. He understood deeply that very young children do not process language as quickly as adults. They need to have ideas presented to them in short segments, and slowly enough so they can actually think about what is being said to them.

All this verbal stimulation is not necessarily supporting children in their ability to understand and use language. Instead, like a rushing waterfall, there seem to be just too many words of questionable value pouring in too quickly. The need for Communicating with Clarity and Precision is more important than ever in our current social climate. We need to be attuned to what is developmentally appropriate in the amount, speed, and content of the language to which children are exposed if they are to become effective communicators.

The need for Communicating with Clarity and Precision is more important than ever in our current social climate.

Costa and Kallick (2000) consider language to be the foundation of the Habits of Mind. When, for example, we use a metacognitive strategy, we are using our *inner language* to help us through a difficult moment or to help us solve a problem. When we manage our impulsivity, it is usually by using inner language to help us stop and think first (*I don't need to buy that sweater now. I can wait until it goes on sale.*). And we have also considered how Listening with Understanding and Empathy helps us to get to the unspoken feelings behind the words. But to navigate the complexities of life, we need not only the inner language to know our own thoughts and feelings, but also an effective and varied outer language so that we can express ourselves with clarity and precision. We need to be able to say what we mean.

In this chapter, we focus on a more mindful use of language so that we can be more accurate and effective in our thinking and communication. And of course, so we can turn around and help our children to be more precise in their own developing use of language. Because the emphasis in this section is on the benefits of good communication as applied to relationships, we pay particular attention to expressing feelings and expectations clearly and succinctly. Because children do not learn just from *hearing* what it is you have to say, we also suggest some strategies to ensure that they really will "get it." We suggest ways to turn down the volume and turn on the lights with our choice of words.

Tools of the Trade

Conversation

There are many ways to enrich our child's understanding and use of language, but the first and most important way is, of course, to *talk*. Unhurried and companionable conversation between parent and child is the most organic way of developing language. When taking a walk, cleaning up after dinner, or riding in the car, we have great opportunities to catch up on the day, plan for tomorrow or speculate about the wealth of interesting phenomena that surround us. In our busy, time-starved lives, it is challenging to eat dinner together regularly, but that is probably the best time to reconnect with one another, to tell our stories about our day, and to refuel—not just with nourishing food, but with emotional support. The dinner table is a fine place to reaffirm our own family values, to tell little in-jokes, to give each person a chance to talk and listen. It is a perfect time to bask in the shared pleasure and pride in being part of *this particular* family.

Parents often find bedtime to be the best time for a reflective private conversation with each child. It is a time to wind down, to be comforted by a snuggle, to soothe bruised feelings, to develop a plan for tackling tomorrow's challenges, and to send a child off to sleep secure and optimistic. All of these conversations develop a child's language skills. The experience of listening and being listened to at home provides a strong foundation for the academic demands for language that children face every day at school.

A Rich Vocabulary

One prerequisite of Communicating with Clarity and Precision is, of course, that we have the vocabulary to do so. This doesn't mean that you have to use a four-syllable word when a simpler one will do, but we should be looking for opportunities to playfully expand our own and our children's vocabularies. Generations of readers found a feature in *Readers' Digest* magazine, "It Pays to Increase Your Word Power," to be an engaging way to add variety and verve to their own speaking ability. Every week, the column would quiz readers on a few, less familiar words and put them in the context of appropriate sentences so their meaning would be clear.

Similarly, in classrooms, it is common for teachers to put up a "word wall"–lists of interesting words that are posted for discussion and review. Any unfamiliar word that students encounter in their reading or in conversation goes up on the wall to be looked up, discussed, and to be made their own. It is not unusual for students to use simpler language in their writing than they really know because they don't want to make spelling errors. Inspired teachers will brainstorm ideas first with their class, and write on the board all the bright, vivid, descriptive nouns, verbs, and adjectives the children come up with. That way, kids can refer to the board for the right spelling and don't need to be constrained in their written expression.

We want to give our children similar access to words they need to express their ideas and feelings. In addition to various kinds of parent-child conversations, reading is one of the most important ways that children develop a good vocabulary and begin to appreciate the power of words. Even babies of a few months respond with joy and excitement when you hold them on your lap with a picture book. "Oh, look, there's Peter Rabbit! See the bunny?" For the very young child, being held on your lap as you read to her can give her tremendous feelings of being secure and cared for. The expression and warmth in your voice, the way you point to the picture as you say the word, and the shared enjoyment of the story, are powerful ways to develop language skills. Perhaps more important, they create lifelong positive associations with reading and literature.

School-age children are initially focused on their developing decoding skills. Until they are reading fluently, the printed words to which they are exposed will be simple and predictable. This is another reason why continuing to read aloud to them is so important. You can choose great stories of fantasy or adventure that are within your child's ability to understand but above his reading level. By modeling your own interest in the story, stopping to speculate on what might happen next, or why the character behaved as she did, you are coaching your child to experience reading as the great interactive process that it is.

At first it is a three-way interaction between you, your child, and the story. As your child's reading skills develop, she will engage in her own internal dialogue with the author through the stories and characters and, later, through the many new ideas and information she gets from reading. These early, rich conversations that take place as you read together are powerful ways of expanding your child's vocabulary and her thinking. As you encounter unfamiliar words, you can provide a definition if you don't want to break the flow of the story. If you are reading on an electronic device, you can access the dictionary function instantly.

WHAT PRECISELY DO YOU MEAN?

Too often we use vague and general terms such as stuff, thing, nice, good, etc., which are easy to access but don't pack much meaning. Costa and Kallick (2000) identify several categories of vague language that interfere with clear and precise communication. These are words that fail to convey the specifics that a particular situation calls for. Here are some examples:

- **UNIVERSALS**: Always, never, all, or everybody. Everybody is going to the party.

- **VAGUE ACTION VERBS**: behave, be nice, settle down. I wish you would be nice to your brother.

- **COMPARATORS**: Better, newer, more. He always gets more than me.

- **UNREFERENCED PRONOUNS**: They, them, we. They say that too much Vitamin D is bad for you.

- **UNSPECIFIED GROUPS**: Teachers, parents, teenagers, things. Teenagers just have no work ethic.

- **ASSUMED RULES OR TRADITIONS**: Ought, should, must. You should never go to bed angry.

Or, you can keep reading for a few more lines and give your child a chance to infer the meaning from the context—from what comes after.

Even as children develop a richer vocabulary, they will still struggle to come up with that one right word or phrase—either because they just haven't learned the word yet or because their "filing system" for words is not yet as well organized as an adult's would be. Make sure you give enough wait time for your child to access that word on his own, and then, if it looks like he just doesn't have it, you can acknowledge his frustration. "You look like you know what you want to say but you just can't think of the word! It's on the tip of your tongue! Could it be _____? Or ____?" As you assist him in his effort to express himself, you can let him know that it happens to all of us.

By using open-ended questions, parents can gently challenge their children to substitute more precise language for these overly general terms. Here's an example:

Parent: How was the movie?

Child: It was good.

Parent: What was good about it? What did you especially like about it?

Child: It was exciting.

Parent: What was exciting about it?

Child: I liked the way they showed people's dreams.

Parent: I wonder how you *would* show a dream. How did the director do that?

Child: Well, the colors were brighter, and the music was different in these scenes. It sounded magical. So, even though the scene was about something that could never happen in real life—the boy jumped off the mountain and started to fly—it felt so real that you did believe it. And the music was beautiful, too.

You can see how the parent's questioning brought out a wealth of detail from this child. Not only did the child then communicate more effectively, but in so doing, she probably also increased her own understanding and awareness of what it was she had so enjoyed about the movie. These kinds of conversations help our children *differentiate* their experiences. Instead of a vague sense of "liking" the movie, the child became aware of the mood that was created with music and special effects and how those aspects especially appealed to her. When we have these kinds of conversations, we help our children to make the most of their experiences—they become more vivid and more memorable. We also help our children develop a more differentiated sense of self through a clearer awareness of what they like and dislike and why.

Parents can apply similar strategies to challenge their child's use of vague language, especially when they are trying to convince you of something they want.

Ten-year-old Andre is campaigning to be allowed to play a new videogame that is rated "Mature." "All the guys have it," he tells his parents. "I'm the only one not allowed. It's not too violent. It's fun. It's just so much better than my stupid old games." Andre really wants that game, and he is hoping that his reference to "all the guys" will push mom and dad in his direction. It is up to his parents to lead the conversation toward more clarity and specific information. They might start by inviting him to sit down with them and have a real conversation about what he wants. You've probably noticed that kids often adopt a tone a great urgency and hurry when they think they're on shaky ground with a request. If you can carve some time and space out to actually *discuss* the issue, and convey a willingness to listen to their arguments, it may create a more reasonable atmosphere. The conversation might go something like this.

Dad: So you're telling us that you think you're ready for "Morning Mayhem."

Andre: Yeah, it's just a great game, and all the guys are playing it.

Mom: All the guys?

Andre: Yup. Harry and Joe play it. They said it's great.

Dad: Anybody else talking about it?

Andre: *Everybody's* talking about it.

Mom: So Harry and Joe's parents bought that game for them?

Andre: (pause) Well, not really for them. Their older brothers have it.

Mom: Oh. Their teenage brothers actually own the game. And their parents allow Harry and Joe to play it?

Andre: (another pause) I don't know for sure, but they've seen it, and they said it's great.

Dad: You mentioned that it's not violent, and you've said you think it's "great." Tell us more about that.

Andre: Well, I know you don't like violent stuff for me and, um, well, this does have some explosions and stuff, but it's really fast and the special effects are awesome.

Dad: You really love those special effects, I know. Andre, what other stuff besides explosions are in the game that you think mom and I might not like?

(Andre is quiet.)

Dad: (gently) You're right that Mom and I don't like violent games or shows for you. We don't like you having those images in your mind, and we don't like you spending your precious time pretending to create mayhem!

Andre: (whining) Dad…

Mom: I'm pretty sure we're going to stick to our rule about no violent games, but just to be sure, I'll call Harry and Joe's moms to ask their opinion about the game.

Dad: Meanwhile, Andre, let's talk a little more about the special effects you like so much. You know I just read about a new program where you can create some of your own. Want to take a look at it with me?

In a tactful and respectful way, Andre's parents asked questions that moved Andre toward being more specific in his assertions. Without ever calling him out on what might have been deliberate shadings of the truth, the conversation brought out a more accurate representation of the real situation. Andre's parents are unlikely to give in on "Morning Mayhem." They have good reasons for not wanting their son to play those games. But they accomplished a couple of important objectives in their conversation:

• *First,* they established with Andre that vague assertions and overgeneralizations would not work with them. He would need to be clear and forthright in making his requests. Although Andre may have felt frustrated and annoyed by their polite insistence that he give them the whole story, their approach is setting a good foundation for his teenage years when the stakes are so much higher. (Just think of future conversations about taking the family car, attending parties with older teens, drinking, smoking, etc.)

• *Secondly,* they reinforced a limit that they had already established, but did so in a way that was supportive and respectful. Dad's offer to explore some new special effects software with his son legitimizes Andre's interests, and gives him a way of appropriately and productively exploring those interests. Perhaps you recall the little boy in Chapter 3 on Managing Distractions who was becoming increasingly preoccupied with video games. His mom understood that it wasn't enough to limit the games; she needed to replace them with something healthier and more compelling, so the two of them started taking long bike rides together. That decision required a commitment of time and energy on her part. Andre's father, too, understands that it isn't enough to say "no." We want to help our children with the difficult beginning steps of developing interests and competencies. We do this by offering our time, expertise, and companionship until they can take off on their own.

What Exactly Are You Feeling?

Use of vague terms is especially true when talking about feelings. A few basic all-purpose words tend to be overused to convey a whole range of human experiences. If you ask a child how he feels about a negative experience that just happened, he might say he feels "bad." But a variety of feelings may be hiding within that word.

"Bad" Feelings

Sad	Frightened	Disappointed	Terrified
Depressed	Worried	Abandoned	Remorseful
Grief-stricken	Ashamed	Lonely	Guilty
Shocked	Embarrassed	Annoyed	Disheartened
Dismayed	Anxious	Furious	Betrayed

Similarly, of course, a child will tell you she "feels good" but what exactly does she mean? Here are just some possibilities:

"Good" Feelings

Excited	Happy	Proud	Ecstatic
Exuberant	Giddy	Passionate	Powerful
Competent	Strong	Energized	Enthusiastic
Appreciative	Moved	Inspired	Brave
Secure	Comfortable	Altruistic	Adventurous

People don't just feel "good" or "bad." They experience all sorts of in-between feelings that might include: *unsettled, uneasy, pensive, wistful, ambivalent, mixed-up, bittersweet.* These are the feelings that tug at the edge of awareness when something feels not quite right, but we don't yet know why. Having access to a wide variety of feeling words helps us to hone in on just what it is that's causing some distress. From there we can use metacognitive strategies to dig a little deeper and bring that troublesome thought to light. An excellent way to help children expand their feelings vocabulary is to use some of the strategies described in Chapter 4, Listening with Understanding and Empathy. Paraphrasing, especially, gives you an opportunity to offer your child's words back to her, but in a slightly expanded or more precise way.

Often children (and adults) first experience some feelings as though they were physical symptoms. Anxiety can be felt as stomach pain or shortness of breath. Worry or depression or a sense of being overwhelmed may *feel* like fatigue. How can you recognize the difference?

Eleven-year-old Rebecca slumped through the front door after school, shrugged off her backpack right there, and threw herself on the couch groaning, "I'm soooo tired." Her mom, Margaret, could have just advised her that she should not stay up so late. Instead, she thought to *expand* on Rebecca's body language and words:

Margaret: You sound *exhausted.* How did you sleep last night?

Rebecca: Okay, I guess.

Margaret: You seem really…*drained.* Was it a rough day?

Rebecca: (Turns her face to the back of the sofa): It was the *worst.*

Margaret: Oh, honey, I'm so sorry. There are days like that when you just feel like you've been beaten up.

Rebecca: (Nods her head but doesn't say anything.)

Margaret: I'm going to get you some lemonade and a little something to snack on. Be right back.

Margaret: (Returns with the snack) Here, Becca. Tell me about your awful day.

Rebecca: Well, for starters, I found out I did get cast in the play. Not the part I wanted, but an okay part.

Margaret: So…I thought you kind of had your heart set on the role of Jenny, no?

Rebecca: I thought I did, but then I looked over the part I got—Millie—and she has some pretty funny lines. I think I could actually have a lot of fun with it.

Margaret: Becca, I love the way you just rolled with it. Sounds like you didn't stay disappointed for long—that you found something to like in the role you got.

Rebecca: I guess I did.

Margaret: (smiling): You know what they call that, don't you? It means you're *resilient,* you bounce back and make the best of a situation. (Squeezes her hand.) You're my resilient girl.

Rebecca: (ruefully): Good thing I'm resilient, because then Arden was upset that she didn't get the part of Millie. She started crying and gave me a dirty look. I didn't know what to say, I didn't even ask for that part. At lunch, Arden and a couple of other girls actually turned their backs on me. They wouldn't even speak to me.

Margaret: I can see why you said it was a rough day. That had to be so awkward. What did you do?

Rebecca: I just felt frozen for a minute. I did feel bad for her. I could see how upset she was. But I had been disappointed, too! And it wasn't my fault.

Margaret: So many different feelings…. Sounds like you could really empathize with her disappointment, but you could have used a little empathy, too. And, what do you think was going on with them shutting you out like that?

Rebecca: I don't know. We've never had a problem before, but they were acting like I did something wrong, and I didn't. I don't even know if I want to do the play anymore. I don't know if it's worth it.

Margaret: (waits for a moment). It's odd, isn't it? When you go out on a limb like that, to try out for a play, or a team, or anything where you could fail in front of people, it's always a bit of a risk. You might do a bad job, people could be jealous or mad...

Rebecca: (sits up, now, animated). But you *have* to do those things, otherwise nothing good would ever happen! The director must have thought I would do the best job for the play and that's why she gave me the part. I do feel bad for Arden, and I'll probably try to talk to her about it tomorrow. But I don't think I should drop out because of that. It wouldn't be fair.

Through conversation, Margaret helped her daughter clarify and sort through a difficult day that held many strong emotions. Rebecca's apparent exhaustion was not so much physical fatigue but more a reflection of being stuck with some uncomfortable feelings without a road map. Margaret's introduction of the word *resilient* at the appropriate time gave Rebecca an idea of herself that she could call on to help her through her dilemma: *I am a resilient person, I can bounce back, that's the kind of person I am.*

Praise such as Margaret offered, given in a sincere and low-key way, can make a real contribution to a child's self-concept—when it is an honest expression of the behavior you see in front of you and not perceived by your child as you just trying to make her feel better (see Willingham, 2006).

Meaning What You Say

Sometimes kids just don't listen. You have tried the strategies suggested in Metacognition, Managing Impulsivity and Listening With Understanding and Empathy. Your child is still not responding. What do you do next?

Vanessa vividly recalls her first horseback-riding lesson taken when she was in her early forties. Feeling awkward, anxious, and self-conscious on top of what seemed to be an absolutely enormous animal, she concentrated on just staying on the horse at a slow walk. "Okay, Vanessa," her instructor, Amy, called out. "Now you're going to look to the left, press a little with your left leg, and gently pull the left rein to make Lady turn toward me." Vanessa thought she followed the directions, but Lady blithely turned right, instead, toward the barn. Embarrassed, Vanessa laughed, "Well, I guess right is an OK direction to go." But Amy was emphatic: "NO! NO! NO! When you are riding, you have to make the horse do what you want her to do. If you say left, right is not acceptable!" At that moment, Vanessa remembers thinking, Where is Amy when I'm at the playground or the mall with my kids and they ignore me? I really could use someone to coach me then! Vanessa eventually learned to ride fairly well, in part because she came to accept the necessary authority she needed for riding safely. But she also thought a lot about the necessity of following through with her own children if they, as Lady did, decided to just ignore a directive she had given.

It is common for children to ignore requests they don't like and for parents to repeat themselves as if they believe their child did not hear them.

The embarrassment that Vanessa felt when Lady ignored her and went her own way probably did evoke similar feelings to when our children ignore or disobey us in public. Especially when children are in a crowd of other children or other stimulating situations, parents may feel uncertain of their own authority. Not wanting to cause a scene, or trigger a meltdown, or have their authority flouted publicly, parents may sometimes avoid taking the actions necessary to ensure their children are safe and well behaved. This can result in scenes where parents might appear to be unconcerned or unaware that their children are behaving inappropriately. Parents may be unwilling to take decisive action because they don't want to embarrass their child or they themselves don't want to be further embarrassed. This is a difficult spot for a parent to be in, and is a dilemma almost all of us have experienced at one time or another. We have already discussed how using metacognitive strategies before and during over-stimulating situations can prevent or lessen the intensity of misbehavior. Sometimes, however, the stimulation is just too much for the child, and things spiral out of control. Or, if agreed-upon expectations about some behavior have been handled inconsistently in the past, the child may feel compelled to test limits in order to determine what exactly you mean by "settle down" or "use an inside voice, please."

If you have already tried the metacognitive strategies, those for managing impulsivity, and have listened with understanding and empathy, and you still are not getting cooperation, then it is time to move to the next level. These are times when you need to teach your children that your words *mean something*, that they are not vague wishes or hopes, and that you expect cooperation and compliance. Parents are most effective in doing this when they use actions rather than more words.

It is common for children to ignore requests they don't like and for parents to repeat themselves as if they believe their child did not *hear* them. Robert MacKenzie (1998) writes about the "dance" that takes place as well-intentioned parents ask nicely, explain, cajole, or lecture, to little avail. They become so frustrated as they find their child does not respond until the fourth or fifth reminder or until they yell or erupt in anger. This dance is exhausting and disheartening for parents. They are left feeling indignant that their kindness and patience are responded to with such disrespect and lack of cooperation, and they feel remorseful and guilty after they have reacted angrily.

Although the larger topic of setting effective limits is beyond the scope of this book, there are some basic principles worth considering.

- First and foremost, *it is important that you have your child's attention before you start speaking.* Refer to the section in the Chapter on Listening with Understanding and Empathy re: teaching basic listening skills.
- *It is important to be clear in what you are requesting.* "It's time for dinner" does not convey what you want your child to do. Instead, you might say something like, "In five minutes dinner will be on the table. When the timer goes off, you need to turn off the TV and come to the table."
- *Follow up verbal requests with "action messages."* If you state an expectation, your child has to be held accountable. So, for example, if your child does not comply with the request to turn off the television, and you are certain that she heard you, then it is necessary to calmly go into the room and turn it off yourself, and escort her to the dining room. If your son is playing with friends and is too close to a busy road, you

need to go over there physically and bring him back if he does not heed your call.

- ***If your child does not comply, there have to be consequences.*** Think about it: If you have a family rule about not hitting, and your eight-year-old daughter continually is punching her sister on the arm, what do you do? A verbal apology is not enough to teach her not to do it again. There needs to be an appropriate and related consequence that will convey that you are serious about the no-hitting rule. While she sits in time-out, she should be expected to come up with some strategies to help her "remember" the rule. Appropriate consequences should also include some "reparations" if someone has been hurt or property damaged.

Some consequences just naturally follow: If Jamie leaves his baseball glove outside, it may get stolen or ruined in the rain. It's sad, but hopefully his experience of loss and regret will teach him to be more careful with his belongings (that is, if parents do not rush out to buy him a new one). More often, parents have to think of a consequence that will help the child to remember the next time that we mean what we say. This is especially true when coming up with appropriate consequences in the heat of the moment.

In order for consequences to be effective in teaching the desired behavior, they must:

- ***Follow logically from the misbehavior.*** In school, a child who repeatedly fails to bring in his homework may be helped to remember by having to spend his recess doing homework instead of playing with his friends. The homework has to be done because it supports learning. The teacher can't let him lose valuable class time doing it, so recess is the only discretionary time left. It is a consequence that follows logically from the behavior.

The parents of six-year-old Henry told him to stay with them and not run around the grocery store, picking out his own items. The first time they turned their backs, he disappeared to the toy aisle and returned with a water gun. The toy was put back, and he spent the rest of the shopping trip having to hold his father's hand. Henry was embarrassed but never again ran off on his own at the store.

- *Be given in a calm and non-punitive way.* Parents have a better chance of achieving this if they have anticipated problems ahead of time and are prepared to act. Thus, if you know your child tends to get over stimulated and out of control at birthday parties, you can rehearse with him proper party behavior before you leave. Have a plan for dealing with misbehavior if it should occur. You might try removing him temporarily from the scene and sitting with him until he regains self-control, or you may have to just go home before the cake is served. If he knows the expectations and understands when he has crossed the line and he still misbehaves, then it is appropriate and right to follow through with the consequence. If you feel sorry for him or rationalize that the behavior is not that bad, he will have no way of knowing what the limits are. If you have this plan worked out ahead of time, you will be less likely to react in an angry way. Once the consequence has been imposed— whether it is five minutes in time-out or we have to go home now—avoid any further explanations or lecturing. Allow the consequence to do its work all by itself.

- *Be imposed as soon as possible after the misbehavior.* The longer you wait, the less impact the consequence has.

- *Be short and simple.* It can be difficult to come up with logical consequences. Days or weeks of "grounding" or no television or play dates usually do not provide any added value to the learning experience. If your son does not adhere to the time limit for video games, he loses them the following day, no further discussion needed. If Sally jumps in the basket of clean laundry with her muddy shoes on because she thought it would be fun, she needs to re-wash that load of laundry and fold it when it is dry. (*See MacKenzie's book for excellent ideas for choosing and imposing consequences.*)

To be honest, it can be tiring to consistently enforce our expectations. Sometimes it may not seem worth it to follow up with an action message or to risk a melt down on the playground, and we just want to let it go this one time. But following up with action messages and consequences is a crucial investment in our children's development. It helps them understand that basic rules are there for a reason: They are guidelines that ensure that we can live together safely, peacefully, and productively. When children get the message early on that there is no pay-off to breaking rules, they will be less likely to test other rules later on, such as those governing speed-limits, academic cheating, or financial misconduct that carry much more serious consequences. Better to put the time and effort in when children are young and more eager to please than when they are adolescents and consequences are so much more difficult to impose.

In this chapter we demonstrate how Thinking and Communicating with Clarity and Precision involves two important aspects of language. First is to model and encourage a love of language, to help children develop a rich and varied vocabulary, not so much for getting better grades or test scores, but to unlock meaning. The better command of language we have, the better we can understand, describe, and feel that we have some control over our own experiences. Second, we acknowledge that even children with exceptionally well-developed language skills may not yet have learned that we mean what we say. Children who can rely on their parents' word—even if it results in some temporary discomfort or unhappiness when a consequence is imposed—are securely grounded in their parents' rightful, kind, and compassionate authority. In the long run, this will help them understand that there has to be some structure, some common understanding of how we behave toward one another. In a confusing and contradictory world, this will give them a reliable guide for the decisions they will have to make.

Four More Tips

Keep explanations brief and to the point

Sometimes, perhaps, we say too much. Maybe our explanations of why certain behaviors are or are not acceptable go on so long as to cause children's eyes to glaze over and their ears and brain to tune out. Keep your explanations clear, brief and to the point: "It's not safe." "Hands are not for hitting." "It's not acceptable to say mean things to your sister." To ensure understanding, ask your child to explain the rule back to you in her own words. Keep your praise and acknowledgment simple and to the point. Saying something like, "Thank you for helping your little sister when she fell down. We all appreciate how kind you were to her," is more effective than a lengthy speech.

Refrain from "bad words"

Bad language has broken through the border between the adult world and the world of childhood. It is everywhere, on television, in song lyrics, in overheard cellphone conversations, and at Little League games. It can be such a habitual part of many adults' speech that they are completely unaware of what they are saying.

If children hear their parents using bad language, they will use it also—sometimes at a most embarrassing or inappropriate time. Children will use the language they hear and not even know what it means or how offensive it can be. Try to think of it this way: Bad language is basically spewing. It coarsens the child's mind and forestalls the development of language that can more accurately express what a person is thinking or feeling. It certainly does not contribute to any positive remedy. Bad language is a poor substitute for a *real* vocabulary of feelings.

Try to monitor the language your child has been exposed to. If you catch yourself in a moment of anger, saying things to your child that you shouldn't, back up and try again. "You know what? I shouldn't have said that. I feel very frustrated, but that's not a reason to use bad language. I'm going to try to catch myself next time and use better words instead."

Teach the art of giving a compliment

Because we live in a time when put-downs, complaints, and sarcastic comments roll so easily off the tongue, children have few role models or guidelines for giving compliments. In addition to being clear and specific in our own praise, we can explicitly teach our children how to offer a compliment to someone else. A nice conversation starter at the dinner table is to go around the table and have each family member say one thing they appreciate about each person there. Many people feel awkward and embarrassed when receiving a compliment. Be sure to say "thank you" or "that made me feel happy" when your child compliments you, and teach him to do the same.

Be a role model

A friend's father made his living as a radio announcer. In part because he wrote some of his own copy, and partly because he was so careful to pronounce words correctly, he delighted in researching new words, which he shared with his children. "Where do you think that word comes from?" he would ask them with a smile. "What does it remind you of?" To this day his adult son continues to be intrigued by unfamiliar words he may encounter in his reading. He enjoys looking up their meanings and incorporating them into his own vocabulary. The delight that parents take in continuing to learn new words or in finding just the *right* word to express that thought or feeling will be a value that is automatically absorbed by their children.

Chapter 6

I Believe in You:
Questioning and Posing Problems

In Chapter 4, we touch on the importance of questions for effective relationship building. We expand on those ideas in this chapter so that you will have a well-equipped "communication toolbox" to see you through many different types of conversations.

Well-constructed questions are good tools that open up the possibility for deeper understanding and allow us to really hear the thoughts and feelings that underlie behavior. Using questions effectively involves engaging your metacognitive strategies as your inner voice prepares you for the encounter. It involves issues of timing, phrasing, and tone of voice. We also look at how we can increase the clarity of the questions we ask to improve the quality of the discussion and move things further along toward good problem resolution.

Let's start with the role of Metacognition, because, as always, Metacognition keeps us from jumping to conclusions and, instead, focuses us on questions about what might really be going on. In their book *Difficult Conversations*, Douglas Stone, Bruce Patton,

Questioning and posing problems

How do you know?

Having a questioning attitude; knowing what data are needed & developing questioning strategies to produce those data. Finding problems to solve.

and Sheila Heen (1999) of the Harvard Negotiation Project explain that "Certainty locks us out of their story. Curiosity lets us in" (p.37). An attitude of curiosity acknowledges that there are usually *many different* contributing factors to a situation, and that we don't *yet* know all of them. Such an attitude increases the complexity of our thinking. It opens up thinking and communicating to permit a fuller understanding of one's self and others. That fuller understanding—of feelings, beliefs, and events—is what enables us to get to a more satisfying resolution of the problem.

If we approach an encounter with curiosity instead of certainty, we are automatically predisposed to ask questions of ourselves. Here's how the difference between an attitude of certainty versus one of curiosity might look when compared side by side:

CERTAINTY	CURIOSITY
He's always trying to push my buttons.	I wonder what he's thinking and feeling to make him behave that way? I wonder how I might be contributing to his behavior?
I am so fed up with her attitude.	Why is this getting on my nerves so much?
He is so ungrateful.	What is making me feel so unappreciated? Is there some part of this that I am not aware of?
I am going to give her a piece of my mind!	I wonder if she is aware of how I feel? How will she react if I tell her? Is it possible that I don't have the whole story?
I will not tolerate this behavior!	What is the best way for me to approach him on this? What is causing him to do these things? Is he aware that it is inappropriate? Has he been taught the right behavior?

One important aspect of asking good questions is that they should be supported by our *positive suppositions.* Costa and Kallick (2000) write about the importance of positive presuppositions in the classroom: "Positive presuppositions assume capability and empowerment" (p. 41). For parents, positive presuppositions are simply our best beliefs about our children. They embody our acceptance and delight in exactly who our children are. Positive presuppositions are the convictions we convey to our children that they are good people who we know to be well-intentioned and capable. Positive presuppositions also imply a can-do attitude about fixing problematic situations. They imbue the conversation with a conviction of hope rather than discouragement. When questions are supported by positive suppositions, the wording and tone of voice create conditions that lead us to thoughtful solutions. When our questions are framed in a way that conveys positive presuppositions, we avoid the zingers, sarcasm, and barely concealed anger or disappointment that so easily spoil communication. Consider these two questions:

1. Why aren't you able to share your things when your friends come over?

2. *What would help you feel more comfortable about sharing with your friends?*

The first question implies a lack of capability (Why aren't you able….) and likely puts the child on the defensive. The second version acknowledges, without judgment, the child's feelings of discomfort and implies that a solution is possible. Try to identify the positive presuppositions—or the lack of them—in the following pairs of questions. As you read them, think about how your child might react to each one.

1. Why do you two always have to argue?

2. *How can we solve this problem so that both people are happy?*

1. Why do I always have to nag you to brush your teeth and put your toys away?

2. *How can we help you keep track of what you have to do?*

1. Do we have to get you a tutor so you can get good grades?

2. *What do you think is getting in your way of doing better in math?*

Notice that many of the negatively loaded questions start with the word *why*. "Why" is a perfectly respectable word and has many good uses, but when used to demand accountability from our children, it invites defensiveness and tends to close down thinking. "Why" places the child in an uncomfortable spotlight, exposed and vulnerable. Starting off with the word "how" or "what," especially when you include yourself in the team of problem solvers addressing the issue, is more likely to lead to a productive effort to resolve the situation.

Costa and Kallick (2000) describe several attributes of questions that give us a better chance of opening up thinking about a problem situation. In addition to infusing our questions with positive presuppositions, we also want to make them *invitational*. There are several ways of doing this. First, we want to monitor our tone of voice to make sure that it conveys warmth and optimism. This may require us to delay having the conversation until we've had a chance to work through our feelings of irritation, disappointment, or discouragement, so that our voice is scrubbed clean of the undercurrents those feelings create. No matter how artfully you construct your sentences, if the tone of voice conveys something else, your chances of success are diminished. We are not saying that you need to be "Stepford parents" who never show any negative feelings. Of course you are going to feel annoyed or even angry at times. Maybe your emotional reaction (if it is under control and not too intense) can be a good reality check for a child who is repeatedly stepping over the line. Children need to learn that their behaviors have an impact on people. But, just because of the power differential between you, any conversation about problematic behavior needs to be held in an atmosphere of trust and support.

Costa and Kallick also suggest phrasing questions in a way that conveys tentativeness. This is done with tone of voice and by choice of words. This is something you already have been practicing when you Listen with Understanding and Empathy. When you *paraphrase*, you speak in a tone of voice that almost humbly asks, "Is this what you're thinking? Am I getting this right?" When you convey tentativeness in your questions, you also convey that you are not claiming to have all the answers. You are inviting your child to engage with you in trying to figure something out.

Your choice of words can also be invitational. Instead of saying, "I'll tell you what we're going to do," you could ask, "How might we work this out?" The use of *plurals* stimulates thinking. When you structure a question with plurals, such as, "What are some *ways* we can solve this problem?" you make it clear that there is no one right answer and that creative or unconventional solutions are welcome. When children are encouraged to come up with lots of possible solutions—even if they seem silly or far-fetched—they are usually able to select at least one or two that have a chance of working. (More about that in Thinking like a Problem Solver.)

What we hope to accomplish by an artful use of questioning is to reach the greatest possible clarity about a situation in a way that stimulates productive efforts toward a solution. Too often, we rush to settle on a solution before fully exploring the different dimensions of a problem. The problem-solving part comes only after good questioning has enabled full exploration of the problem. Questioning and Posing Problems, particularly when simultaneously used with Metacognition and Listening with Understanding and Empathy, can make this happen.

Let's listen in on a conversation with 10-year-old Gabriela and her mother to see how this might unfold:

Gabriela: I'm quitting soccer. I can't stand it any more.

Mom: (Quite taken aback as there have been issues about
          Gabriela wanting to quit things before. Nevertheless, she
          decides to let her curiosity take the lead, and activates her
          empathic listening skills.): You sound like you've just had
          it. You feel like quitting?

Gabriela: I've got better things to do with my time than put up with
           that bunch of mean girls.

Mom: You sound really fed up. *What's going on with you and those girls?*

Gabriela: I'll tell you what's going on! Valerie, Sherri and Janice act like they're the only ones who know how to play the right way.

Mom: Well, that can't be easy to take. *What is it that they say and do when they act that way?*

Gabriela: Well, Janice yelled at me in front of everyone. She said I was out of position and I got in her way. When I was running downfield like I was supposed to, Valerie actually knocked into me.

Mom: She knocked into you?

Gabriela: Well, I don't know if she did it on purpose, but I fell down and Sherri started laughing.

Mom: That sounds like a horrible soccer practice you had. Did you get hurt?

Gabriela (pause): No, actually, that part was pretty funny. I didn't really mind Sherri laughing. She helped me up. I just felt so frustrated. I didn't know if I was where I was supposed to be or not, but I hated when Janice yelled at me. I don't think she knows what she's doing either!

Mom (slowly and thoughtfully): So…it sounds like there might be two main things bothering you. Could it be that maybe all the girls are kind of confused about exactly where they should be and what they're supposed to be doing in their positions? And it sure doesn't help the situation when some of them start turning on each other.

Gabriela: Exactly! It is so frustrating when you're trying to do a good job, but you don't know just what it is you're supposed to be doing. And Janice *acts* like she knows it all, but I think she's mixed up, too. Instead of helping each other, we're all kind of arguing about it. It just doesn't have that good team feeling we're supposed to have.

Mom: I wonder if the other girls—even the girls who are acting mean—are having some of the same feelings you're having about this?

Gabriela: I could ask some of the other girls what they think. Maybe we could talk to the coach about it. Maybe she could help us work this out.

Mom: It sounds like you are putting so much thought and effort into this. I'm proud of the way you are sticking to it and trying to make it better, even after such a hard practice.

Gabriela: Yeah, I want it to be more fun. I'm going to give Sherri a call.

In this scenario, Mom's questions helped Gabriela work through some of her frustration and embarrassment and enabled her to clarify a possible source of discord on the team. The questions Mom asked helped Gabriela eventually begin to think of some possible ways to begin to address the problem. She did not directly confront Gabriela's assessment of her teammates as "mean girls" but, as Gabriela was helped to figure out what actually happened that day, her perceptions of them began to soften on their own. Notice that Mom's acknowledgement at the end cited Gabriela's persistence and effort—this from a girl with a history of quitting!

Keeping the idea of positive presuppositions in mind can help parents through those times when they feel tired, discouraged, and frustrated. All parents sometimes feel like their best efforts go nowhere; that there must be something very wrong when they keep repeating themselves, and the same problems keep cropping up. It is at those moments when we are most likely to lose it and perhaps say things we regret. Those are the moments when we will most appreciate that "communication toolbox" that Habits of Mind can provide.

Children at Work
Achieving Meaning
and Success with
Habits of Mind

*Think of learning as a moving
target in which we travel along a
continuum, starting as a novice,
becoming an expert, then becoming
novice again until we reach another
point of mastery and the process
repeats itself.*

Children learn persistence when they are successful at a challenging task. The art in building persistence is in offering a task that is just challenging enough, but not overwhelming.

National Association of School Psychologists

Courage doesn't always roar. Sometimes courage is the little voice at the end of the day that says, "I'll try again tomorrow."

Mary Anne Radmacher

Chapter 7

The Art and Science of Persistence

A five-year-old, after days of failed attempts, finally balances on her two-wheeler; an eight-year-old spends hours putting together a complex Lego construction; and an eleven-year-old saves part of his allowance until he can buy his own video game.

Children often persist in achieving what they want—without cajoling or badgering and despite falls, bruises, setbacks, and sacrifices. The challenge is how to encourage this same drive, not only when kids are motivated, but also when their enthusiasm has faded or their good intentions never get past go. Through persistence, children learn to play the piano, turn in their homework every day, perfect their keyboarding skills, or master the intricacies of a good soccer defense. Persistence makes it possible to experience firsthand the benefits of practice and to fully develop talents and competencies. Only with persistence can one enjoy the satisfaction that comes with a task well done. We open this part of the book, Children at Work, with Persistence because this Habit of Mind is the first step to a child's success.

Persisting

Stick to it!

Persevering in a task through to completion; remaining focused. Looking for ways to reach your goal when stuck. Not giving up.

Prerequisites for Persistence

Most people think of persistence as only "never giving up." If you try hard enough, you will succeed. In fact, this definition only guarantees the likelihood of coming upon a dead end at some point in time. A persevering child who does not understand the process of long division will not be able to do his homework despite his best efforts. A motivated but novice runner won't get through a marathon without more training. Most kids will need some help "unpacking" what goes into this Habit of Mind if they are going to make it their own. A hybrid of attitudes, conditions, and skills play a vital role in our ability to persist, all of which need to be in sync for a person to be able to stick with the hard work of achieving a goal.

Just Challenging Enough

Particularly with children, "just challenging enough" is the all-important condition—a just-right goal—within reach but requiring a stretch. Kids need this balance of learning new concepts or skills and also having the time and experience to practice, express, and enjoy what they are learning. This is how mastery develops. Think of learning as a moving target in which we travel along a continuum, starting as a novice, becoming an expert, then becoming novice again until we reach another point of mastery and the process repeats itself. Persistence may keep us on track, but it is the positive benefits of gaining mastery that will also pull us forward. In a study of best teaching practices by the National Research Center on English Learning and Achievement, Richard Allington (2002) describes the impact when kids were given books they could successfully read. They got better at reading. Some challenging texts were useful for instruction, but level-appropriate books gave the children the opportunity to use and master the new skills and strategies. "Simply put," he says, "students need enormous quantities of successful reading to become independent, proficient readers." They need practice reading books they can comprehend and understand with accuracy, whether they are high or low achieving.

Parents won't be able to custom fit all of the events in their children's lives, but they can ensure that their children experience some activities in which they will encounter the need for and the rewards of this Habit of Mind. The child for whom school is a constant struggle will benefit from some activities in which he can more readily see the connection between his effort and successful results. At one school, a ballroom dance program provided that opportunity. At the end of the year, when the 5th grade students performed for a group of adults, many of them commented that their positive experience learning how to dance taught them what they had to do in school to achieve and inspired them with the confidence that they could do it. Similarly, children who easily ace everything they do need to be challenged out of their comfort zone to get some practice as a novice.

On Your Mark, Get Ready

Basic organizational skills give us a head start with this Habit of Mind. Planning ahead of time can mitigate the natural reaction to give up at that first realization that we don't know the next step or don't have what we need. People have a better chance of persisting through a difficult task if they come prepared–if they take the time to first size up the problem (*see Managing Impulsivity, Chapter 8*) and then develop a plan of action (*see Metacognition, Chapter 9*). This means thinking through what we want, the goal; what we have to do, the challenge; and how we are going to achieve it, the means.

An adult might think: "Okay, finishing this report is going to take me at least two weeks, not two nights, and I need to get the marketing department to run some figures right away." With some self-evaluation—an honest look at our own strengths and a willingness to make provisions for our limitations–an adult will make strategic decisions. "I know how to do the target goals but have a hard time with scheduling. I will ask Jack to help me."

But most kids won't have this level of self-awareness or a memory bank of experiences to draw from to put the pieces of the persistence puzzle together. Tasks such as completing long-term assignments or cleaning up a messy room can be overwhelming. Kids procrastinate because they don't know where to start. Or they think, "I have plenty of time. I can do it later." Children need help at home, like they do in school, breaking down a task into manageable steps. The idea is that gradually they will learn to master each step and eventually achieve their goal. It is the small goals that give kids a sense of accomplishment and motivate them to take the next step. The little victories are what allow children to look around, take stock, and revel in the fact that they have come a bit farther toward their ultimate goal.

Navigating the Roadblocks

Even with the best of planning, roadblocks are inevitable, and so are the negative emotions they trigger. We may have back-up plans and alternative routes, but adults and kids alike are apt to get frustrated or anxious when encountering those small and big bumps to the finish line. People who have mastered this Habit of Mind recognize obstacles as a natural part of the process. They expect to face moments of frustration and discouragement or even despair. They anticipate having dark moments along the way. They are more willing to ride them out, give themselves a pep talk, or use the emotional discomfort as a stimulus to come up with a better plan. If we are unprepared for these negative reactions, however, they can shake our confidence or cause us to doubt the validity of our ideas. We may become convinced we will never get it right and give up.

> ...we want children to learn to pay attention to what their feelings are telling them and to think about what to do.

Kids will need strategies to manage a host of uncomfortable feelings as they weather the lows that are part of achieving all worthwhile goals. It helps to name some of the feelings that can sweep over them as they struggle to focus and stay with a task. By naming such feelings, we normalize the experience: "Yes, it can be frustrating when you're trying to understand something so difficult." Or, "I know it can feel boring to practice your multiplication tables over and over, but you'll feel proud when you can zip through them quickly." Or, "I know you want to be on the team like your brother, but he is two years older and has been practicing a long time. It is hard when you are just beginning to learn a sport." Your empathic restating of how your child feels at those moments is a lifeline. It helps her to feel not so all alone with a daunting task.

Over time, we want children to learn to pay attention to what their feelings are telling them and to think about what to do. "Okay, I am frustrated and tired. I know I am making progress, but I need a break." Or, "I am stuck. I need some help." Or it may mean acknowledging their anxiety and teaching them a way to relax, perhaps through simple breathing exercises. Bright and confident children can be particularly vulnerable to succumbing to these feelings. At the first hint of things not going as planned, they feel threatened. They may claim to lose interest when, in fact, they are just not used to the challenge and are afraid they will fail. Kids need to know these feelings are a natural part of grappling with learning and any achievement.

It Comes Down to a Mindset

A group of 5th graders were given a set of puzzles. At first, all the kids enjoyed them, but, as the puzzles became more difficult, some quickly lost interest, while others became more intrigued in trying to solve them. The one distinguishing feature the researchers could find between the two groups was their mindset—their attitude about intelligence, talent, and skills, says Carol Dweck (2006) in her book *Mindset: the New Psychology of Success*. The kids who believed that brainpower is "fixed"–you're born with "smarts" or you're not—assumed that they lacked the ability and then gave up. The students who persisted had what she calls a "growth mindset." They had an expansive view of intelligence akin to what Costa and Kallick (2000) ascribe to–that through effort, you can improve your skills, talents, and abilities.

The growth mindset doesn't mean that with lessons and practice, you can be another Beethoven, says Dweck. It means that "a person's true potential is unknown and unknowable; that it's impossible to foresee what can be accomplished with years of passion, toil, and training." It means that with a just-right challenge and with the right tools and support, persistence can make a difference in achieving those tasks that always seem out of reach. Parents have to believe in the growth mindset and convey it in their expectations, in their day-to-day interactions with their children, and in their support. In this way, their children can come to believe in and act on their potential, too.

Kids' View

Eight-year-old Elena was full of good intentions in 3rd grade but had a poor track record for getting her schoolwork or chores completed without a lot of badgering. She procrastinated often and would then cut corners to make a deadline. Her parents were more frustrated than she was. Their hope for their daughter's maturation didn't seem to be happening on its own. A note from her teacher indicated that Elena was beginning to fall behind in school and the teacher thought she would likely need some help with the more challenging curriculum and demands of 4th grade. With summer break soon approaching, the teacher recommended that they use the long vacation to give Elena some practice in persisting. She suggested that they ask Elena to choose one project she wanted to do over the summer break and that they choose another task that she had to do, a chore, for example. Persisting with both experiences would lay the groundwork for a better start when school resumed in the fall.

Because her grandmother had recently taught her to crochet, Elena decided to make her a scarf for her birthday. Hands-on activities like making a gift allow children to experience time-on-task in a positive and meaningful way. Elena was also highly motivated. She was very fond of her grandmother. Making the scarf was something she wanted to do.

To keep Elena on schedule, her parents cut out a paper pattern and hung it in her room and had Elena figure out how much she would have to complete each day. They also asked Elena to choose how she wanted to be reminded when she went off schedule. Elena made a birthday card for her grandmother and said her parents could just point to the card that they attached to the bulletin board in the kitchen.

For the second task, her parents decided to hold her accountable for cleaning up her room. They were specific about their expectations. During the week, she would have to make her bed and keep the floor of her room clear rather than covered with her possessions. By noon on Saturday, everything would have to be in its proper place. To help her achieve this goal, they all examined the things in her room and decided to purchase two colorful bins and a second bookcase. Elena wanted to put her dolls, arts supplies, and board games in the new bookcase. She decided to use one bin for her "big stuff" like sports equipment and use the other one for things she didn't have a chance to put away during the week. She said it would be easier to clear out one bin on Saturday than a whole room.

Elena had several meltdowns during the summer. The first week she didn't notice a mistake in her crocheting and had to undo ten rows. By the second week, she said crocheting was boring. She was on the verge of giving up. Fortunately, her parents were prepared for setbacks. Instead of getting upset and exacerbating the situation, they listened to her frustration and asked her what she could do to get back on track. Elena decided to divide her crocheting time up –do some with her mother while she knitted after dinner, some in the morning, and some while she watched television.

By the end of the summer, Elena finished the scarf for her grandmother and was better at keeping up with her room. And her parents had learned how to respond to her meltdowns and setbacks more effectively. They were all more prepared for 4ᵗʰ grade and looked forward to working with the new teacher on setting goals for Elena to keep up with schoolwork. (See Chapter 9 for more on Elena.)

The Persistence Tool Box

We like to think of persistence as a large toolbox containing useful strategies that can be pulled out as needed. Just as we wouldn't climb a high mountain without a trail map, good hiking shoes, drinking water, and other specialized equipment, we shouldn't think of starting a difficult job without a variety of equipment found in

our persistence toolbox. For adults, of course, the toolbox is a mental one. But we know that children benefit from and enjoy visual cues. In one school, each classroom was provided with a decorated photo box labeled "Persistence Toolbox." Each toolbox contained laminated strips of paper with a different persistence strategy written on each. Children were encouraged to go to the toolbox when stuck, so they could get some inspiration. Some of the strategies included:

- Believe in yourself. *You can do this!*
- Make a plan to solve the problem or achieve your goal.
- Take time to think it through.
- Have a back-up plan.
- Assemble all the materials you will need to achieve your goal.
- Break the problem down into smaller pieces.
- Check in regularly – how is my plan working?
- If one strategy doesn't work, back up and try another.
- Take deep breaths to help you relax.
- Take short breaks from the problem when you are tired or frustrated.

- If you are stuck, remember that it's okay to try a different way.
- Picture yourself as successful.
- Remember: Reaching success is a bumpy road.
- Know in advance whom you can call on for help.
- Give yourself a pep talk.

It may be helpful to consider for a moment something challenging you had to do. What were some of the strategies you used to get you through those difficult moments? Did you visualize a successful outcome? How did you know when your plan wasn't working and you had to go back and rework it? What did you say to yourself to keep going? How did you know when it was time to reach out for help? Some strategies will be helpful in the *preparation stage* (e.g., make a plan; make a back-up plan; make a list of everything you might need; think of who might be helpful to you in getting this job done).

Other strategies will be helpful in the *execution* (e.g., break the overall job into small, manageable tasks; keep tabs on how you are progressing; check back frequently to your original plan to see if you are on track). Still other strategies are essential to keep your *motivation* up and your emotions working for you (e.g., celebrate incremental successes; give yourself a pep talk; take a break when you are frustrated or tired). Be as specific as possible in visualizing all the many facets of persistence you have experienced. Keep this in mind when encouraging your child with his challenges.

Work Is Hard

It seems too obvious to point out, but an often-overlooked fact of life is that work is hard! We may need to remind ourselves and our children that, yes, it is hard to do a long-term project, practice a musical instrument regularly, compensate for a learning disability day after day, spend time doing drills before you get to play a sport, keep on weeding the garden even after you feel hot and tired, take the puppy outside for the hundredth time until he learns not to go in the house, write a good essay instead of the bare minimum, etc., etc., etc. It is hard to do all those things because they are often tiring, boring, and, at the time, may even seem

It may be helpful to consider for a moment something challenging you had to do.

pointless. Because we do not always get an immediate payoff for our labor, it is a leap of faith to accept that there will be a reward at the end.

Our job as parents is to instill confidence that effort will indeed bring successful results, but that it often takes time. We need to help our children learn to choose and use the tools that will get them through the labor, boredom, fatigue, and discouragement; to point out the progress they are making so they will believe that it is worthwhile. *You worked so hard on that scarf, and I can see how it is coming together. It is just beautiful! Those sugar snap peas will thrive because you weeded around them. Look how big they are getting. Let's taste how sweet they are. I think our puppy is beginning to get the idea. Thank you for all your hard work in helping him learn.* (See Chapter 8, Managing Impulsivity, and Chapter 9, Thinking about Thinking.)

Encouraging Kid-Size Persistence

Build on success. Remember, kids are not starting from scratch when it comes to persistence. Build on their positive experiences. Make them aware of their own success stories. Direct your praise to their effort and the process leading to their achievement. "You put a lot of time into this science project. You thought through every step and worked on it throughout most the day, even when it meant you couldn't go out with your friends. It was hard work and you had to give up having some fun, but you did it. Great job."

Share your own experiences. Tell your child about some incident in which persistence, or its lack, was the game changer for you. Or simply talk out loud about your own efforts as you try to accomplish a task—as simple as paying bills or as complicated as completing a major project in the house or for work. Talk about the steps and strategies you employ. Acknowledge when you make mistakes and how you correct them. Let your children hear about your frustrations or need for assistance. Show them how you deal with the stress and challenges. "I am so fed up with this project today," or "It takes me a long time to get started. I have to spend so much time making sure I understand the directions. I know I will feel more confident once I begin to see it take shape." Familiarize them with all aspects of this Habit of Mind.

Tell stories. Take advantage of the stories involving persistence that fill the media, literature, and history. But be sure to balance your selection of super stars with quieter heroes, the fleeting moment of glory with the effort and the missed foul shots. The slow, plodding tortoise in Aesop's Fable is an unlikely winner of a race. The confident, spunky hare is also an unlikely loser. That's what makes this fable so perfect. With the superstars, talk about their strikeouts, their long hours of practice as well as their home runs. For older children, the true story of how Ernest Shackleton endured unspeakably harsh conditions when his ship was crushed by Antarctic ice will surely inspire. Against impossible odds, he fought his way across nearly a thousand miles of the roughest seas in the world, in a tiny open lifeboat, to secure help to go back and rescue his stranded crew. That story sets a high standard indeed for what it is to persist.

Tell your children about the value of practice. Malcolm Gladell (2008) cites a study by K. Ander Ericcson that identified 10,000 hours as the amount of time people need to master their art. Ten thousand hours of preparation and hard work are behind what often appears as natural talent in the spectators' eyes. Even exceptions, such as a child prodigy, often fit this rule upon closer analysis. Gladwell quotes psychologist Michael Howe from his book, Genius Explained (1999) who says Mozart's earliest compositions were largely arrangements of work by other composers. His true genius was not fully realized until he was in his 20s. After "10,000 hours of practice," Mozart began creating his most masterful, original compositions.

Ask your children about their experiences with persistence. Is managing time or knowing where to begin easy or difficult? Ask them to tell you about a time when they are glad they persisted. Praise the process more than the product or the intelligence of your child. Praise can encourage, but it also can inhibit a child.

Practice Persistence

Do it together. A family project is an opportunity for you and your children to go through the steps together. Make explicit each stage, from preparation to execution. "Okay, we will need to get two rakes to clear up the back yard. Let's work for 20 minutes and see how far we get. Then we can estimate how long it will take us to finish the job. We will build in time for some breaks, too. This is going to be hard work, but we'll make it fun."

Accept Your Role as Coach. Kids learn by doing. Think of yourself as coach and your child as the player. It is your child's chores, homework, or scales to practice. He is the one who is responsible for doing the work, not you. Be sure to check your own anxiety about your child's performance. Kids are quick to pick up on our feelings. Talk, advise, and guide but remember, it is not your project. You are the coach.

Break the Big Tasks Into Small Steps. This can't be said often enough. It is the successful completion of each small separate step that teaches children to be persistent. For those extra challenging tasks, set up markers along the way, points at which your child can step back and appreciate her work.

Increase stamina gradually. With younger children, start small, gradually building up their ability to stay on task. "You have read for five minutes. Do you want to try adding another two minutes?" Or "I know answering 20 long-division problems is a challenge. You could try doing half before dinner and half later. What works for you?" Or "I know this is a difficult math problem. What have you figured out so far? What makes sense to you? What if you give it another five minutes?" When high school students were monitored for the time they spent on a difficult problem, it took an average of two minutes before they gave up (Gladwell, 2008). At the very least, we want our children to be clear about what they know and don't know. While five or ten minutes more may not solve the problem, it can result in more clarity about what to ask when seeking help from a teacher.

Begin with the end in sight. Visualize the finish line with your children. Point out some of the benefits of getting there. "When you do your chores, I will have more time to play games with you in the afternoon." "Think of how proud you will feel when you bring in this report on Monday."

Make sure they understand the purpose of the task. Chores are what you do when you are part of a family. Showing up for practice goes with being part of a team. Homework is a requirement for school. It's your job.

Liven up the routine. If your children find raking leaves boring, think about how to make it more interesting. One family played music. Their children were younger and happy to sing along. Another family with older children told a story, each person taking a turn to add a scene. One father wisely scheduled the deadline for chores just before going to the mall. "The sooner you get this done, the sooner I can drive you." Or, simply ask for their ideas.

Make time for persistence. Like a good sauce, ideas take time to brew. Anything requiring persistence may not be able to be completed on demand, sandwiched in between ten other activities. Honor the time each step requires as well as the time required to draft, rehearse, test, and finally put together all the pieces.

Plan for problems ahead of time. It is often helpful to observe your child at work first. Quietly watch him doing homework or at Little League practice. Is he focused and paying attention, or distracted? Does he understand what he has to do? Is he clear about the expectations? Does he need help in breaking down the task into more manageable steps? You may discover useful information, so don't rush it. Be sure to see the situation through your child's eyes, too, taking into consideration his work style and temperament, interests and aspirations. (*See Making a Plan* in Chapter 9.)

Help your child anticipate some of the hurdles she may encounter and some ways to deal with them. Robert Brooks, coauthor of *Raising Resilient Children* (2002), suggests, along with setting realistic expectations and preparation, asking your kids, "what if your plan doesn't work?" This question prepares kids in advance for possible setbacks. Forewarned and forearmed, you want your children to view frustration as a signpost, not a dead end. "This way is not working. I need to go a different way." "I'm stuck. I need some help." Make sure your child has a persistence toolbox he can turn to in a jam. Identifying people he can go to for assistance, for example, will defuse some of the anxiety when he needs help later.

If the hurdles seem insurmountable to your child, acknowledge his feelings and find out what he thinks. "Let's take a break and figure out what's getting in the way."

You can also seek help. Talk to your child's teacher for additional insights.

Do Some Self-Reflecting: What's Your Response?

Robert Brooks (2011) came up with a list of questions that can help reveal our own capacity to persist:

"What do I typically tell myself when I make a mistake or don't reach a goal?"

"When goals are not reached, do I tend to back away from the challenge or do I engage in creating more realistic goals?"

"Do I have backup plans that do not fall in the category of self-fulfilling prophecies?"

"Do I recognize that mistakes and setbacks are not indicative of my being a failure but rather provide information for future success?"

"Do I often make excuses to avoid challenging tasks that I believe may lead to failure?"

"What is one instance when confronted by a setback that I displayed self-compassion? What followed from the self-compassion?"

The Motivation Factor

That we must motivate our children is a myth. Rather, we must create conditions that liberate and sustain children's natural, internal motivations.

Art Costa, 2007

A key concern expressed by many parents is that their children lack motivation. Some seem to lack interest in schoolwork or practicing their musical scales, for example. Without motivation, they fear their children are destined to be mediocre at best in what they do. How, they ask, can they promote persistence or any Habit of Mind, when their children seem so unmotivated to begin with?

Motivation has been the topic of research for decades as psychologists, educators, and scientists seek to identify its magical ingredients. Writer Daniel Pink (2009) synthesized four decades of research and studies about motivation and in his book, *Drive*, he offers helpful insights for families on this topic. What motivates most successful people to work hard and persist centers on three conditions, he says: their desire to control their lives, which gives them a sense of *autonomy*; their desire to learn about their world, which helps to build *mastery*; and their desire to accomplish something that endures, which gives them a sense of *purpose*. This is true universally, from preschoolers to adults, from factory workers to artists.

These conditions affect motivation in several ways:

- **Autonomy**. Having a say in what we do, when, how, and with whom empowers and energizes us. This is evident in employee-run companies where morale and effort are usually higher because employees have an important stake in their own actions. It is also seen when students are given a choice in what they learn and how they go about doing it. For example, all 3rd graders may study rain forests, but each child may select an animal to research and become an expert on. This choice increases–and builds on—children's interest and curiosity.

- **Mastery**. When we are doing what we have to do, we typically are complying. When we have a choice, we typically are engaged. The more engaged we are, the more time we are likely to invest and the better we become at what we are doing—and the more motivated. We reach that state that Mihaly Csikszentmihalyi called "flow," in which we are immersed in those "optimal experiences" when challenges are perfectly matched to our abilities; when our goals are clear; when we are focused and committed; and for this moment or task, we are in control (Pink, 2009.)

But such moments are not sustainable indefinitely, nor do they guarantee mastery. Mastery requires hard work. The musician reaches a point where she can create inspired music with others or improvise beautiful compositions. But she wouldn't have gotten there without laying the groundwork with practice. "Mastery is a pain," says Pink (p.123). It demands effort, grit, and deliberate practice. "Mastery often involves working and working and showing little improvement, perhaps with a few moments of flow pulling you along, then making a little progress…" (p 125.) While most children won't have a realistic perspective on how much hard work goes into achieving excellence, the prerequisites for persistence–just challenging enough, step-by-step approach, targeted praise—go a long way to creating the conditions in which children's motivation can thrive.

- **Purpose.** Autonomous people working toward mastery perform at high levels, but that is not the whole picture of what drives them. We are also purpose seekers, says Pink, and studies confirm this. Those with "purpose goals" — to help others improve their lives, to learn, and to grow, for example — report higher levels of satisfaction than those striving for wealth or recognition. Encouraging children to help set the table because they are a contributing part of the family rather than to simply earn part of their allowance may prove a better motivator in the long run. Many children have shown they are capable of great effort and sacrifice as they do chores to earn money for charity, or make sandwiches to distribute to homeless people. When struggling through a difficult chapter in science or social studies, children may be encouraged to persist when we remind them that, despite the difficulty, their efforts now will make a real contribution when they are older. Our country needs citizens who understand their world, who can think and reason for themselves. The hard work they are doing right now is vitally important in helping them to grow into well-informed citizens.

Creating these conditions for motivation on an everyday basis is what the Habits of Mind are all about. Each habit provides one more tool for children to develop autonomy, engagement, mastery and a sense of purpose. (*See Chapter 13, Creating, Imagining, and Innovating for more on motivation.*)

Chapter 8

Slow Down: Managing Impulsivity

As we read in Section I, the impact of impulsivity and distractions on our relationships can be profound. Our ability to fulfill responsibilities in the world of school and work also depends on this key Habit of Mind. Refraining from jumping to conclusions, taking time to gather information and advice before making a decision, setting clear goals, and working with purpose and intention all begin with the ability to stop and think before acting—the habit of Managing Impulsivity.

When it comes to work, children who can manage their impulsivity have a decided advantage over those who are more easily distracted. They pick up information more effectively. They are more likely to listen to or read directions before beginning a task, and thus work more accurately. While these children are paying attention to the teacher as she explains a new concept, their more impulsive classmates are less able to regulate their attention. They can't tune out the interesting noises coming from a nearby construction site or from down the hall, and soon their thoughts are not focused on what they are supposed to be learning. Instead, they are hijacked by distractions. Because their

Managing Impulsivity

Take your time!

Thinking before acting; remaining calm, thoughtful and deliberative.

113

attention was fleeting and intermittent, they have only a vague sense of what the assignment is all about.

When it comes to work, children who can manage their impulsivity have a decided advantage over those who are more easily distracted.

In addition, when it then comes to actually putting pencil to paper, impulsive children tend to charge right in, often missing key words in the directions. They might work a whole page of problems before discovering they did it incorrectly and must do it all over again. Picture yourself laboriously erasing and redoing as the rest of the class moves on, and you get a sense of the costs of impulsivity in terms of frustration, boredom, and corrosion of motivation on a young learner. It is not uncommon to see very bright impulsive children who never quite produce the level of work their verbal skills would predict they are capable of doing. In large part, this is because they are simply not focused on learning. Children who are more skilled at managing impulsivity are better at tuning out distractions and sustaining effort toward learning. They are better able to reflect on their work, to go back and improve it when necessary and so bring it to a higher level of mastery.

In this section we look at some strategies for modeling and teaching the Habit of Managing Impulsivity as it applies to work and responsibilities. Although it is beyond the scope of this chapter to specifically address children with ADHD, we borrow some of the excellent strategies developed by experts in this field, as we believe they benefit all children. We consider some ways of helping children reduce their susceptibility to internal and external distractions. We also suggest some ways of increasing focus on the task at hand, as the ability to focus on what you are doing is a necessary precondition for task commitment and persistence. We are building on the strategies already covered in Managing Impulsivity in the Communications Section. *(See Chapter 3)*

Start With Structure, Expectations, and Routines

Just as we teach our children to take turns on the playground or wait until after dinner to enjoy dessert, we want to be equally clear about our expectations for them in meeting their responsibilities. These expectations will need to be evident not only in what we say but most importantly in our family's daily routines. Beginning teachers are advised that life in the classroom goes much more smoothly if, from Day 1, they establish routines and procedures for all the basic activities such as unpacking backpacks, turning in homework, lining up to go to lunch, taking a spelling test, raising your hand, putting your name on your work, and so on. What these procedures establish is a sense of purpose and serious endeavor that takes place within the walls of the classroom. Establishing routines clears the deck for the more important aspects of learning and ensures that time will not be wasted on housekeeping details. When you observe a well-run classroom, you can see that the majority of children know exactly where things go and what is on the schedule. You notice that they are able to select the right notebook or text, turn to the right page and begin to work with more independence and less teacher talk than in less organized classrooms. Structure and routine minimize the impact of distractions and opportunities for impulsive behavior.

Establishing a few key procedures at home can go a long way toward minimizing some of the frustration and confusion that often accompany homework and other chores and commitments. We *always* clear our plates after dinner, *always* read for at least 20 minutes before bedtime, *and always* do homework before watching television or playing video games.

The Backpack–or the Class Web Page

Since so much important information from school gets delivered via backpack or the class web page, it is important that a parent or responsible adult takes time to check in soon upon arrival home. This is a great transitional activity that can trigger lots of spontaneous conversation: *I see the school is sponsoring a food drive. Let's choose some good things from the pantry to send in. Look at these handwriting sheets. They are done so neatly. Do you remember when it was so hard to remember which way the 'b' went? You didn't eat much of your lunch! What happened? A new library book. This looks great! Let's take a look at your planner and see what needs to be done for tomorrow.* This little ritual makes the handover from school back to home more explicit. Consider it the baton in a relay race. It's as if you are saying to the teacher, "I'll take it from here." It establishes a connection and common purpose in the education of your child.

Think about Everyone's Schedule

Scheduling has to be one of the most challenging aspects of modern

> **Establishing routines clears the deck for the more important aspects of learning.**

parenting. There are so many demands on everyone's time, and the sheer complexity of fitting everything in between arrival home and bedtime is mind-boggling. Nevertheless, addressing schedules may reveal some ways of reducing the stress. You might want to make a list of all the extracurricular activities in which your child participates. Many children do at least one seasonal sport and an additional activity such as karate, dance, gymnastics, art, or a musical instrument. Many children attend religious instruction after school once or twice a week, and many also participate in boy scouts or girl scouts. Most children also enjoy play dates after school. Some children would do this every day if possible. Others sadly turn down invitations because they are booked solid with other scheduled activities.

Life for children is very different now than a few decades ago when we were told to "go out and play" and would happily meet up with other neighborhood kids for bike riding, roller skating, building a snow fort, "exploring," or whatever other free form play we happened to think of. For a variety of reasons, we may never get back to those less structured times but a child who has some time to let off steam and unwind may be better able to concentrate on what has to be done later. Parents need to take a hard look at the family schedule and ask themselves:

- Have we built in time each day to decompress and just enjoy a little time together?
- Is there time for us to eat dinner sitting down together, even if it is take-out?
- Does my child have some time for free play?
- Does my child have opportunities to be outside and get some exercise in the fresh air?

These should be happening pretty much on a daily basis. Of course, if your child is playing soccer or baseball, the fresh air and exercise is taken care of, but participating in a team sport, with its rules and expectations for performance, does not necessarily qualify as "down-time." In addition, you have to build in time for homework and reading. Scheduling this can be tricky, as schedules vary so much from day to day, and so do children's styles and preferences. Some children just have to have a snack and decompress after school before sitting down to do homework. Others are better off getting it done early, as they are too tired after dinner.

Make scheduling part of the family conversation. When there are too many activities crammed into the schedule and too little time, you have a recipe for stress, irritability, and, yes, impulsivity as a natural response to being rushed and overloaded. Sit down together with the calendar, talk about what each family member needs in order to be healthy, productive and happy. Color-code each child's activities so it is readily apparent who is doing what. As the adult in charge of everyone's well-being, you may have to make some hard decisions about which activities can stay and which might have to be cut. Using your empathic listening skills, you may gain some insights into how each child feels about his or her workload, and together you can brainstorm ideas for making things better. You also have to take care of yourself. You might realize that taking two children to eight different activities during the week, monitoring homework, preparing nutritious meals, making sure that they have clean clothes to wear, and taking care of your own work responsibilities, is beyond reasonable expectations. The idea is to slow down a little bit. There are so many enticing choices out there, but your child doesn't have to try absolutely everything and doesn't have to do them all at once. Through these family conversations, you can help your children to prioritize and to make decisions. While you must necessarily take the lead in these conversations, by including your children in the process, you are also teaching them how to manage their time, so eventually they can do it on their own.

The Homework Routine

Your child hasn't seen you all day, both of you have just gotten home and are tired and hungry. You've already agreed as part of your established routine that she would start homework in the kitchen as you prepare dinner, so she sits at the counter and starts to unload her backpack. You hand her a snack and review with her what she has brought home. Together you look at the planner and you see she has a page of math problems, a spelling assignment, a review of science vocabulary words, and a social studies worksheet—about 45 minutes of work altogether. It doesn't seem like much, but you know that she can be distracted by so many things. That 45 minutes can easily stretch to twice that time. You might chat together for a few minutes just to reconnect and then you both need to get busy.

Younger children in the primary grades naturally will require—and are more receptive to—adult supervision. As your child matures, she should begin to internalize this approach and be able to take on this responsibility more independently. Her track record for completing homework will guide the kind of monitoring required. She may eventually prefer to move homework operations up to her room. That's fine as long as she continues to get things done in a timely way. As kids get older, their need for independence grows but, remember, so do the opportunities for distraction. Rather than creating and enforcing an older child's schedule, parents will want to gradually hand responsibility over while still keeping tabs on what they have to do and how they plan to get it all done.

Suggestions for structuring homework:

1) Ask your child to estimate how long she thinks it will take to do each assignment well. Check to see that she understands what she has to do. (It will take practice to get good at estimating but your child will learn a valuable skill.)

2) Help her to establish the order in which she would prefer to tackle each task. Some children prefer to do the easier assignments as a warm-up before going on to the more difficult tasks. Others prefer to get the harder assignments out of the way while they are relatively fresh.

3) Number the assignments in the order he wants to do them, either in the planner or on a checklist you make.

4) Break the work into manageable parts. You can do this by task or by time spent. You might set the timer for, say, 15 or 20 minutes and then allow a short break. Or get math and spelling out of the way before your child takes a break. Caution: Try not to let your child get involved with another interest or activity during the break or it will be difficult for her to return to the task. Best to use that short time as a way to restore energy. Give her a little shoulder rub, do some jumping jacks, have him play with the dog for a couple of minutes, then it's back to work.

Continued on next page

Powering Down Distractions

The 21ˢᵗ century may have ushered in a new era in which we are connected to and inundated by electronic media to an unprecedented degree. For those of us raised before the advent of cell phones and Internet, the ability of younger people— "digital natives"— to multitask and to control an array of devices with speed and precision, seems mind boggling. Some have suggested that this new era of information processing is a monumental step forward in human capabilities. Others acknowledge the benefits but are concerned about the costs.

5) Use incentives. For each segment of work accomplished, make sure you note it with a sticker for younger children or checkmark for older. It is very motivating for children to see the progress they are making. Some children need more incentives: Remind them that when they are done, they are free to play, watch television, play a game with you, or whatever motivates them.

6) Children who are more distractible may need more help in "getting into" the assignment. Anything you can do to make it more interesting or understandable will help. Help your child make connections from the assignment to something meaningful in his own life. Give your child a highlighter to emphasize key words in the directions or read them out loud with lots of emphasis. Sometimes textbooks are written in very bland language that is uninteresting or difficult to understand. If that is the case, take turns reading it aloud, with you providing lots of vocal color and commentary to make it more meaningful to your child.

7) Take a look at your child's work occasionally to ensure she's understood the directions and is on track, but don't micro-manage. If she is really struggling with a concept and your explanations don't help, just write a note to the teacher indicating that you worked with her and she is still having difficulty. Don't insist on perfection; don't give out answers or do it for him; and don't insist on perfect neatness (readability, yes).

8) Celebrate a job well done. Finishing homework deserves a smile and a high five. Make it clear that completing a responsibility like homework pays off.

The Down Side of Ubiquitous Media

In Chapter 3 we mentioned the *New York Times* (nytimes.com/tech) series called "Your Brain on Computers", and considered how being so "plugged in" might be affecting the ability of adults to concentrate and to recall information. Series author Matt Richtel (Nov. 21, 2010) also looked at the effect of texting, instant messaging, and computer gaming on student learning. The implications are alarming. Studies show children spending more time consuming media than any other single activity except sleeping. The most recent Kaiser Family Foundation study on media usage (Rideout, Foer & Roberts, 2010) concludes that "over the past five years, young people (ages 8 to 18) have increased the amount of time they spend consuming media by an hour and seventeen minutes daily, from 6:21 to 7:38. (p. 2). That figure does not include multitasking in which children are simultaneously texting, surfing the net, and watching TV.

...as kids become accustomed to switching back and forth between activities at lightning speed, the capacity for sustained, focused effort withers away.

An accumulating body of evidence demonstrates that the brain needs a period of "down time" to consolidate and commit to memory new learning. Richtel quotes Dr. Michael Rich of Harvard Medical School and of the Center on Media and Child Health (CMCH) who says, "Downtime is to the brain what sleep is to the body. But kids are in a constant mode of stimulation." (www.cmch.tv.) There is no downtime as children simply switch from one electronic activity to another. The concern is that as kids become accustomed to switching back and forth between activities at lightning speed, the capacity for sustained, focused effort withers away. Being distracted and shifting attention becomes the preferred and then only way to function. Many teachers are now finding that even very bright children from well-educated homes are finding it more difficult to sustain attention to reading, and that the only way to guarantee students have read an assignment is to read it orally in class.

Children, with their still-developing brains, are especially vulnerable to the disintegrative effects of too much stimulation. Dr. Rich (2010) notes that heavier media users tend to get lower grades and are in trouble more frequently than those who are plugged in less often. One intriguing study described by Richtel was done out of the University of Cologne in Germany. Boys from the ages of 12 to 14 played video games for one hour after homework and before sleep. On alternate nights they watched an exciting movie instead of playing video games. The researchers found a significant difference in both the quality of sleep and in the boys' ability to remember vocabulary words depending on which activity they engaged in before sleep. Playing video games was much more disruptive to sleep and to academic progress than watching a movie.

Even before this technological revolution, humans found it difficult to concentrate and pay attention. Russell Barkley, (2000) a renowned expert on ADHD, acknowledges that all of us are continually shifting focus as different sounds and sights conspire to pull our attention away from the task at hand. In order to accomplish anything, we have to find ways of continually redirecting our attention and our efforts to the report, bills, letter, homework, or other job that needs to be done. (We suggest a few strategies for encouraging focus and sustained attention a little further along in this chapter.)

What can possibly be done? While the genie may indeed be out of the bottle in terms of our kids' expectations for and dependence on electronic stimulation, experts seem to agree that the answer lies in achieving a healthy balance of activities with parents establishing appropriate limits. In a speech he gave to the American Academy of Pediatrics (October, 2010) Dr. Rich delineated "5 C's to a healthier family." Among these were controlling time spent consuming media. The CMCH website goes into further detail, including the idea of creating a "screen budget." If you agree that total screen time should be limited to no more than two hours per day, you would have to work out with your child how that time should be divided up between video games, television, the Internet, and texting friends. You might have to specify whether research done for a homework assignment counts toward that total. Expect considerable resistance from your children as you establish a new set of expectations regarding media use. Dr. Rich suggests that you can explain to your children that we now have new information that was simply not available before on the negative effects of too much screen time.

As we advocate throughout this book, we suggest that you may first want to look at your own media consumption with an eye toward understanding the messages you may unwittingly be conveying to your children. Is the TV always on? How many times in the course of an hour do you check for email? Text? Check

Facebook? How much time do you spend playing online games or use your cell phone apps to fill empty time? Do you feel agitated and impatient when you have to wait for something and have no electronic distraction to fill the time? Have you given up on conversation during long car trips and instead just load up the DVD player for the children to watch? (One little boy, when asked how far away his brother's college was, replied that it was seven Scooby-Doo DVDs away!)

The Habits of Mind approach is very conducive to becoming more intentional and mindful about the use of technology. The idea is to bring it under conscious control, and to help our children do so as well. Dr. Rich includes this idea as one of his 5 C's: *Create and Model Media Mastery.* If you are to put your children on a media diet, it is one the whole family will have to buy into if it is to succeed.

The bottom line is that when you use media, use it intentionally. Rather than having the TV on constantly, have a family movie night when you choose a DVD to watch together. Make a point of turning off the cell phone and computer except for specific tasks that have to be accomplished. Schedule a period of time to respond to emails, rather than checking frequently throughout the day. You may be surprised at the amount of time that gets restored to you by these simple actions.

Use Metacognition to Increase Awareness of Distractions

We have seen before how Metacognition increases our awareness of our own thoughts, feelings, and tendency to behave in certain ways. You can also use metacognitive strategies to help your child gain a better understanding of how impulsive responses to distractions are affecting his work and time. David Rock in his book, *The Brain at Work* (2009), describes in detail the split-second chain reaction of our response to a distraction, starting with a signal the brain picks up, to a subjectively felt desire, culminating in a response. To deal most effectively with a distraction, he advises us to nip it in the bud. If you pull away from your work to check your email or check on the latest baseball score, you make it that much harder to recover your attention.

If these things are difficult for us, imagine how much more so they are for our children. To help them take those first steps in managing their responses to distractions, Rock suggests we work on increasing their awareness. We gain more veto power over distractions when we know how they work their magic on our brain. Parents can help their children develop what Rock calls "explicit language" to describe their effect on them. Using words to describe the experience of being distracted breaks down the mystique, puts it on the table, and makes it possible to begin to deal with it more effectively. If our children are going to gain mastery over their distractions, they will have to recognize them for what they are. Our goal will be to get our children to stop and think in advance, to intentionally clear the deck of distractions, and to focus on the task at hand.

> **Help your child develop a list of top 10 distractions. You might be surprised at what they are.**

First, model your own thinking about distractions. You can easily point out moments when you get distracted: by a funny commercial on TV, a telephone call, the cat's antics, the limousine that pulled up in front of your neighbor's house. Make it clear that, by definition, a distraction can be hard to resist, but resist it you will! Comments such as, *Well, that was certainly interesting, but I have a job to do.* Or, *I could watch this silly cat all day, but if I do that, there will be no dinner, so back to work for me.* Tell your child that distractions are normal. They happen all the time, but they are not a reason to break off attention and effort. When you define "distraction" (what does it look like, sound like, feel like?) you take distractibility out of the realm of a character flaw and begin to make it manageable.

You can talk with your child about what you find most distracting and ask her to help you monitor your own tendency to get off track. Help your child develop a list of top 10 distractions. You might be surprised at what they are. Often children are completely unaware of when they have been distracted. For example, in one elementary school, the 4th grade teachers decided to work on increasing their students' stamina for reading lengthier passages. During the daily half hour of "Drop Everything and Read" time, one teacher quietly took notes on how often students became distracted from their reading and what the nature of the distractions were. She tallied up all the trips to the bathroom, students out of their seat to throw something in the wastebasket or to look out the window, and books put aside for a whispered conversation. The following day she shared her "data" with her students. They were shocked to learn how little of the reading period was actually spent reading. The teacher noted with some wonderment that, following that debriefing, the students spent noticeably more time with their books. Awareness of their own distractions sparked some improvement.

It is also common for students to like to talk with friends on the phone or online while they are doing homework under the guise that they are working together. When they do this, chances are that they too are unaware of how much time is not spent on schoolwork.

One mother, Brenda, decided to take on this issue while in the car with her 11- year-old daughter and her best friend, both of whom spent at least an hour each night talking with each other on the computer or phone. The girls were great friends and did in fact sometimes discuss their assignments, but most of their talk was social. Brenda made a deal with them that they couldn't resist. Both agreed to have no contact with each other on school nights from 7:00 to 8:30 p.m.—the time they were supposed to be doing homework–for a month. If they stuck to the agreement and turned in all their homework assignments during the week, Brenda would take them to the mall or ice rink or a place of their choice each Saturday afternoon.

Brenda's goal was to get her daughter to be more aware of the need to devote quality time to her work. In the short term, her daughter might chafe a bit at having to limit her friendly talks to certain times, but the incentive of the Saturday outing would make up for that. More important, Brenda was hoping that her daughter would begin to realize more meaningful rewards from putting in uninterrupted time on her work. She hoped that her daughter would be better prepared for the next day's class work and start to do better on quizzes and tests. Those intrinsic rewards would help her begin to lay down a habit of improved concentration and focus for schoolwork.

Age and temperament have to be considered when helping children deal with distractions. Younger children may require a more hands on approach.

Cal was only seven and his life was an open book. He blurted out every thought that crossed his mind as he sat down to do his 20 minutes of homework. His friend was having a birthday party. What was for dinner? When was his brother coming home, and could he have the first turn on the video game? He needed to go to the bathroom. When could he take a break? Like many seven-year-olds, after being in school all day, he had little patience for sitting still once he got home. In between his chatting, he would get up for a drink, get the dog a drink, check on the goldfish, and play with a rubber band he found on the kitchen counter.

Cal's teacher said he was doing fine in school, so his parents didn't want to come down too hard on him. First of all, they made sure he had more time to play after school, not only doing sports through an after school program, but also giving him time to play and unwind at home. They had a schedule posted on the refrigerator, and when it was time for him to do homework, they were consistent about adhering to the schedule. To make it feel less burdensome to him, they broke up his math and reading time. They set a challenge that Cal agreed to: No talking or getting up for five minutes or until four problems were done correctly, whichever came first. Cal enjoyed this routine and viewed it as a game. When it came to reading, one parent would silently read along with him, and then discuss what they had just read to keep his attention focused. Even so, Cal would sometimes interrupt with an unrelated thought. When that happened, his mom or dad said gently, "We're not going to get distracted by that now. We can talk about it later, after you're done with homework." Cal's parents made sure they acknowledged his concentration and effort. They also looked for ways to bring into the conversation things he was learning at school or stories he was reading at home so that he would feel his parents' warm interest in his learning.

Transitions

Getting down to work represents a *transition*. We have already suggested that by establishing routines and procedures for homework, you can help your child settle in more easily. Acknowledging the difficulty of settling down to work is important, too. *Yes, it is difficult to stop watching television and do your homework. I know you want to stay outside and play but we agreed that you would get your math homework done before dinner.* By coaching your child through those first difficult moments, you help him to transition to an engagement with the task. You then open a door for the good feelings that accompany us when we are working productively.

We can also make the transition from play to work go more smoothly by having a little ritual that serves to clear the mind of what went before and get ready for what lies ahead. Just as mindful breathing can be helpful when we're faced with a stressful situation, teaching children to take two or three deep breaths as they sit down to do homework can help them to shake off the distractions of their busy lives and focus on what they have to do. In fact, this technique can be useful for all kinds of transitions. In her book, *The Mindful Child* Susan Kaiser Greenland

125

(2010) suggests that everyone take three deep breaths before leaving the house in the morning in order to start the day with a calmer mind. Author David Rock practices the breaths with his family before dinner. If your children think this is silly, have them observe athletes as they get ready for their moment. Note how the pitcher or batter breathes before taking his position, how the swimmer shakes her arms and breathes deeply to get ready for the starting bell. The breathing helps them get focused and ready.

The transition from home to school in the morning is often a difficult one. You can ease this by helping your child develop a mental set that makes him feel ready for his day. We suggest keeping the television off during this hectic time, so everyone can focus on getting ready. You can casually mention what he was working on with his homework yesterday and suggest that he should feel well prepared for the work he will be facing. By keeping up with the curriculum via the class websites, newsletters, and other communications from school, you can—-even in a very general way—help your child anticipate what he will be learning about. By expressing your own interest in the content of what she is learning, you strengthen her interest and her ability to focus in on the material when she is at school.

The Importance of Time on Task

The ability to become immersed in a problem or task or to practice for an extended length of time is one of the hallmarks of "giftedness" (Renzulli & Reis, 1997). Managing our susceptibility to distractions is a first and necessary step to increased mastery over work and school demands. It is a truism that the more time you spend actively working on improving your skills, the better you will be at it. How could it be otherwise? Time and practice are necessary for excellence, whether we are talking about pitching a baseball, playing guitar, or learning a new language. Talent helps. It might draw you to one area of endeavor or another, and it might make the early going a little easier, but without sustained and disciplined effort, talent alone will not get you very far. The dilemma is to stick with a task long enough so that it becomes intrinsically rewarding—so rewarding, that you can't wait to work on it some more.

Many early readers face this dilemma as they huff and puff, trying so hard to sound out the words that they completely lose track of the story. Until they "break the code" and can begin to read on their own, it often just feels to them like a difficult chore. Wise adults keep these young readers immersed in literature through conversation and stories read to them until they can begin to get up to speed with their own independent reading. (Hopefully, parents will continue reading aloud, long after that period, as long as their children will allow.) In this way, children are motivated to keep working on those basic skills by the powerful idea that they will soon be able to access a world of literary treasures all by themselves.

Think about the earliest stages of learning to play a musical instrument: The hand positions may be unfamiliar and uncomfortable, the musical notation is a foreign language, and the sounds that emerge can be almost painful. (One retired music teacher described beginning strings teachers as the "Mother Theresas of the music world"!) So many people give up in the early stages because there is not enough payoff; they can't visualize ever being successful; and, yes, there are so many easier things to distract them from their efforts. But, oh, the rewards for those who can sustain focus and effort. One eight-year-old girl, Ashley, was overheard in a school corridor talking with a friend. The friend told Ashley she didn't have to bring her viola home since the holiday concert was over. "But I want to keep practicing," Ashley replied, "I like doing it." Now a year older, Ashley lights up when talking about how much the viola means to her. She starts homework as soon as she gets home, so as to leave sufficient time to practice. She loves the music she is learning, loves how the instrument feels in her hands, and feels sustained by the competence she is gaining from her increasing skill. She has just discovered that her grandmother also played the viola as a girl, and she is looking forward to talking about it with her on their next visit.

Increasing Focus

Russell Barkley (2000) in his guide for parents, *Taking Charge of ADHD*, offers many useful suggestions to help children increase focus that can be very useful to all kids. One suggestion (p. 256) is to help your child "Think aloud and think ahead." In other words, encourage her to say out loud what the task entails: "Okay, I have to solve this page of math problems, and for each one I have to explain how I got my answer." Ask your child to explain to you what strategies she plans to use. "I think I'll read the questions at the back of the chapter first, and then I'll take notes about where I see something about each question as I'm reading. That will make it easier for me to find the answers when I'm ready to start writing." Saying this out loud provides a little extra feedback to help your child remember and to stay on task. You can suggest that she give herself verbal reminders to stay focused, and to give herself a compliment when she succeeds in doing so.

In their book, *Smart But Scattered* (2009) Peg Dawson and Richard Guare recommend that parents note how long their child can usually stick with a task before needing a break. Treating this amount of time (say, five minutes for a six- year-old) as a baseline, they suggest using a kitchen timer or other device to gradually stretch out that amount of time by two or three minutes until they reach a new, higher baseline.

It is always a good idea for you and your child to evaluate together which strategies work and which do not. Doing this helps her to become more aware of her own learning preferences and how she performs best. It is an important step in becoming a more independent and self-directed learner. When we help children improve their ability to focus, we create the conditions that allow them to develop their talent and skills to their fullest.

TIPS FOR MANAGING EXTERNAL DISTRACTIONS

- Assess and monitor your own media use.

- Model intentional use of devices for your child. Let your child see you turn your computer or cell phone off when you are working. Let your child see you resisting distraction, and then explain what you were doing and why.

- Create a family schedule for "screen time" and stick to it.

- Plan interactive family activities to replace videogames, TV watching, etc.

- Label distractions and problem solve with your child specific strategies he can use to resist them.

- Create some little ritual to help transition from one activity to another to clear the mind for the task at hand.

TIPS FOR MANAGING INTERNAL DISTRACTIONS

- Help your child recognize the moment when she becomes distracted and nip it in the bud.

- Label internal distractions; create a visual image, e.g. My thoughts are like a little puppy, running all over the place. That's okay; I'll just gently bring her back.

- Give your child a strategy he can use to "put" the distracting thought somewhere else for the time being, e.g. Just push that thought to the back of your head. Or, Let's push that thought down into your shoes.

- Allow time later to talk about whatever was on your child's mind that was distracting him.

- Compliment her when you see her successfully resist a distracting thought and getting back to work.

TIPS FOR INCREASING FOCUS

- Provide supervision and support, especially for younger children.

- Break tasks into manageable segments, with incentives for completed work.

- Gradually increase the amount of time spent on-task. Use a timer to make it fun and challenging.

- Encourage your child to "think aloud and plan ahead."

- Help increase focus by using an expressive tone of voice when reading directions, or by providing visual stimulation such as highlighting key words.

- Be sure to acknowledge your child's efforts to focus.

- Engage your child in assessing how well he thinks he was able to focus and sustain effort.

Chapter 9

Thinking Like a Problem Solver: Metacognition

Try to solve this problem in your head: How much is one-half of two plus two? (Costa, 2007).

Did you hear yourself talking to yourself, trying to decide between adding two plus two vs. taking half of two first? If you were having this kind of inner dialogue, you were experiencing metacognition, thinking about your own thinking.

Metacognition is what enables us to know what we know and what we don't know. It is our ability to make a plan, know the steps to solve a problem, and reflect on and evaluate our progress. The habit of Metacognition helps us become more systematic and structured in our approach to work. Instead of feeling lost at sea with each new work challenge, Metacognition helps us to develop a *way* of working that is efficient, practical, and well suited to our own personal strengths and weaknesses. More than any facts we can teach, Metacognition is the Habit of Mind that gives our children what they need to tackle challenges. When children have a healthy and robust sense of themselves as problem solvers, the following thoughts

Metacognition enables us to know what we know and what we don't know.

course through their minds: *This looks hard but I can handle it. Let me think of how to begin and I'll be on my way. Okay, I'll give it a try! Where do I start?* Such children are confident and optimistic. They are intrigued and energized, rather than discouraged, when difficulties arise. They have learned a variety of ways of approaching problematic situations.

Over the years, we have observed that students who have received special education services early in their school career often go on to become very strong students in high school, precisely because they have been taught strategies they can apply to increasingly difficult work. They also have developed a more mature perspective on their own learning. Having struggled from the start with reading or writing, they have come to understand that patience and applied effort really do pay off. Teaching Metacognition early on, before bad habits become entrenched, can go a long way toward ensuring that all children make the best use of their abilities.

Think Out Loud: Allow Your Child to Witness How You Make Decisions

By definition, Metacognition requires us to be more *thoughtful* and *intentional* in our actions. Before running out the door for a morning of errands, you might ask your child to help you make a list of what has to be done (dry cleaners, grocery store, gas station, garden supply shop, pharmacy). Engage your child in thinking about the best *sequence* of those activities. Which route would be quickest and most direct or the most energy efficient? In what order should you make your stops? (If you go to the grocery store first, what might happen to the ice cream you've bought?) What do you need to bring with you to achieve your "goals" for the morning? (Cell phone—check. Coupons—check. Grocery list—check.) In a game-like way, you can demonstrate the value of planning ahead and being organized.

This same exercise can be enacted for what is often a stressful time in families—getting ready for school. If you establish a routine for having everything prepared and ready to go, you will avoid many of the frustrations and delays that go along with this time of day. The schedules you created in Chapter 8 can be posted so you can—with your child—check for what is coming up the next day and help your child to plan accordingly. *You have phys ed tomorrow. What do you need?* Get your children to put their sneakers in their bag. Music lesson? In goes the clarinet. Develop the habit of frequently checking the schedule with your child so there are no surprises. Do as much as possible the night before in order to preserve the morning time for a good breakfast and a peaceful send-off.

If you have a decision to make (what kind of car to buy, where to spend a vacation, whether to adopt or buy a new pet), have a family conversation about the pros and cons of each possibility. Draw a vertical line through a piece of paper, and have your children brainstorm all the positives and all the negatives they can think of. If they have already settled on one choice and are defending it staunchly, have them give their reasons why.

All of this helps children understand that things don't just magically happen. Approaching a decision in a systematic, thoughtful way is the better alternative to impulsively following a whim.

Metacognition Is About Becoming More Reflective

Maybe you recall the story about Dan from the earlier chapter on Metacognition in the Communication section. Dan had put considerable thought into what kind of coach he wanted to be for his son's Little League experience. He anticipated that there might be some difficulties because of his son's lack of focus and tendency to fool around, and he had already come up with some ideas on how he would react when the inevitable happened. Children also can be guided to develop a more reflective approach to fulfilling their responsibilities as a student. Some children seem to show up at the door of the school with all their school supplies, but with very little awareness of what mental attitudes they will need to be successful.

Remember Elena (from Chapter 7 on Persistence)? By helping her to set goals, break down tasks into smaller pieces, and monitor her progress, her parents helped her to improve her ability to stick with tasks till completion. Now in 4th grade, it soon became apparent that Elena still needed some work in meeting her responsibilities. Her teacher, Mrs. Mackie, noticed during the first few weeks of school that most of the other students followed through on the basic morning tasks of unpacking their backpacks, putting lunch bags in their proper place, turning in their homework folder, and getting their writing journal out and ready to go by 8:30 a.m. Elena, on the other hand, came into the room happily chatting about the baseball game she attended the night before or a movie she watched with her parents. She seemed unaware of what she was supposed to do next. She was nearly always the last one to hang up her backpack and usually had to make a return trip to retrieve a forgotten item. Mrs. Mackie needed to remind Elena frequently about what she was supposed to be doing and had to continually monitor her to ensure that she stayed on task and completed her work. It was one thing for Elena to stick with cleaning her room and crocheting the scarf over the summer. It would be another leap for her to stay on task throughout the school day.

Mrs. Mackie met with Elena's parents to discuss some goals and how to build on what Elena had begun to experience over the summer. She wanted Elena to come to school with a clear sense of herself as a student with a "job" to do. In the course of their discussion, her parents realized that their daughter was much more interested in the social aspects of school and did not have much to say about what she was learning. Mrs. Mackie suggested that they start by helping Elena increase her awareness of the kind of attitudes and behaviors that she would need to develop to be a more effective student, one of the missing pieces in her ability to persist. Mrs. Mackie told them that she would meet privately with Elena and share some of her observations, emphasizing the things that gave her confidence in Elena's ability. They would identify two or three behaviors that could make a big difference in her becoming more independent, and establish those behaviors as learning goals.

Elena's parents, in turn, said that they would help increase her awareness of herself as a student. They agreed that it was necessary for Elena to experience more connection between home and school. They decided to make a point of reading some of the same books she was reading in school, and talking about them with her over dinner or before bedtime. They decided against going out on weeknights whenever possible. Elena's parents also began to acknowledge the same behaviors at home that Mrs. Mackie was working on at school: good listening, following directions, and so on. Finally, they made a point of previewing her day with her at breakfast. In a warm and casual way, they would talk about the day's schedule and ask her what she was especially looking forward to. This served two purposes: First, it helped her establish a mental readiness for the school day. Instead of

> **Some goals can be long-term and inspire a lifetime of effort and achievement.**

thinking about all kinds of other things, her thoughts would be focused on what she would be doing that day. Second, by showing interest in the details of her day, they helped her to feel their support even when they were apart.

As the school year progressed, Elena began to develop a much clearer idea of what she needed to do as a student. The feedback from her teacher and parents helped her to recognize when she was doing things right. The feelings of pride she enjoyed when earning their acknowledgement motivated her to continue improving. Just as she experienced her parents' interest in what she was reading and learning in 4th grade, she was able to bring back to the classroom enriching experiences she had with her family. As a result, she gained a satisfying feeling of connectedness between home and school. Elena became more motivated. There would still be times when she would want to talk about sports with her pals at school, and she realized that there were plenty of times during the school day when it would be fine to do just that. As the year went on, Elena became more aware of what was expected of her and more confident that she could perform accordingly. She became more connected to and engaged in what was happening in the classroom, and within a few months had shown enough improvement that she was able to stay on track without such intensive support from her teacher.

Set Goals

Some goals can be long-term and inspire a lifetime of effort and achievement (*to climb the highest mountain on every continent; to write a novel; to become an archaeologist*), or they can be simple and immediate (to finish dinner and clean-up by 7:30; to get two pages of my report done) or they can fall somewhere in between (*to follow the recommended oil change schedule for the car*). Goals are helpful in clarifying what needs to be done and motivating you to do it.

When Mrs. Mackie sat down with Elena to establish a few goals that targeted areas she wanted to see improve, she didn't just hand her a sheet of paper with the goals already written down. Rather, she began by talking with Elena about some of the behaviors she was seeing and how they were holding Elena back from making progress. She encouraged Elena to talk about what she could do differently. She knew that key to success in setting goals is that the child feels some "ownership" of those goals and believes that they will make a difference. Together they settled on three "alternative behaviors" or goals that they both thought would make a difference:

- Listen carefully to the teacher's directions and ask for clarification when unsure.
- Be in your seat and ready to work by 8:30.
- Participate more in class discussions.

These goals were specific behaviors that Elena could understand. Mrs. Mackie took care to emphasize Elena's positive attributes and to convey confidence that the goals were not only achievable, but that she would definitely feel better about being in school as she made progress towards achieving them.

Another important element of setting goals is spelling out the steps to their successful completion. Each goal should have at least two or three specific strategies that describe what the goal behavior looks like and how to accomplish it. For Elena to be in her seat by 8:30 and ready to work meant that she had to hang up her coat, empty her backpack, and turn in her homework before sitting down. To improve listening skills, she should look at the speaker and be able to repeat back what she heard. Also, just as adults often rely on "punch lists" or other ways of keeping track of a multitude of tasks, children will need specific steps and visual reminders such as calendars and checklists. Their working memory is typically not yet developed enough to allow them to hold on to many details or steps in a process without the help of visual cues.

Again, don't forget to acknowledge even small steps toward achieving goals. To be effective, the acknowledgement has to be *sincere* and *specific*. A low-key, quiet comment to the effect that you saw and appreciated the desired behavior can be a more powerful motivator than effusive praise. The more specific you are, the clearer the child's understanding will be of what exactly he is working toward. A comment such as "you did a good job," while positive, conveys very little useful information. Better to say something like, "I noticed that you checked back to your planner to make sure you had done all your assignments. That's really being responsible and organized!" When your acknowledgement is given with a warm smile and an appreciative tone of voice, your child internalizes your pride in his efforts and feels encouraged to keep trying.

Finally, in the spirit of the Habit of Metacognition, we will want to occasionally reflect with our child on how he has experienced the process of goal setting. Was it helpful? Why or why not? What could improve the process? How could *we* be more helpful? Remember we are always aiming to get ourselves and our child thinking, thinking, thinking.

Show Them What Success Looks Like

Kids need to be shown what success looks like, whether it be a demonstration of a good curve ball, a clean room, or an example of an exemplary essay. They also benefit from clear indicators of what progress looks like as they work to achieve success. School children don't just arrive at the middle school door suddenly able to write a good essay. Expressing your thoughts in writing in a clear and organized way is a complex skill that starts in kindergarten as five-year-olds laboriously learn to recognize and write their letters. Step by step, children move from letters to words to sentences to paragraphs and beyond. Each one of those foundational skills requires breaking down the larger skills into small achievable parts. Little by little, the parts come together and the child is able to apply those skills to reading and writing. This approach makes a difficult and daunting task manageable.

"Rubrics" is a relatively new term in education to describe scoring guides that many schools use for this purpose. A rubric provides descriptions of what finished projects look like at different levels of proficiency, ranging from *not yet accomplished* to *satisfactory*, to *mastery*. Rubrics serve as guideposts so children can see for themselves where their work meets expectations and where they may have to develop their skills further. The use of rubrics encourages children to become more in charge of their own learning. They have a clear sense of what progress looks like.

This is exactly what one 2ⁿᵈ grader, Jackson, needed. He had twin 11-year-old brothers and was always trying to do just what his brothers could do. Sometimes he was successful. He was quick with the soccer ball and a wiz at computer games. But his preoccupation with keeping up with his brothers and, by extension, competing with his classmates, meant that a lot of his energy went to keeping tabs on what everyone else was doing instead of focusing on his own learning. Rather than concentrating on the lesson, or remembering what he had studied for a test, he was watching to see who was raising their hand or finishing the test first, and then rushing to be first. As the work became more demanding, his skills began to slip.

Jackson's teacher wanted him to take pride in his own progress and to be less concerned about where he stood compared with everyone else. She met privately with Jackson and showed him what level he had attained in his math and writing so far, and what skills he would need to move up. The rubrics were very specific, showing him what he needed to do in spelling and punctuation and different ways to convey ideas to improve his writing. His teacher started by helping him set realistic goals about what he could accomplish each week and the kind of progress it would mean over the month. She broke down the levels into smaller increments in the beginning to encourage him and to keep him focused on the skills he was learning. Knowing how competitive he was, she set it up as a personal challenge for him to be able to monitor and keep track of his progress. She told him that she would enjoy "coaching" him through this challenge. At home, the teacher asked Jackson's parents to make use of rubrics, which she posted on her website. These guidelines helped the parents be more specific in their responses to his assignments, to acknowledge what he was learning and the progress he was making.

Setting goals and providing rubrics both help to give children a sense of purpose and focus along with a detailed roadmap. While you're probably not going to want to make up a set of rubrics to cover chores and responsibilities at home, you could inculcate a little more "quality control" into your child's efforts. For chores such as cleaning up the kitchen after a meal or cleaning one's room or playroom, or for responsibilities such as caring for a pet or keeping track of what papers and materials have to go back to school in the morning, you might engage the children in a discussion and simple charting of what goes into each job. You could map out the minimal expectations, what the expected level of job performance is, and what a really great job would look like. Keeping in mind what children of different ages are developmentally capable of doing, you would tailor your acknowledgement and any rewards to what constitutes a good job for the child's age.

Goals and rubrics introduce children to one of the main functions of metacognition and a key component of persistence: the ability to monitor their own progress, assess how they are doing, and determine what else they need to do in order to get there.

Let's Make a Plan

A plan is a detailed roadmap that helps you and your children break down challenges into manageable steps. A plan gives children something tangible to hold onto when they feel discouraged or overwhelmed. The process of making a plan is valuable in and of itself. It prompts you right up front to think through both the advantages and disadvantages of your ideas. Since part of the process is to anticipate possible obstacles, no one is shocked or dismayed when setbacks inevitably arise. Having a contingency or backup plan in your pocket for when things don't go well allows you to keep going instead of staying stuck. It also takes some of the negative emotion out of setbacks. Typically when things go wrong (missed homework assignments, a failed test, wasted music lesson because of failure to practice), parents naturally become anxious and upset and can't help but pass those feelings right on to their child. The whole enterprise then can become emotionally loaded. Once that happens, children tend to avoid the activity that caused the anxiety in the first place, which cascades into *further* anxiety and upset. A good plan, developed together and then written down, will neutralize some of this anxiety and provide a structure to move you forward.

When Do You Need a Plan?

If you have a recurring problem that creates tension, is disruptive or interferes with a family member's growth, progress, or well-being, then you need a plan. Typical problem areas include fulfilling school responsibilities such as homework, projects, and reading; fulfilling home responsibilities such as setting the table, cleaning one's own room, taking care of a pet, being ready for school or after-school activities on time, and getting along with siblings well enough (no physical aggression and no bullying or destructive teasing) so that parents don't have to provide constant supervision.

What Makes a Plan Good?

To be effective, a plan needs to have the following characteristics:

- It has to be collaborative. All parties have to work it out together and agree to it. It cannot be imposed or it will be sabotaged.
- It has to be clear and simple.
- It has to be comprehensive; that is, address all the issues that cause the problem in the first place or interfered with solutions in the past.
- It needs to be written down so that when there are disagreements—and there will be—you have the document to refer to.
- It has to be flexible enough to allow for the reality of family life, yet strong enough to set an expectation that it will actually be implemented. You can never know if a strategy works or not unless you actually *try* that strategy over a period of time.
- It has to be periodically reviewed and updated. How is this working? Are there any problems with it? Are we seeing progress? If not, how do we change it so that we do?

How Do You Make a Plan?

There are many variations on this theme, but the problem-solving process is actually very simple, with some basic steps:

- Identify the problem.
- Have everybody think of as many possible solutions as they can. Encourage creativity. Don't criticize suggestions that might seem unrealistic; just try to come up with a lot of them. Write them down. Even the silly ones.
- Review the list of possible solutions and consider which ones might work, which ones wouldn't, and why. You might find yourselves laughing as you discuss the more outrageous suggestions, and that is a good thing. It breaks the tension.
- Narrow down the list to two or three possibilities that everyone can agree on. Decide what each person will do and write down the agreement.
- Make a date to review how the plan is working and if changes need to be made. Give it a trial period of a week or so before trying something else.

1. Identify the Problem

You will want to use your empathic listening skills during this process—especially when you are trying to figure out exactly what the problem is. We adults often think we already know what the problem is and how it should be solved. Often, though, there are other issues simmering beneath our radar that need to be brought to light before the *real* problem can be addressed. Defining the problem clearly, accurately and fully is essential to its resolution. Children often need encouragement to express their feelings and perceptions about a problem situation. It is important to listen empathically, ask questions for clarification, and check in with them to make sure you're "getting it." (This doesn't mean you have to totally agree with their version of the "facts" of the situation; just that you are accepting how they perceive and feel about it.) You can encourage your children to speak first, but if you start, make sure you begin with a simple, non-accusatory explanation of how you see the problem. Acknowledge that other people might see it differently and that you are interested in hearing from everybody so that, together, you can find a solution that makes everybody happy. Children often will interrupt and argue (especially if siblings are involved), so it is a good opportunity to model good listening and to let them know that you expect it of them as well. And, yes, they may find fault in everyone but themselves, but this is part of the process. Generally, when they realize they will be fully heard, the pressure to dominate and to get the last word in dissipates.

Parents sometimes worry that they are relinquishing all control by allowing their children to participate in the problem solving process. That can be avoided right up front by making sure your child is clear about your expectations, what is negotiable, and what is not. Bedtime is nine o'clock. Homework must be completed.

2. Brainstorm Solutions

This step can be a lot of fun as children often vie with each other to come up with the most or the most outrageous ideas. Just keep writing them down. Key to success with this step is to keep the creative juices flowing while also being realistic. If the goal is to make a plan to get homework done on time, be specific: Some assignments are long term, studying for a big test requires extra time, etc. Talking to their friends at night and taking breaks need to be factored into the schedule. Soccer practice means late suppers. Go back to the definition of the problem if you get off track. If the brainstorming list has too many blanks, think about similar situations and how you dealt with them. Or talk to a teacher, friends, or a reliable older child who succeeded in a similar task. Searching the topic online may also trigger some ideas.

Don't permit put-downs or criticism of any solution, no matter how implausible. You never know what will work. The most effective solution is not always the one a sensible adult would necessarily have chosen.

3. Evaluate the Possibilities

When children evaluate their own ideas, they come face to face with the reality of what it takes to put an idea into practice. The more children discover these nuggets of truth through their own thinking, the better. Go through the list, one at a time, and ask your child to imagine what would happen if he tried this particular solution. Try to stimulate thinking about positive and negative outcomes. Questions like "What about…?" and "What would you do if…?" work better than "Why?" These types of questions help children to create a realistic picture of the situation. Again, don't jump in right away with your opinion. You may be surprised at how well even young children can do a cost/benefit analysis.

4. Choose a Solution or Three

Many problems are multifaceted and require a number of different interventions, so you may end up with more than one solution. Perhaps the solution requires each person involved to contribute something different in order to solve the problem. Your child needs you to stop nagging. You need your child to be more responsive to your requests. The most important aspect of this step is that there is consensus. Each person, including you, has to feel that they can follow the agreement. Remember, your original stated goal was to solve the problem so that *everybody is happy*. If your child feels that she was truly heard and understood and if she feels that she had a significant role in crafting a solution, she'll be much more motivated to try to make it work. When you go through this process with children, you may find it difficult to not impose your own solutions on them. You can certainly suggest a solution in the brainstorming step, but try to allow the children to choose the solution they think will work best. You will be assessing how it worked in a few days, so there will be an opportunity to make adjustments if necessary. Often, however, just going through the process is enough to set in motion positive changes.

5. Build in a "Review of Progress"

Agree to meet again in the next few days for a quick review of how things are going. Make sure that you acknowledge everyone's efforts in trying to come up with some ways to solve this problem. Encourage metacognition by asking them what they liked about the problem-solving process. What worked for them and what didn't? What could you do next time to make it go even better? Celebrate that you came up with a plan.

When you do meet again, be specific in asking each person involved how the solutions seem to be working. Often, you will find that the problem has faded into the background and is no longer an issue. There may be disputes about what was agreed to or how each person is adhering to the agreement. (This is the advantage of writing everything down!) When this happens, redirect them away from blaming each other, and try to engage in the process again. You could ask questions such as, "What seems to be getting in the way of making this plan work? Remember, we're trying to find a way to solve the problem so that each person is happy."

A Few Additional Thoughts

This protocol may feel awkward and artificial at first. This tends to happen whenever we try something new. If you can stick with it and approach it with humor and a light touch, it will soon begin to feel more family friendly. This problem-solving process is a proven winner. These same steps are followed by 10-year-old peer mediators resolving playground disputes and by heads of state negotiating a peace treaty. The content may vary but the process is the same. Also, our interest is not just in solving a particular problem that may arise. Our larger goal is to teach children an effective approach to solving all different kinds of problems that they will face in the future.

Chapter 10

Life's Lessons:
Applying Past Knowledge to New Situations

We only have to think about our own experiences to know why Applying Past Knowledge to New Situations works so well with children. What sticks with us? What makes a deep enough impression that we find ourselves more attentive and willing to actually change our behavior or our thinking about some issue? Most often, it has less to do with what someone *tells* us than what we *discover* to be true because of our own personal experience. That is the intention of this Habit of Mind: to make the most of one of the best resources we always have on hand–our own life lessons.

Applying past knowledge to new situations

Use what you learn!

Accessing prior knowledge; transferring knowledge beyond the situation in which it was learned.

Applying Past Knowledge to New Situations is useful in all kinds of circumstances. Committees of experts are often formed following natural disasters and political or economic debacles to assess what went wrong, how to solve the problem, and how to prevent it from ever happening again. On a personal level, individuals (hopefully) learn to choose a mate wisely based on thoughtful consideration of positives and negatives from past relationships. We learn to manage money, drive safely, and get along with coworkers by actively thinking about both our mistakes and our successes in these different arenas.

A variation of this process is also repeated in classrooms each day. To counter the tendency of students to see each new lesson as an isolated activity, lacking meaning and unconnected to what they learned yesterday, teachers often begin by setting a context. They might launch a new topic from the previous lesson, start with a relevant story, or reference a current event or news item. This not only engages the students, creating this kind of framework—educators call it a scaffold—grounds the new learning. It helps children *make connections* between what they already know from their own experiences or studies and the new material they are about to learn. This is the first step in ensuring that they will eventually own the new knowledge, integrating it into cohesive concepts they understand.

> **Our starting point is to consciously make use of what we know from our previous experiences.**

Think of the real work of this Habit of Mind as the prep stage to becoming an expert. Writer David Brooks describes expertise as "forming internal connections so that little pieces of information turn into bigger networked chunks of information. Learning is not merely about accumulating facts. It is internalizing the relationships between pieces of information" (2011, p. 89). This Habit of Mind fuels that process. When we need to do our best thinking or learning, rather than being on automatic pilot, we need to be intentional. Our starting point is to consciously make use of what we know from our previous related experiences.

Here are two common situations when using past experiences will benefit us:

- **When you encounter a problem or new situation**, take a moment to think about past similar experiences. If nothing comes to mind right away, try broadening your associations. When was a time that you had similar *feelings*? Was there a situation in which you felt discouraged or overwhelmed like you are feeling now? How did you handle it then? What comes to mind? Success? Mistakes? Regrets? You have to take it all in, what worked and what didn't. Then, after considering what you learned from those situations, think about how you can better prepare for the new opportunity before you.

- **W*hen you are about to learn a new topic or skill,*** think back to what you already know about this subject. Like students recalling the previous lesson before beginning the next one, are there questions that you want answered? If you are watching a special series on a particular topic, just before the first show, recall your intentions for wanting to know this information, what you don't know and what you hope to learn. With each show or article or book you read, anticipate what is to come by reflecting on what you already know

This Habit, in particular, gives parents a structure for helping their children think about and use their own experiences in positive and concrete ways. It is the perfect antidote to our natural tendency to want to tell them what to do, to protect them from making the same mistakes we did or, when we are feeling rushed and harried, to simply give a direct order. Asking a few questions at an opportune teachable moment can get them started.

For example, if your 3rd grader is overwhelmed by a new unit on fractions and ready to give up at the onset, first use your listening skills to empathize with how daunting learning new terms, concepts, and procedures can seem. Wait for your child's response and then ask if he remembers ever feeling this way before when he was learning something new. Then ask what happened. Maybe he recalls that learning the multiplication tables also seemed impossible at first, but now they are easy. Encourage him to think in a detailed way about all the steps he took to master the multiplication tables. See if he can select one of those steps and apply it to beginning to tackle this new skill.

You can go one step further by talking about what he already knows about fractions, reinforcing the scaffold that his teacher is building in class. Use the pizza you order for dinner every Friday or the cake you had for dessert. Show your child how each slice is a fraction of the whole.

This versatile Habit of Mind can also help when it comes to making the many decisions that come up in the course of a day with children. Whether big or small, from a child's perspective each decision typically looms large and is the only matter of concern. By incorporating time to examine past experiences, you inject a little breathing room into the situation, diverting the child's attention from the quick answer she expects to a more thoughtful analysis. Both of you get to share viewpoints and think through all sides of the issue at hand. Children get to hear their parents think and reason out loud. They participate first hand in some good decision-making practices.

Consider the common question of whether a child is ready to assume responsibility for a pet:

Grace was a 6th grader and was clamoring for a kitten for her birthday. The first inclination of her parents was to say no. They thought she already had enough commitments. They viewed getting a pet as one more thing to do, a responsibility that would inevitably fall on their shoulders. They remembered when she had brought home the class pet—a salamander— in 3rd grade and how they ended up caring for it over the summer. They raised both concerns with Grace, her busy schedule and her past record with pets.

Grace saw it differently. She agreed that she was busy but pointed out that she was keeping up with schoolwork and after school activities. She talked about how her grades were good and she didn't miss practice for music or sports. She said she was looking forward to coming home and having the kitten to play with and care for. She thought it would be "nice company" before her parents got home from work each day.

As for the salamander, Grace explained that she only volunteered to take it home because no one else did. She felt bad about neglecting the salamander, but the experience made her realize that she wanted a pet "with personality" as she called it. Salamanders were boring. She also researched caring for cats on the Internet. She understood that the cat would need to be fed and played with, its litter box cleaned out, and she was ready to get up 20 minutes earlier in the morning to do just that.

Grace's parents acknowledged that she had done very well this past year and they appreciated what she learned from the salamander. They also were struck by her comment about a cat being good company, and realized that the time before they arrived home might be a bit lonely for her. Her research and goals made sense to them and they were willing to seriously consider the possibility of a pet. But her father had one reservation. He questioned Grace's assumptions about the kind of pet a cat would be.

Cuddly kittens can grow up into aloof and independent cats. Could a cat offer what she was looking for in a pet? He reminded her of her aunt's two cats, who hid every time they went to visit. He suggested that they open up the conversation a little to consider a variety of different animals before deciding. Grace was defensive at first but her father kept bringing the discussion back to what she was really hoping to have in a pet. Eventually the idea of a dog came up. Grace was thrilled that her parents would even consider a dog. There were indeed concerns about the amount of extra work a dog would entail, but both parents recalled happy memories of their own childhood canine companions, and felt that Grace should have those experiences also. They reached a compromise to research rescues dogs that were already trained but to wait until the summer when Grace would have more time to give the new pet the attention it deserved.

When we are willing to look back before we go forward, it enriches our understanding of the present...

In the course of this discussion, Grace's parents began to see the situation differently than when they started. Had they just said no as they were tempted to do, they would have failed to recognize Grace's increased maturity and sense of responsibility since the salamander incident. Had they cut they conversation short with a quick decision, they would have missed the loneliness underlying their child's wish for a pet. Their acknowledgement of these two facts validated Grace's feelings and encouraged her growing sense of responsibility. The detailed conversation that ensued established a template for a thoughtful systematic approach to decision making. Her past experience with the salamander was a platform from which to learn about the responsibility involved in taking care of an animal. Even more important, her parents' willingness to engage with her in that conversation contributed to her conviction that she is understood and cared for.

When we are willing to look back before we go forward, it enriches our understanding of the present, and provides a guide for the future. *Mistakes become opportunities. We are ready to make the most of the situation at hand.*

But not all children will be as thoughtful as Grace. And many may not be receptive to a different point of view. Personality and temperament, an impulsive nature—or some particularly negative experiences—will make some children unwilling participants, at best. We like what Carol Dweck suggests in *Mindset*. Parents can take small steps to changing their child's fixed, negative reaction to a more positive attitude of "what can I learn from this situation" (2006). Rather than waiting for a teachable moment, parents can make this Habit of Mind a daily ritual with the goal of taking the sting out of mistakes. Dweck suggests everyone have an opportunity to answer these three questions at dinner:

- What did you learn today?
- What mistake did you make that taught you something?
- What did you try hard at today? (p. 229.)

Adults will have to take the lead in this discussion. Dweck says "dramatize" the tale of your mistakes so that your child feels every aspect of your saga, your struggles and your progress. And when your reluctant child with the fixed mindset, (*see p. 101, Chapter 7*), comes up blank, telling you that he learned absolutely nothing or that school is boring or too hard, then be ready to point out all he is missing. "Oh, that's too bad that you're not learning. Can you find something hard to do so you could learn more?" Or remind him that the real champions "are the people who work the hardest."

Reuse and Recycle:
Tips for Applying Past Knowledge to New Situations

Jump-start school connections

You don't have to be walking encyclopedias to help your child see the bigger picture when it comes to a homework assignment. If your child is about to learn a new topic or skill, encourage him to reflect on what he already knows about this subject. A quick scan of chapter headings in the textbook is one technique. Remember, the attitude of curiosity can go a long way. A question, a simple comparison between then and now, a quick search on the Internet may be all that is necessary to trigger a conversation and help your child make a few connections.

You can also plan some family outings based on your child's studies for the year—a trip to a colonial museum to go with history class or a trip to the planetarium for science. Or, try some armchair adventures like reading a novel or watching a movie set in the colonial period. These activities give children something on which to "hang" their new learning as they make sense of the world.

Adopt a family credo

Many a successful person has made learning from mistakes their life credo. Tennis champion Billy Jean King says, "For me, losing a tennis match isn't failure, it's research." Inventor Thomas Edison took a similar approach, "I've never made a mistake. I've only learned from experience." His inventions were not luck or accidental, he said, but the result of hard work and an inquisitive and open mind always making connections.

Ask your children to help you come up with a family saying to use as a gentle reminder. For example, "Mistakes are opportunities for the Donnelly family."

Tap into your child's memory bank

When deciding how to handle a situation, sit down with your child and try filling in the blanks:

- This situation sounds like….
- This situation reminds me of…
- What I really don't want to happen again…
- What I would like to happen again….

Even a seven-year-old has a history of first times, past mistakes, memorable moments. Encourage your child to reflect on these events when confronted with a problem, when anxious about an upcoming event or feeling insecure. Make a book of your child's first experiences as a keepsake and reminder of her accomplishments as well as efforts and hard work.

Make lemonade

In the heat of an unsettling situation—for example, your child has just showed you a test he failed because he didn't study, or your daughter is upset because she didn't get the part she wanted in the school play—it is difficult for children or adults to think clearly. Time is needed for emotions to settle down. Depending on the incident and the temperament of those involved, this may take hours, a day, or longer. Revisiting past episodes from a safe distance, however, is important. It gives a family a chance to calmly examine what lessons can be learned from the situation. With a supportive and empathic parent at their side, children can turn a mistake into an opportunity.

How Is Your Child Doing?

Try tracking your child's progress in mastering this Habit of Mind.

- When starting out, your child may need you to provide the memories of past experiences for her. Chances are you are much more aware of her early struggles and successes than she is.

- In time, she will make simple connections when you remind her. With your help, she can make sense of early experiences. She can see her progress, whether it is her ability to read or dance. She will become more aware of how she gets frustrated when she first learns something new.

- As your child begins to apply past knowledge more independently, she will be able to conjure memories of similar situations more readily and apply them to what she is learning. This will enable her to become better able to take in and make use of new information.

- As she progresses with this Habit of Mind and as she matures, look for her to modify her ideas as she considers past experiences. In school, encourage her to make connections, to identify similarities between ideas in different subjects: a formula in math and a scientific phenomenon, or a particular historical period and the experience of a fictional character in a novel. Eventually, she will become naturally reflective, able to modify old ideas as she creates new ideas.

Chapter 11

What's Your Hunch?
Questioning and Posing Problems

We start this chapter, appropriately, with a question of our own: Why is it that, as soon as our children learn to speak, they bombard us with questions about everything they see, hear, touch, taste, and smell, yet, by the time they reach middle school, the torrent of questions has all but dried up? How can this be? Do they really believe they have already learned everything? Have they just lost interest? What happened? Po Bronson and Ashley Merryman (2010) assert that children don't stop asking *because* they lost interest, "it's the other way around. They lost interest because they stopped asking questions." If that is so—that asking questions keeps children's curiosity and interest in their world alive—then the Habit of Mind of Questioning and Posing Problems is the powerful tool we need. This habit should enable us to help jump-start our children's thinking and "get them to a place where ideas can find them," as Eleanor Duckworth, professor of Education at Harvard University (Meek, 1991), says.

In Chapter Six, "I Believe in You," we demonstrate how a well-constructed question can enrich relationships. In this chapter, we

Questioning and posing problems

How do you know?

Having a questioning attitude; knowing what data are needed & developing questioning strategies to produce those data. Finding problems to solve.

look at ways good questions can make kids more alert to their environment as well as enrich their understanding of what goes on around them. We see questions as the route to a life-long passion for learning. Each well-placed question begets another and another and takes us further down the road to knowledge and understanding.

What Do You Notice?

Questions need a context to engage children and are best when asked in a way that sounds less like a quiz and more a reflection of our own curiosity and desire to hear what our children have to say. We want to invite children into our conversation, not put them on the defensive. One of Duckworth's favorite conversation starters is "What do you notice?" It is open-ended, kid-friendly, and can be used in almost any situation—while watching penguins at the zoo or helping children with homework. "What do you notice?" engages kids directly and immediately. Even their smallest observation is a valid answer. This is important because children, like adults, need to feel that their ideas are worthwhile. This gives them confidence in their perceptions and encourages them to stay open to learning. "Noticing questions" also put the adult in the role as listener rather than arbiter of what is a right or wrong answer (Meek, 1991).

Parents point out and name objects and events with their children, starting in babyhood.

Parents point out and name objects and events with their children, starting in babyhood. It is part of a child's "apprenticeship," Peter Johnston reminds us in *Choice Words* (2004, p. 18). Parents start by naming every object their infant sees–the ball, the bus, the flower, etc. Then they add descriptors. "The ball is big, red, and rolls. Catch it." With school age children, the process moves to the next level as conversations make room for a child's emerging ability to think concretely and grasp more and more attributes about different phenomena.

"Look at these tomatoes from our backyard. What do you notice about them compared to the ones from the store?" a parent asks while preparing dinner. "Yes, they are plumper and redder, but not so pretty. Now, taste them and tell me what you think." And so a conversation begins. Together a parent and child speculate about what it is that makes a homegrown tomato so sweet and juicy. They wonder about where store bought tomatoes come from, how they are shipped, how long it takes to get them to the store. More conversation unfolds about what happens to the tomato plants when the weather starts getting cold; what to do with all the tomatoes that get ripe at the same time; and what gets in the way of our having fresh juicy tomatoes in the winter. Think about all that a child could learn from a conversation like that.

Starting with a child's own observations has advantages when it comes to schoolwork, says Johnston. Adult and child begin with a common focus of attention. He describes one 4th grade teacher using this practice for a lesson in handwriting, "without actually doing a lesson." The teacher explained that she was having difficulty reading some of her students' handwriting and invited them to help her plan some instruction to improve their writing. She took notes as they talked about what they noticed when comparing their writing to the chart of alphabet in cursive. They discussed which were the difficult letters and why, which letters were easily confused and which letters had a lot in common. This, too, took place as part of a conversation, this time among the students and their teacher.

At home, parents can follow a similar process with homework. Asking a child what he notices about a poem he doesn't understand, for example, can open the door just wide enough to let him in. He may notice that the poem mentions a lake and that it rhymes. "Okay, what else?" A boat is in the lake and a little girl and mother are standing nearby on the shore. Gradually, the child builds a picture in his mind from which he can understand and write about the poem.

Listening carefully to our children's responses is key, particularly when they may be stuck with an assignment. Does she understand the question? Does she not know enough about the topic to answer it? Is she unsure how to put all the information together?

Ten-year-old Kate was struggling with an essay on the circulatory system. Her father saw her fidgeting at the kitchen table. "You seem restless tonight. Is there a problem?" As they went over the assignment, it was clear to Kate's father that she understood the question and she had her notes and review sheets. But she didn't know where to begin. Her father looked at the notes along with her and asked her to tell him what the notes said. Resistant at first, she read the information methodically, but in time Kate began to get into the process more and more. She began to notice similar themes and the big picture came into focus. Her father had her look at the textbook, specifically the headings in the chapter. This confirmed that she was on the right track.

Three Levels of Questions

To appreciate Kate's initial difficulty, it is helpful to understand three levels of questions and thinking, which Costa (2007, p. 200) modeled after a poem by Wendell Holmes called the *Three-Story Intellect*. Children's ability to answer questions depends on where they are in their intellectual development or, as we saw with Kate, their mastery of information, concepts, and skills that they need to know. Just as children must crawl before they walk, there is no way of getting to the top floor of the Three-Story Intellect without first going through the other two levels.

Fact collectors reside on the first level of intellect. This is where children *gather* information they need to know. Basic questions like *who, what, when,* and *where* are useful in focusing their attention at this stage. Assignments that ask students to identify, list, match, or describe are all designed to ensure they are learning the material. Kate got stuck because she tried to bypass this level and go directly to the second level, leaving her with that "I don't know where to begin–or where I am– feeling." She may have read the text and taken down the notes in class, but she didn't know the material well enough to recall it when she had to do her essay. Once she read through her notes carefully, she was ready to move to the next level.

The second level is where children *process* the information they have acquired. Here questions like *why* and *how* become important as students use the information they have learned. Rather than just copying or paraphrasing, they may be asked to analyze and synthesize what they know. Comparing and contrasting, making analogies, or explaining why are common strategies at this level. Depending on how well students understand the information, they may even go beyond an assignment. If they really understand the information, Costa says, they may raise their own questions, triggering their own inquiry. Kate was ready to compare the circulatory and respiratory systems in her essay but not to go beyond the assignment.

The highest level is when children are ready to *apply* what they know. There is a skylight in the Three-Story Intellect, because this is when students are able to use what they know to create new scenarios. Here they evaluate what they have learned and then move on to their own ideas in which they idealize, imagine, and predict. Questions like *What do you imagine or hypothesize?* and *What if?* invite them at this stage to think creatively and hypothetically, to use imagination, to expose a value system, or to make a judgment, says Costa. These questions prompt them to make sense of the material in a way that really makes it their own.

Like Kate's father, parents will want to guide their children's movement through these different levels, helping them to understand where they may be stuck and why and then how to resolve the problem. If your child has completed an assignment, asking "How did you figure that out?" invites him to think about his process and become more aware of his own steps and strategies (Johnston, 2004).

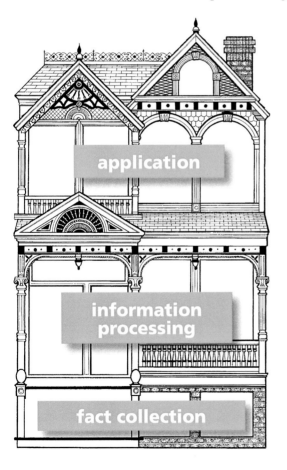

Questions for Thinking:

- **Highest Level**—The child evaluates and can apply what he knows. Ask: What do you think would…? and What if…?

- **Second Level**—The child makes sense out of the information. Ask: Why? and How?

- **First Level**—The child gathers information. Ask: Who?, Where?, and When?

Moon Watching: Getting Kids to Ask the Questions

It should be clear by now that, of course, we want children to ask questions. Lots of questions. For that, you don't need much in the way of special equipment. A magnifying glass or a cheap pair of binoculars can often stimulate their curiosity. A trip to the lake or seashore, or even a little creek running through the park, is more interesting with a small net and a pail to catch and observe critters. Flashlights are great fun for children and make nighttime adventures possible. While we always think that a trip to the museum can be inspirational, your own backyard or neighborhood park can also yield profound opportunities for learning.

Duckworth thinks that "moon watching" is a perfect way to stimulate important questions. While most people think they know all about the moon and its habits, those who have tried observing it very soon notice things that surprise them. At some point, they begin to recognize that what they thought they knew about the moon is different from what they are actually seeing. Then the questions begin. Sometimes you see the moon shining earlier in the evening but can't find it a few hours later. Where did it go? Sometimes you see the moon in the day. Does that mean the moon rises? Or you see it in a certain place one night but not the next night (Meek, 1991). Eventually, a child may come to the realization that the moon does not actually disappear during the daytime but can still sometimes be seen. Although she had surely seen the moon out during the day prior to this moment, it hadn't actually registered as such, because of her assumption from stories and nursery rhymes and pictures that the moon is a nighttime phenomena. This sudden realization makes her think in a new way about the moon.

Duckworth has given this assignment to her graduate students, but it is also an excellent one for school age children. Observe the moon every night and keep a journal about your observations, jotting down every detail you can think of, such as where the moon is located in the sky, how bright it is, the time, where you are standing, and what it looks like. Children can also draw pictures of the moon. This is a great activity for kids during a summer holiday, but any time of year is fine. It only takes a few minutes each evening. A special notebook and the adventure of going out in the dark can add to this experience.

We suggest you do not research information on the Internet until you have gone through at least one cycle of the moon first. Parents can take their cue from

Duckworth about their role. She does not provide answers. She listens intently to her students. "What did you notice?" and "Tell me more" are her standard responses. If the student is closing in on something important, she will encourage him to stay with it. Duckworth's adult students—who presumably had learned about the moon in their science classes all through school—found that going back and observing, staying with the moon night after night, gave rise to thoughts and questions that had never before occurred to them. They discovered that the more they observed, the more they realized they didn't know, and the more motivated they were to find

...your own backyard or neighborhood park can also yield profound opportunities for learning.

out. The very act of discovering that there were still unexplained mysteries about this thing they thought they knew so well was, to many of them, awe-inspiring. Children are very open to this kind of learning experience. The point is not to tell children what they are seeing or to explain it, but to create situations in which they discover it. "I found that the more interest I took in what they were saying, the more interest the children themselves took. I saw that they were willing—even eager—to keep thinking about the question, and to work on developing a degree of understanding that they found increasingly more satisfactory," said Duckworth. (Duckworth, 2009, p. 186)

What If? Turning Young Spectators into Inquiring Participants

Six-year-old Sammy loves bubbles. He even has a motorized bubble blower, which he dug out from the bottom of his toy bin when his friend Timmy was visiting. But the batteries were no longer working and they couldn't find the jar of commercial bubble-blowing liquid.

This story could have gone any number of ways. Sonia, Sammy's mother, could have put the bubble blower back in the toy bin and told them to try something else. They could have all gone to the store to purchase more liquid and batteries or, as happened on this day, Sonia decided to challenge Sammy and Timmy to make their own bubble-blowing liquid. She recently read an online recipe for making bubbles, but instead of just telling them what to do, she told them to come up with their own recipe. Both boys jumped at the opportunity.

"What do we know about bubbles?" Sonia asked to get them started. Sammy said they were fun and broke when you touched them. Timmy said his mother sometimes blew bubbles at him when she was washing dishes. He said they should try using dishwashing soap. And so Sonia got out two jars, her liquid dishwashing soap, a measuring cup and two spoons for stirring. Sammy looked around for substitute wands to blow the bubbles. He found an old wire egg holder from a kit for dying eggs and got Timmy a pasta spoon with a hole in the middle.

If we want children to know what to do when confronted with complex problems, giving them the answers to predictable questions is not enough, say Costa and Kallick (2000, p 7). What did Sammy and Timmy discover that day? In the course of their playing, making a mess, and having fun, they learned to think about things they took for granted—soap and water. They had a hunch and made something of their ideas. They eventually looked online for a recipe and read that sugar would help, but neither thought it did when they added it. What did make a difference, however, was how they blew the bubbles. They decided that was the most important discovery in their experiment. If they blew gently, they got bigger bubbles. They experienced a great deal of satisfaction finding that out through their own trial and error. Instead of passing their time with a predictable toy, Timmy and Sammy were encouraged to experiment with their own wonderful ideas and to come up with their own discoveries.

There are plenty of variations to *What if?* Older kids typically are more scientific about their experiments, carefully measuring and making detailed observations. Let kids pursue what interests them. For kitchen chemists, there are safe online experiments. For mechanics there are flashlights to take apart, and egg drops for physic buffs. Young naturalist can never get enough outdoors. Do ants prefer bread or cookie crumbs? Programs like Science Olympiad and Odyssey of the Mind also offer kids opportunities to test their problem-solving skills. In her book *Raising Lifelong Learners* (1998), educator Lucy Calkins lists questions to inspire kitchen and backyard scientists: *What's your hunch? How can you find out? What could account for that? How could you see if that's a reasonable expectation?*

And for young writers and poets, there are stories and puppet shows and many what-ifs to explore: *What if you lived a hundred years ago? What if you rewrote that story? What if people could fly?*

How's School? Getting Beyond One-Word Answers

How was school? It is a question asked by generations of parents, to which generations of children have responded with a grunt, a shrug of the shoulders or "fine" at best, and "boring" more typically. Instead of accepting this fate, vary the question. Acknowledge their boredom but don't settle for it. Lucy Calkins says to acknowledge how kids feel but seek an explanation. "It may feel like you learned nothing and that everything you did was boring. Why do you think that it was boring? What would you do differently?"

Calkins advises taking on the attitude of a journalist. "The more you know, the more you can learn." She advises parents to find out what is going on during their child's school day. Check the online class page or your child's backpack or take a quick visit to the classroom to find out about some activities or events going on in school; let these become topics to talk about with your child. Is there a special assembly or a visitor? Is the class reading a special book or learning about woodland animals? Is there a class pet? Better to ask a specific question such as following up on a project they did for class, or what they did during lunch or recess, or what they made in art class. Or think back to what happened in your child's life yesterday and follow up: How did it go on the playground? What did your teacher say about your project? These are the questions to engage your child (Calkins, 1998, p. 19).

You can also make questions a family affair. Hold your question about your child's day until everyone is home and can talk about their day, perhaps at dinner or bedtime. Adults can share first. Some parents pick a question for everyone to answer. Remember Dweck's suggestions:
- What did you learn today?
- What did you try hard at today? (Dweck, 2006, p. 229.)

Itzak Rabi, Nobel Prize winner in physics, attributes his career to his mother's question when he came home from school, "What question did you ask today?"
And don't forget to ask:
- What made you laugh today?
- Did you do anything that made you feel proud?

Chapter 12

Taking Responsible Risks:
Go For It! (But Think About It First)

When you think about very successful people or remember times when you have achieved something you've been most proud of, you are likely to discover a strong element of responsible risk-taking in those reflections. In almost every culture it seems the stories we love best are those of ultimate triumph over seemingly insurmountable odds: the tale of the ordinary person who dares to *try*; of the unlikely hero who finds himself in a tough situation and takes on the challenge anyway—not because he's certain to win, but because it is the right thing to do.

We love those stories because they speak of what is possible within each one of us. The Habit of Mind of Taking Responsible Risks calls on us to "venture out," to attempt more than we thought we could do, to get past our comfort zone, and to "live on the edge of (our) competence" (Costa, 2000, p. 34). There is an implied energy, a forward propulsion in Taking Responsible Risks. No matter what their profession or endeavor, responsible risk takers are seekers, explorers, doers. They have a restless urge to push past the limits of what was thought possible, into new territories of

Taking responsible risks

Venture Out!

Being adventuresome; living on the edge of one's competence. Try new things constantly.

knowing, doing, and understanding. Any time an individual meets a daunting new challenge, it is understood that there is no guarantee of success. After assessing the risks and taking a chance, you may indeed accomplish what you set out to do. If so, you are likely to become more confident and more capable of tackling future challenges. If success eludes you that time, hopefully you will reflect on what went well and what didn't and put what you have learned to good use. Without such a repertoire of experiences—sometimes successful, and sometimes not—we risk stagnation and failure to grow. Individuals might hope that they are staying "safe" by not venturing out and trying, but that is not likely. The demands of the world don't stop because we have stopped growing—they just become more difficult to manage.

Parenting can sometimes make us feel that we are *falling off* the edge of our competence. In fact, it can feel like a pretty harrowing undertaking at times. Every day parents are faced with new situations that can stymie their best intentions and for which their own upbringing provides no answer. Teachers, friends, and experts may all have differing opinions. Just to add a little more stress, how could the stakes possibly be higher? What else could be more important than to make good decisions on behalf of your child? As a way of managing this anxiety, some parents seek to have complete control over every possible contingency. They may feel that without their intense involvement in every aspect of their child's life—academic, social, nutritional, athletic, and more—their child won't have a chance. They assume responsibilities that should, increasingly over time, belong to their child. This can result in the phenomenon commonly known as "helicopter parents" who hover about and micromanage, even as their children are off to college. With so little practice in problem solving and dealing with obstacles independently, these children are apt to have some difficulty functioning on their own.

At the other extreme are parents who permit a greater degree of autonomy than is really safe or helpful to their child. They may underestimate the degree of danger in the environment or overestimate their child's maturity. Perhaps they are preoccupied with work or relationship difficulties, or maybe they feel overwhelmed by a strong-willed child who keeps pressing for more freedom, which they grant, just hoping for the best. These children may navigate their world as though they are free agents, but they seldom have the judgment or maturity to make good decisions. They take risks, but the element of *responsibility* is missing. They often learn the hard way, by bumping up against rules and expectations and discovering that there are indeed consequences. We acknowledge the difficult balancing act parents perform in assessing how much freedom and responsibility a child can handle. There are so many variables to consider: the child's age, maturity level, the "norms" of the school and the neighborhood, and, ultimately, what you yourself feel you can live with. Decisions such as when a child is ready for her first sleepover at a friend's house, when he can walk home from school by himself, when he can stay alone in the house for a short period, when she can have her first cell-phone all present a number of different factors to consider.

> **The demands of the world don't stop because we have stopped growing—they just become more difficult to manage.**

Taking Responsible Risks is also relevant to your child's learning. Teachers often express concerns about a child who doesn't ask questions, who wants the security of the *one* right answer, and who seems to have a hard time formulating his own opinions of things. Such a child seems to shrink from actively engaging with the subject matter. His basic skills might be just fine, but when it comes to drawing inferences, imagining different outcomes, thinking outside the box—he just doesn't want to risk it. With these children, teachers find it a challenge to encourage the child to begin to look within himself for possible answers—to *think*, rather than just recall what someone else has said.

Because they encourage a more reflective, thoughtful, and intentional approach, activating the Habits of Mind should reduce the ad hoc quality of responses to different situations. Along with Applying Past Knowledge to New Situations (*see Chapter 10*), the habit of Taking Responsible Risks provides a more structured and considered way of approaching decision making. Other Habits of Mind, such as Metacognition and Managing Impulsivity, should help parents manage some of the stressful emotions that accompany decisions for which they have no precedent. In addition, when families have done some of the work suggested in Thinking Interdependently to create a shared family vision, they may have already clarified certain values for their family, such as going out of your way to help others, thus making some decisions easier. And, as mentioned in Chapter 10, you can try to recall previous situations that were similar in *some* way to the current dilemma for clues as to how to proceed.

In this Chapter we suggest ways to balance out the *responsible* and the *risks* parts of Taking Responsible Risks.

Temperament and Risk-Taking

As with many of the Habits of Mind, temperament (parent's *and* child's) will influence a person's willingness to take responsible risks. From infancy, we can see temperamental differences along a continuum from the child who is very cautious, watchful, and perhaps clingy, to the child who charges ahead into a situation with no hesitation (see Chess, S.& Thomas, A., 1987). Each extreme presents its own concerns to parents. The child who tends to withdraw in the face of new experiences, takes a long time to warm up to new people, or who is reluctant to try new foods, can be frustrating to parents, who urge her to "just try!" This child sees a reason to worry in every new situation and requires a lot of coaching, coaxing, and handholding for every new milestone. At the other end of the continuum is the youngster who may be *too* unafraid. This child needs close supervision because impulsivity and lack of forethought may put him in harm's way. To complicate matters, parents' own temperaments influence how they react to their child. A father who is dynamic and outgoing may feel impatient, annoyed, or embarrassed if his son is reluctant to join in the games. A mother who tends to be cautious may be unduly alarmed at her daughter's bold and adventurous approach to play. Problems can also arise when parent and child are similar on some dimensions of temperament. You sometimes hear people saying, "We don't get along because we're too much alike!"

There is a very wide range of what is "normal" in temperament. Knowing that a child comes into the world with basic temperamental tendencies already in place may help the way you think about and react to her. As you begin to form a picture of her on the temperamental continuum—is she slow to warm up, or does she approach new stimuli with a high activity level and intensity?—try to reflect also on what those characteristics mean to you. Were you also that way as a child? If so, did you get criticized or find yourself in trouble without knowing why? Or were you considered shy? Did you miss out on some experiences or opportunities because of that? More important, did you feel accepted and appreciated for who you were? If so, what did your parents say or do that helped you feel secure and cherished? If you recall clashes because of temperament, what do you wish they

There is a very wide range of what is "normal" in temperament.

might have said or done differently? If you were shy and withdrawn, what might they have done that would have helped you? If you were a child with a high activity level and tendency to be impulsive, how could they have kept you safe and responsible without dampening your spirit?

As you develop a clearer picture of your own and your child's basic temperamental traits as they apply to risk taking, now try to identify your own emotional reactions to these manifestations of temperament. If you find yourself frequently reacting with frustration or impatience to behaviors that may reflect a child's basic "wiring," then perhaps it is time to recalibrate those reactions. Putting the Habit of Metacognition into play is a good place to start. You could ask yourself, *why does this bother me so much? What does it remind me of? If she really can't help reacting this way, how can I best help her?*

You can also take a moment to collect your *positive pre-suppositions* about your child. Assume that his intentions are good. Understand that he doesn't enjoy feeling anxious about going into new situations or getting into trouble for being too intense and impulsive. Metacognition can also be very helpful in *reframing* the way you think about your child. Does your child have a rather high activity level? That's good. He is a lively child who will be well served by his energy. Is he cautious and tentative in new situations, and does it take him quite awhile to feel comfortable? Well then, you don't have to worry about his impulsivity getting him into trouble. Our point is that there is adaptive value to all these manifestations of temperament. When we find our child falling toward one extreme or another, we will love them for exactly who they are and, together, figure out ways to minimize any deleterious effects.

Model Your Own Responsible Risk Taking: Do a Cost-Benefit Analysis

This is your opportunity to demonstrate how this important Habit of Mind works. If you are faced with a decision to make—let's say you've been asked to organize and direct the annual talent show at school—you could use this as a teachable moment for your children. How do people even make decisions like this? Do you just go by feelings? If so, how do you know which feelings take precedence? You might initially feel anxious and overwhelmed by the very thought of the time commitment and responsibility involved. Yet, as you think about it, you begin to feel excited, and a happy anticipation bubbles up at the chance to put your creative energies into a worthy project. Taking Responsible Risks means we take all of our feelings into consideration as we begin to do a cost-benefit analysis. Following your feelings, *all* of them, is a sure way to come to your own personal truth about the decision. One of the ways to do this is to ask yourself, *What would be the best possible outcome from this venture? What would be the worst possible outcome? What are the implications for each outcome? How serious would a failure be? How fulfilling and satisfying would success feel?*

With a decision like this, it might be helpful to check in with the whole family to think it through interdependently, hashing out all the combinations and permutations. Children as young as seven or eight respond well to the simple decision-making strategy of putting a vertical line down the center of a paper and labeling one side "Pros" and one side "Cons" (or "good" and "bad" for younger children.) As you go through the process, your children might express concerns about the time commitment: Will you still be as available to them? Maybe they have concerns you would not have imagined; for example, what will it mean to their friendships if their mom is in the position of deciding who gets into the talent show? For each concern, the family can problem-solve possible ways of managing. It may be that some aspect of what you have discussed is a deal breaker, and you decide you just can't do it. Better to realize it now than two weeks into the project. Or, by having discussed the decision thoroughly and systematically, you decide "it's a go." If so, you are in a much better position than if you had simply said "yes" to begin with. Why? Because going through this process gave everyone in the family a stake in the outcome. Together, you all considered the possible negatives and how all of you might deal with them. You're not as likely to be ambushed by problems you hadn't considered.

> **Taking Responsible Risks means we take all of our feelings into consideration as we begin to do a cost-benefit analysis.**

There will always be unknowns. There is still an element of risk to the undertaking—there always is in anything slightly challenging. But it is a *responsible risk.* You have considered as many contingencies as possible and are going forward. And if, despite doing all that, the venture turns out to be unsuccessful? Well, you gave it your best shot. Success is never guaranteed despite our best efforts. You will be comforted by knowing you went into it with open eyes, you tried your best, and surely you learned something valuable from the experience. And if you succeed, which is more likely, you will enjoy the pride of accomplishment, a whole new set of skills you have learned, and the confidence to tackle another new challenge. Priceless. Now let's take a look at how you can help your children have some of those priceless experiences for themselves.

Encouraging the Reluctant Child

This child tends to be unwilling to try new things, does not adapt well to sudden change, and needs extra time and support to get used to unfamiliar people and situations. When things are handled well and accommodation is given to the child's temperamental need to take it slow, this kind of child generally adapts just fine. Knowing this, here are a few strategies to move your child toward being more amenable to Taking Responsible Risks:

Plan Ahead. For any new experience, your child will appreciate lead time to prepare himself. Provide information ahead of time that is likely to allay concerns. If you are going on vacation, provide pictures or view the destination online so she can visualize what it will be like. Explain how you will be getting there, how long it will take, and so on. Involve your child in the planning by having her make lists of what she will pack.

Preview new experiences. Is he dreading the new school year, worried about what the teacher will be like and if the work will be too hard? Find out if you can take him to visit the new teacher in the summertime as she is preparing her classroom. That will likely reassure him that his teacher is really nice; he can see how the room is set up; and the teacher can give him an enthusiastic preview of some interesting things they'll be doing in the upcoming school year. That will give you some positive things to talk about as he gears up for September. There are also many good children's books that cover situations that typically cause anxiety. Reading a relevant book together and then talking about it can help normalize the experience for your child.

Allow more time to adjust to new stimuli. Some children need to watch the ocean waves go in and out for quite awhile before they'll stick a toe in. Try to honor their own timetable.

Break the experience down into small, manageable steps. A new experience such as swimming lessons or going off to camp can be overwhelming for a child who is slow to warm up. Try to set up the experience so that your child can master his anxiety one small step at a time. Allow your child some control over the process, so the anxiety is not overwhelming.

Talk about it. If your child is reluctant to do something new or expresses worries about it, ask "What's the worst thing that could happen?" Try to help her identify the key aspects of what concerns her. Is she afraid she won't know what to do or how to do it? Is she worried about feeling stranded or alone? As you both work to identify what it is that worries her, assess with her how likely or unlikely it is that those worries would actually come true. Then, together, build a back-up plan. "Well, if you feel stuck and don't know what to do, what do you think the first step would be? Who could you ask?" You could also role-play some of those scenarios to try out alternative strategies and help her feel more empowered.

Recall past successes. "Remember when you started skating lessons? You wanted to do it, but you were so nervous about falling. Remember, you were surprised that it wasn't really a big deal when you fell. And now you love to skate. You say it feels like flying. What if you had let your fear of falling keep you from starting lessons? You would never have known that beautiful feeling." You can point out that lots of people tend to be cautious about new or challenging experiences, and there is survival value to that. But remind your child how good it can feel to push past that comfort zone.

Master your own anxiety. Sometimes we push too hard. We imagine that it will be like this forever, and we panic. Remind yourself that this is the child you *have*, and your goal is not to change who he is but to give him the support he needs to make the best of his own personal constellation of strengths and weaknesses.

Help your child evaluate the experience afterward. Ask questions, such as "How did you do that? What did you tell yourself when you were getting ready to jump in? How do you feel now?" The idea is to increase your child's awareness of the thoughts she had that enabled her to take that risk so she can call on them again in the future.

Celebrate small successes. Convey your quiet pride, that, *even though it was difficult*, your child did it anyway. Remember, in Chapter 5 how Rebecca told her daughter she was *resilient*? You can define "courage" for your child as something all people have, just by pushing themselves through those difficult moments. Affirm your child's courage.

Strengthening the *Responsible* Part of Taking Responsible Risks

Children who approach new situations eagerly don't always put much energy into worrying about what might go wrong. You love their optimism and enthusiasm but, when combined with a tendency toward impulsivity, you know they can sometimes get themselves into hot water. With these children, we want to strengthen the *responsible* aspect of Taking Responsible Risks. In addition to the strategies covered in Chapter 8 on Managing Impulsivity, we offer here a few *suggestions specific to responsible risk taking*.

Plan ahead. This is not so much to reassure your bold child—no need of that—but to introduce the idea of slowing down and considering possible decisions she will have to make. When planning that vacation, for example, encourage your enthusiastic child to spend some time with you to gain a realistic understanding of what's in store. Will you be going hiking? Make sure she understands it could get tiring or tedious at times. What are some things she can do to help her through those moments? A family reunion with lots of cousins? How will he handle it if the older cousins propose some activity that may not be safe for someone his age?

These conversations are not intended to put a damper on the happy anticipation but as preparation for some possible contingencies.

Preview experiences. Again, the purpose is a little different than for the reluctant child. Here, you want to encourage your child to expand his thinking about what is coming up. Partly, this will be to establish expectations; for example, "Fourth grade is just filled with so many interesting things to learn, so many projects and field trips. I remember your brother was a little surprised, though, that he had quite a bit more homework than in 3rd grade. What are your thoughts about that? How are you planning to manage the bigger workload?" Children who fall toward the impulsive end of the continuum go into new situations eagerly, but are sometimes surprised by what they face when they get there. Any time you are able to stimulate their thinking about situations ahead of time, you give them a better chance to handle the new challenge effectively.

Work on wait time. These children are often chomping at the bit, ready to charge into a new situation. Try to establish the habit of pausing, taking a deep breath, and stopping to think. What do they plan to do when they first enter school, a party, a scout meeting? Get them thinking about what the expectations are and what their behavior will be.

Talk about it. Children who fall a little short on the *responsible* part of risk taking need more explicit modeling and practice with the thought processes that go into decision making. Since these kids tend to get corrected a lot, you don't want them to feel lectured or criticized. Rather, you want to frame it in a way that is comfortable and interesting to them. As we mentioned earlier, you might ask your child to help you with a decision you have to make. We have already suggested ways of having conversations with children to enhance the likelihood they will learn from their experiences. Use some of those empathic listening skills to let your child know that you understand it's not always easy for him when he's "in the moment." You may also want to help your child increase his awareness of those little feelings he gets that might be telling him, *Whoa, slow down here, this might not be safe.* As he gets better at recognizing and paying attention to those feelings, he will see them as trusted allies. When you have these conversations with positive presuppositions in the front of your mind, your child will feel your acceptance and emotional support. He should then be more open to working on strategies to improve the situation.

Recall past successes. Children who tend to be impulsive don't automatically refer back to past experiences—positive or negative—to guide them in the moment. They'll need to rely on *your* memory to encourage them that they have in the past, and can now, make good decisions.

Master your own anxiety. Kids who tend to "go for it" may push back if they sense a parent's own anxiety is holding them back. Try to think through your emotional reactions and assess whether they are based on realistic concerns. Again, if you ask yourself, "What's the worst thing that can happen? What are the chances of that happening? What steps can we take to make it even less likely?" you help yourself think more clearly about the situation. You want to try to find ways of safely meeting your independent child's need to develop her autonomy. However, the bottom line is that you are the one responsible for your child's safety and well-being. There may be times when you will legitimately have to say "no" or "not yet" for no other reason than you just don't feel they are ready yet. If that happens, try to work out a plan with your child in which she can accomplish interim steps *toward* her goal. If you are convinced that she is safe and behaves responsibly at each interim step, then she will have earned that increased autonomy.

Help your child evaluate a situation afterward. Something like, "I saw you start to follow after those bigger kids climbing that tree. It looked to me like you were trying to decide if it was safe or not, and then I noticed that you climbed up, but just to the first big branch. I was wondering what thoughts ran through your mind then?" The child might not even be aware of that sequence of events. Your witnessing it gives him an opportunity to replay it in slow motion and consider the decision making that went into his calibrating just how far up that tree he could safely climb. Whether a child is successful or not with any specific incident, a little debriefing afterward clarifies what he did well and how he might improve things next time.

Celebrate small successes. You want to acknowledge any evidence that your child put some thought into the decision, that it was, in fact, a decision and not just an impulsive response. Your acknowledgement that it is not always easy to stop and think, and your appreciation of her efforts should create more awareness and openness for your child to keep trying.

Taking Responsible Risks in School

We mention above that teachers sometimes express concerns about children who appear reluctant to offer an idea if they are not already certain it is the *one* right answer. They often raise their hand to ask, "Is this right?" or "Is this what you wanted?" and seem focused more on not making mistakes than on learning. Of course we want children to strive for accuracy, and we want them to follow directions. But excessive concern about being correct can constrict children's interests and diminish their intellectual vitality. Our overall goals for children are much loftier than just getting it right. We want them to be curious about their world, to *think* about what they see and encounter and feel. We want them to understand that there are many routes to getting to "right." We want them to have confidence in their own minds, to know that their own thoughts and perceptions are just as valid as anyone else's, and that there is value in sharing them. We want children to *try* even if something seems very hard.

> **...excessive concern about being correct can constrict children's interests and diminish their intellectual vitality.**

If your child's teacher mentions this to you, we recommend that you ask first whether there may be any learning difficulties getting in your child's way. If the teacher does think there may be a learning issue, he should guide you to the next steps in identifying and remediating whatever learning difficulties might be present. If, however, you and the teacher both agree that a child's difficulty in Taking Responsible Risks in learning is more a matter of temperament than anything else, you can then work out with the teacher a collaborative plan to encourage this habit at home and at school. Initially, children who are reluctant to take responsible risks in their learning may need some support in developing a more robust sense of themselves as capable individuals with their own unique preferences and opinions.

- Encourage your child to express personal preferences in a variety of ways. From a very young age, give children choices in clothing, food, room décor, or activities. Notice what she seems to be drawn to and, without overwhelming her, support those interests in small ways; e.g. "I noticed you were really interested in the baby pigs at the petting zoo. I saw this adorable book about pigs on my way home and picked it up for you. Let's read it tonight." As children develop their own tastes and preferences, their sense of self is strengthened.

• As you go places with your child, or even just sitting on the back porch, ask him, "What do you notice?" Get in the habit of just chatting together about what you both see, hear, and feel. What we are looking for is a *non-evaluative* kind of conversation, where he is encouraged to share his perceptions without any worry about being right or wrong.

• Make sure your risk-averse child is not overwhelmed by strong siblings or friends who may make fun of any failed efforts. When children are embarrassed or made to feel inadequate for not living up to someone else's standards, they are not likely to take the risk of being wrong again and may prefer to keep a low profile.

• Help your child manage the uncomfortable negative emotions that go along with not being certain. Some sensitive children are afraid of being wrong; it can feel catastrophic for them as they imagine a classroom full of critical eyes upon them. Empathize with those feelings, but help bring mistakes and failure into proper perspective. It may help to ask, "So what's the worst thing that could happen if you are wrong (or make a mistake, or get a bad grade?") Whatever they reply, you can then ask, "So what?" and "What do you think will happen then?" Reassure your child that you care more about their *learning* than their *grade*. If he gets a bad grade, the two of you together (and with the teacher) will use it to figure out the best ways of helping him learn. We also want to promote "ego-strength" in our children so they won't be so affected by the negative reactions of others. If you think that's an issue, speculate with your child about why a classmate would even make a critical or derogatory comment, and then come up with some little mantra your child can mentally rehearse, such as, *It doesn't matter what he says; he's not in charge of my learning, I am.*

• Some children are anxious about moving forward in their learning because they fear that, once they demonstrate competence, they will be overwhelmed by new and heavier demands. While conveying confidence in their ability, you can also let them know that both you and the teacher are there to cheer them on—not to burden them. You can explain that, by learning, they are exercising their mental muscles. Mastering each skill in school makes them better able to deal with the challenges that lie ahead.

- At the same time you are helping to dissipate some of the fear, anxiety, and embarrassment your child may experience at the mere thought of being wrong, try to promote some feelings of excitement and happy anticipation about taking responsible risks with her learning. You can help your child through a crisis of confidence by showing your interest in what they are learning.

Maybe your child is just moving up to reading chapter books on her own and is dismayed that they seem so long. Perhaps she is worried that she'll have to read these longer books all in one sitting. Try to discover what her actual concerns are so you can address them. Try to convey your excitement that she is now at a point where she can read some really good and interesting stories all by herself. You can *predict* that it won't be long before she will not even be thinking about the length of the book because the stories are so absorbing.

- Monitor your own reactions to errors and mistakes. Demonstrate tolerance when you or your child gets something wrong. Develop some family sayings such as, *That's why pencils have erasers* or *Nothing ventured, nothing gained* to reinforce the value of learning from mistakes and of taking the chance of giving something your best effort.

No matter where you fall on the temperamental continuum, one expectation that can get in the way is the belief success should be guaranteed if you do everything right. Not so. The possibility of failure is the "risk" part of the endeavor; it has nothing to do with fairness, but is just what life hands us sometimes. However, if you keep an optimistic outlook—not so much for the *outcome*, but for the *adventure* of the endeavor—you will not be daunted. Think of all the dreams out there that were never quite fully realized: The Broadway bound extravaganza that folded in previews; the novel that took ten years to write that never really got attention because a similar one came out the month before; the two teams working toward a medical breakthrough, and one gets there first, and gets all the glory. These things happen all the time, but those who believe in and love what they are doing don't give up. They dust themselves off, soothe their bruised egos, and get back to work. They put themselves "out there." If they're not successful, they find comfort in the value of what they did and what they learned from it, and the fact that they gave it a good try. If they do succeed, it is even sweeter when it comes after a missed attempt or two.

Taking Responsible Risks is the way individuals, businesses, and research move forward and make progress. This Habit of Mind promotes a balance between clear thinking and planning and the energy, initiative, and courage that says, "Let's do it."

Parents are so influential in helping children establish this healthy balance. Just imagine you are rock-stepping across a stream with your child. As you look back at your child hesitating to take the next big step, you reach back and offer your hand. *It is a big stretch, but I will keep you safe, you can do it, let's move on.* That's our job.

Chapter 13

Out of the Box:
Creating, Imagining, Innovating

Let's clear up some misconceptions about creativity.

Many people assume that creativity is a rare commodity that someone is either born with or not and that it is reserved for the elite among us: artists, writers, and composers, or the likes of an Einstein, Edison, or Steve Jobs. One of the liberating aspects of learning about this Habit of Mind, however, is the realization that each one of us is fully capable of creative, imaginative, and innovative thought and that we use it more often than we realize in our jobs and personal lives. Are you a basketball coach who has devised fun and exciting games that keep your players interested in practicing their basic skills? Are you a teacher writing lessons to reach children who may learn differently? Are you an engineer designing new ways to provide clean water? Are you a cook who enjoys substituting ingredients in recipes to come up with something altogether new and tasty? Maybe you do carpentry and can be counted on to make a durable and aesthetically pleasing repair with whatever materials are at hand. Perhaps you work in customer service and find ways to make an irate customer happy again.

**Creating,
imagining,
and innovating**
Try a different way!

Generating new and
novel ideas, fluency,
originality

> **As adults, our job is not so much to teach this Habit, but to create the conditions under which it can grow and thrive.**

All of these people have one thing in common: They are tapping into their creativity, imagination, and the ability to think innovatively. Just as we now recognize that there are multiple styles of learning and many kinds of intelligences, a full range of venues also exists for expressing creativity. This includes people in business, sports, and the social and natural sciences and also those who express what Shelly Carson, author of *Your Creative Brain* (2010), calls our "unscripted improvisations"—how we soothe a cranky child, balance a budget, arrange our garden or juggle the 101 demands of career and family. Each of these examples points to one conclusion: We all have the capacity for this Habit of Mind.

Here is another misconception to clear up—the idea that we can't improve our creative skills. You might be willing to accept that your friends rely on you to write their resumes or that you have a flair for interior design, but you don't believe you have the talent to get to the next level. Not necessarily so. Decades of studies and recent research in neuroscience say otherwise. Our creativity can be improved. Sure, talent helps, but training, practice, life experience, and sometimes just thinking about things a little differently also contribute to the growth of creativity. (Carson, 2010).

Before we go further, we want to point out one difference about how we treat this Habit of Mind. We start off most chapters in this book by showing parents how they can begin to master a particular habit before modeling and teaching it to their child. Most of the Habits of Mind show a developmental progression. We would expect an adult to be more advanced than a child in Managing Impulsivity simply because of her greater maturity and life experience. With Creating, Imagining, and Innovating, however, children often start out with vast potential, which, if not protected and nurtured, tends to diminish over time. As adults, our job is not so much to *teach* this Habit, but to create the conditions under which it can grow and thrive, and to *protect* it from the negative effects of criticism or indifference.

Recognizing Creativity in all
its Manifestations in Children

A 20-month-old girl pulls her father's sock out of the laundry basket, drapes it over her shoulder, and sashays across the living room as though she is modeling fancy evening wear. The rest of the family cracks up laughing, and the toddler discovers she can make people laugh with her imagination. A four-year-old boy, in the throes of dinosaur mania, gets out his wooden blocks and collection of plastic dinosaurs and creates a museum. He is very focused and takes care to arrange the block platforms in a way that he thinks is suitable to each type of dinosaur. When finished, he fetches his mother and, together, they "tour" the museum.

One of the greatest joys of parenting is to witness young children as they venture out to discover the world. *Everything* is new and wondrous at this age. As they sally forth with optimism and curiosity, they seem to be bursting with the stimulation of all that new input. This energy is precisely what preschoolers so ably capture in their paintings with bright splashes of color, in their made up songs with funny lyrics, or their invented tales of pirates, princesses, and star warriors. Is it surprising that adult enthusiasm for a child's creativity at this stage seems to know no bounds? Even the masters want to replicate it. "I used to draw like Raphael; it has taken me my whole life to learn to draw like a child," Picasso once said (Gardner, 1982, *Artful Scribbles*, p. 8).

But the dynamics surrounding creativity—and children's expression of their creativity—change as they grow older. Around the age of seven or eight, their thinking becomes more realistic compared to their more "magical" perceptions of the world a few years ago. Their understanding of the world is increasing. They reason more logically. Their motor skills are also more developed, allowing children to try their hand at more complicated tasks. They want to know how things work, how to play a saxophone or the piano, how to bake a cake or make an electric circuit. A shift in attention is also seen in their art. It too is becoming more realistic, as psychologist Harold Gardner (1982, *Art, Mind and Brain*) points out, and, in the process, it may lose some of its initial spontaneity and appeal. Gardener says it may not be until adolescence that a child can begin to combine the "how to" skills they acquire during this stage with the expressiveness and originality evident when they were in preschool.

Almost simultaneously, the demands of school are increasing along with the pressure to fit in everything else. Parental enjoyment of their child's creative expressions may take a back seat to their concerns about grades and testing, homework, or piano practice. The need to practice, in fact, is often experienced as drudge work and can become a real area of conflict between parent and child. The child who loved to sing and play familiar tunes on the keyboard may now be resisting regular lessons.

Expanding our understanding of creativity, Costa and Kallick (2000, p. 32) define Creating, Imagining, Innovating as the capacity to generate novel, clever, or ingenious products, solutions, and techniques. They talk about behaviors such as thinking outside the box, having an active imagination and a variety of strategies to solve problems, showing a willingness to examine alternative possibilities, and striving to find new and inventive ways to work on a task. In his article "Education for Creative Potential," Mark Runco (2003) also defines creativity broadly, saying that "any thinking that involves the construction of new meaning is creative" (p. 318). He says that rather than concentrating on children's products or performance, we should instead look for evidence of their *potential* for creativity and then nurture those behaviors.

A new thought or meaning does not have to be original in the sense of never having been thought of before. It just has to be new to that person. Consider the following examples: A 1st grader enjoys leaping and tumbling in gymnastics, sometimes creating new routines at home. A 2nd grader working on a math problem independently comes up with two different strategies to solve it, displaying her understanding not only of addition and subtraction but also multiplication. A group of 4th graders initiates a green campaign in which they create slogans, posters, and a logo to galvanize other students. A 7th grader submits his response to a question on the effects of the Civil War in the form of a short story in which he depicts the brutality and impact from the perspective of a young soldier. An 8th grader plays drums, the guitar, and piano. He improvises on what he learns in his lessons, composes, and performs with a band.

Children express their creativity in all different ways and with varying degrees of commitment. Some may have one passion that endures throughout childhood and beyond, while others change interests as frequently as shoe sizes.

Some fully commit and others dabble. Some may show no specific preference for a creative pursuit until high school or beyond. Wherever children fall on the creative spectrum, the best way to nurture this Habit of Mind is to recognize and enjoy their expressions of creativity in all its different manifestations. Look for the things your child says or does or makes that strike you as novel. What we want to encourage is not a future career but children's creative impulses, and there is no better affirmation than for parents to be an appreciative audience. You listen to the stories they write for class or assign to their toy figures or to the lyrics they make up in the car. You take a careful look at the paintings that come home from school or the intricate forts and structures they build in the backyard. You savor their special dish of cookies decorated with funny faces, and you notice appreciatively the way they rearrange the furniture in their room or entertain their younger siblings with magic tricks. And each time your child encounters something new—a mountain range, the ocean, a bird's nest, an art gallery, an old cathedral—you encourage the possibility of some new thought or realization in your child.

Throughout this chapter, we address the kinds of responses and conditions that engage children more deeply in the creative process and foster this Habit of Mind.

Family Attitudes that Support Creativity: Autonomy

A number of researchers have looked into whether there are certain family values, attitudes, or child-rearing practices that are more likely to encourage the development of creativity in children. Teresa M. Amabile (1989) suggests there are indeed. She notes that parents of children identified as being creative tend to promote *autonomy* in the home. Autonomy is taking initiative and responsibility for what we do. (*See Motivation Factor in Chapter 7, The Art and Science of Persistence.*)

The parents Amabile studied viewed their children as interesting and capable of accepting age-appropriate responsibilities. They had confidence in their children. The conversations between parent and child tended to reflect a back-and-forth sharing of ideas instead of a top down, parent-directed approach. Interestingly, it wasn't as though the parents were permissive, in the sense of being hands-off and letting their children do whatever they wanted. Amabile described these parents as presenting "a clear set of values about right and wrong." They "display those values by their own example, and encourage their children to decide which behavior exemplified those values." Amabile added, "They expect their children to act independently but responsibly" (p. 105).

Another study was conducted by a group of researchers from the University of Northern Iowa and published in the *Creativity Research Journal* (2008, Vol. 20, pp. 343-351). Gary Gute and colleagues interviewed a number of individuals who had achieved high levels of creative success in a variety of fields. They asked those individuals to look back to their childhoods and describe the conditions they thought may or may not have contributed to their creative abilities.

The researchers identified "complexity" as a shared characteristic of most people interviewed. In their childhood homes they recalled a balance: Parents provided stability and security, and at the same time encouraged uniqueness and innovation. Parents were said to be responsive to their kids' needs, but if a child was bored or slightly anxious, parents did not rush in right away to make them feel better, but instead challenged them to rely on their own ideas. This suggests that parents somehow set the right conditions for children to learn to "self-regulate." One important means of soothing oneself or restoring equilibrium when upset is to use imagination and to come up with a creative solution to the distress.

Developmentally appropriate autonomy permits children to begin to create for *themselves* crucial aspects of who they are. Individuality is expressed in many ways: by our tastes and preferences in food, clothing, sense of humor, preferred activities, room décor, and more. One seven-year-old girl wore a headband with leopard print kitten ears on top every single day throughout 2nd grade. That was her signature item of clothing that, to her, expressed something special about who she was. Wisely, her mother allowed that very individual fashion statement to run its course, without ever saying a word.

In addition to self-expression, autonomy also provides practice for kids to think and solve problems for themselves, to find out which ideas work and which ones don't. A child who is given his own space at the workbench in the basement and who is allowed to tinker with broken objects, is more likely to pursue a deeper understanding of what makes things work than a child who is warned not to make a mess or told to just throw something out because it's easier to get a new one. The child at the workbench is likely to spend more time with an activity or in solving a problem because he has the experience to know where curiosity can lead.

The Power of Play

We all agree that play is a valuable and necessary part of childhood. Child development texts universally credit the power of play with enhancing language skills, social skills, imagination, and creativity. Pretend play gives children opportunities to "work through" situations in their real lives that may be causing anxiety or concern. It gives children a chance at mastery. They get to write their own scripts, practice situations from different points of view, and give free rein to their imagination. Pretend play is the currency through which preschoolers interact with their environment, but it continues to be an ideal training ground for the development of creativity in school age children as well.

How can parents nurture this kind of creative play? Beyond providing a safe setting and the right materials to pique their curiosity, we suggest that parents consider what William Crain, psychologist and author of *Reclaiming Childhood* (2003), calls an attitude of "unobtrusive presence." Unobtrusive presence means you provide support without getting in the way of your children's exploration.

You provide props and opportunities that encourage your children to become immersed in what they are doing. You are available to play along when your presence is requested, but you take a supporting role. If you watch your child at play, you can pick up themes or interests or worries that may give you some clues as to what's going on with him. If he invites you to join in his play, or if you are spending some special "Floor Time" together, let him control the play agenda. If you are playing with LEGOS', for example, don't compete to build the best building. Play along and, if necessary, help find just the pieces he is looking for to complete *his* vision. If you are playing with dolls, allow your child to establish the scenario.

Pretend play continues to be popular with children, even up to 4th or 5th grade. At school, little knots of children can be seen at recess, gathered around a tree or boulder, intently playing at some spin-off from a movie or book, or their own fairy tale involving families, dragons, horses, or puppies. At home, many still pull out those bins filled with scarves and capes, hats, daddy's shirts or ties, mommy's cast-off evening wear, high heels, and costume jewelry to contribute to their high drama. Many love trains, wooden blocks, and other building materials—some to build with and others to play with. The best toys and games are those that allow the child to take the lead in creating fantasy and fun. The more scripted the plaything (e.g., a talking doll or electronic game), the less opportunity for the child's own imagination to be in charge.

In a comprehensive *Newsweek* (July 10, 2010) article titled "The Creativity Crisis," authors Po Bronson and Ashley Merryman write that preschoolers who spend more time in pretend play, acting out scenes as different characters, are shown to have higher measures of creativity. They also cite a University of Michigan study (2006) that found  a remarkably high number of McArthur Foundation "genius award" winners had created "paracosms" in childhood. Paracosms are imaginary alternative worlds created by children. They are exceptionally detailed and elaborate, sometimes even involving the creation of whole new languages. Some parents might be concerned that their older child still engages in pretend play, but perhaps it would ease their concerns to think of play as a way of developing those creative "muscles."

Somewhat alarmingly, however, Bronson and Merryman write about the decline of creativity in American children, as measured by the well-respected Torrance test, starting at around 1990. What could be going wrong? Although they say that it is too soon to know for certain, they point to the increased time children spend in front of a screen—either television or playing video games—as well as the lack of emphasis in schools on teaching creativity. We might also speculate that the increasingly regimented activities for children, in the form of classes, lessons, and organized sports, make even less time available for them to "just" play.

Appropriate Levels of Support and Encouragement

Amabile (1989) tells the story of a 12-year-old boy named Steven Spielberg. To earn a Boy Scout merit badge, he decided to make a horror movie. For his project, the elder Mr. Spielberg lent Steven his movie camera. Mrs. Spielberg made the costumes, permitted the use of their home as a movie set, put her acting abilities to use in various scenes when needed, and even cooked up canned cherries to use as "blood" for one particularly gruesome scene.

While we all know how this story turned out for this incredibly successful movie director, the real stars from our perspective are his parents. They managed to walk that fine line so critical for Creating, Imagining and Innovating to thrive in children. Their involvement wasn't dictated by their aspirations for their child. Instead they took their cues from him. He wrote the script, literally and figuratively, and they were content to play supporting roles. He chose his goal and they pitched in when and where their help was needed. Spielberg's parents mastered the attitude of "unobtrusive presence" Craine described. When it comes to creativity, it helps to keep in mind that the *child* is the director. Even when children ask for help, or for their parents to participate, adults need to stick to a supporting role.

Spielberg was intrinsically motivated. He was pursuing something for no other reason than that it was intriguing to him. For another child, it may be an entire afternoon drawing figures with art pencils. Children need lots of time to just lose themselves in whatever interests them, with no pressure at all to produce something to show for their time. Amabile (1989) likens creativity to a stew. One essential ingredient is the fire under the kettle that cooks all the ingredients.

That fire is intrinsic motivation: the passion, curiosity, and satisfaction a child experiences when working on a task or problem that she has chosen and in which she has a deep interest. Kids, like adults, engage in the creative process and all the hard work it entails not because someone tells them to do so or because they want to please someone else. They create and innovate because that is what they find interesting and satisfying.

Seven-year-old Ariel prepared a poster board for Family Night. It was all her own doing and she took a great deal of pride in it. She chose "rainbows" for her topic, based on a book she found in the school library. She planned out what she wanted to put on the poster: a picture of a rainbow, a description of what a rainbow is, and something to represent how special she thought these multicolored arcs were. She decided to write a poem about rainbows.

When Ariel greeted her father home from a three-day business trip, she began to describe her project. He frowned. "Rainbows! That's kid stuff. Come on, Ariel, you're in 2nd grade now. Let's do electricity instead." While he was away, he thought about how he wanted to share his own love of science with her, something he had not had time to do since he got a new job. From his perspective, this project was the perfect opportunity. So on Saturday morning he purchased a block of wood, wire, and a flashlight bulb. Despite his best efforts to engage her, Ariel whined, didn't pay attention, and two hours later, he gave up. "Okay, Ariel. I was wrong. I can see electricity is not too interesting to you right now. I am really looking forward to seeing your rainbow project."

Amabile says restricting children's choices to what adults want as well as using rewards, competition, and evaluations—positive or negative—can undermine the creative process. She conducted a series of studies in which different groups of children were asked to write stories, create art or solve mathematical problems under different conditions. Some children were told prizes would be awarded for those who made the best art work while no evaluation or competition was imposed on the control groups. In another study, strict rules were presented to some children in a way that was arbitrary and limited their sense of control over their work. These same rules were described to another group, this time as a way of demonstrating consideration for other children who would be using the room. No rules were given to a third group. When outside evaluators were then asked to judge the children's work, they consistently found the most creative work to be done by children in the control groups with no competition or the children with no specific rules or for whom rules seemed meaningful and not limiting. These children also remained interested in their projects longer. Amabile says *intrinsic motivation* encourages us to put in the time and effort it takes to see a project through to completion. When efforts are fueled by parental pressure, or it's someone else's idea, or there is some other outcome hanging in the balance, such as a reward or a punishment for failure—children lose interest. They take short cuts and the easy way out just to get the thing done.

How do parents walk that fine line of paying attention and being supportive? Intrinsic motivation is fragile. "Coercion" of any sorts can undermine the creativity of children. Even comments such as "This is excellent," or "You are the best" or "Your writing is so good" shift the focus of attention to someone else's evaluation instead of a child's involvement with his work. This kind of praise can be as detrimental as telling a child to "fix" his work. By evaluating children's stories or paintings or performances,

> **Kids…create and innovate because that is what they find interesting and satisfying.**

positively or negatively, we run the risk of taking away from them some of their autonomy in the creative process. For creativity to thrive, the individual has to be the judge of his or her own work. A child must learn to establish her own internal standards for what she is attempting to do. That is part of what we mean by being a self-directed learner. The aspects of the child's work that elicit our praise may have little to do with the child's original intentions.

Praise can exert a powerful gravitational force. Instead of continuing down his original path, a child may turn away from developing his interest further, and instead gear his efforts toward replicating whatever brought that reaction of praise. Where once the child pursued his interests free of any thought of living up to someone's expectations, now, because he cares, an element of anxiety may be introduced: *What if she doesn't like this one as well? I'll never be able to do as good a job as I did on the first one.* Ultimately, those concerns can have a negative effect on a child's creativity. Many children who are praised too much eventually lose interest and give up, just because the original joy of creating gets lost. Criticism, or "suggestions" for improvement, has the same effect. This is especially true with younger children or those just starting out with their creative endeavors.

Feedback that Encourages Creativity

There is a difference between appreciation and acknowledgement and praise or criticism. A young child who proudly shows her parent her artwork is seeking to share her joy at self-expression. Any suggestions for improvement would be missing the point entirely and could result in the child feeling pushed away rather than connected with the parent at that moment. If a child appears to be unhappy or dissatisfied with a project, you can simply ask her to tell you more about it William Crain advises that it's best to try to let the child take the lead in showing how much feedback he wants.

The aspects of the child's work that elicit our praise may have little to do with the child's original intentions.

One way for parents to appreciate their child's efforts is to simply notice and acknowledge what you see (with a tone of voice and facial expressions that say, "Well, this is *interesting* or *just lovely*"). Chuck Jones, creator of Wile E. Coyote, Road Runner, and other cartoon characters, recalled bringing a drawing home. When his mother looked at it, instead of asking him what it was, she commented, "Gee, you used a lot of blue, didn't you?" Jones says "there is always something you can observe about a child's drawing that has nothing to do with judgment" (Goleman, Kaufman, and Ray, 1993, p .66).

Parents can also let their child know how their creative expression moves them. Comments like, "Wow, you really captured the feelings in that song," or "Those colors make me think of that field of wildflowers we saw, remember?" or "When you take your imaginary field trip to the stars, it's fun for me too. Thanks for inviting me!" or "Your story really conveyed how hard it was for the immigrants who came here in the early 1900s. It made me think about our family's experiences in a new way." Your comments don't critique the merit of their work, but instead let them know that you "get it" and appreciate what they have done. Your involvement and evident pleasure in your child's creativity will convey the message that you delight in your child's uniqueness. Your comments will draw your child more deeply into his own creative process.

As children become more proficient with their efforts and more focused on a product, they may seek out helpful feedback from someone they see as having expertise in that area. That kind of feedback is different than praise or criticism. Think of it as coaching. Once a child starts to hone in on an area of creative expression, she may need "technical assistance" to give her the specific skills to actually achieve her creative vision. This is when lessons and good quality instruction can be really helpful. As children reach this stage of their creative development, however, they will inevitably begin to run into comparisons and critiques of their efforts. We want our children to have enough "ego-strength"— confidence in the value of their own vision—to be able to put those critiques in perspective. Feedback from a trusted advisor can be incorporated and used to improve technical skills or knowledge. Criticism from peers or adults who can't appreciate truly original thinking needs to be understood for what it is. You want your creative child to cherish and protect her own originality. History is filled with stories of great artists and inventors who were not appreciated in their own time. If your child is feeling discouraged because someone criticized or made fun of his efforts, remind him that only he can judge the value of his creative vision.

Skills to Foster Creating, Imagining, Innovating

Shelley Carson (2010) teaches and conducts research on the topic of creativity at Harvard University. She suggests that the creative *process* follows a similar route, no matter the content or the field, from business to sports to the arts—whether the creator is writing a novel or history paper, designing a skyscraper, or developing new applications for the web. The process includes four stages first identified by Graham Wallas (1926):

Preparation - specific to each project as well as the continual building of what Carson calls our own "mental library"–all of our life experiences, training, memories of discrete bits of information, mistakes, etc.

Incubation - The brain requires time to digest information and ponder different possible pathways we might take. It takes time to *inhabit* a set of ideas and make them your own.

Illumination - This is when that glorious "Aha!" moment occurs. This is our reward for all our preparation and the frustration of feeling stuck and having to wait it out.

Verification - Carson (2010) says that "this is where the real work begins," as we figure out if this idea is the one to pursue. In this stage we are more systematic and focused as we evaluate the strengths and weaknesses of an idea; we elaborate on the idea and finally turn it into something tangible: a theory, a novel, a scientific formula, or a piece of music. This is when we close in on our goal.

No process is identical for each person or for different projects. Each undertaking will have its unique demands. Sometimes a project is a good match for an individual's set of strengths, skills, and interests, *and sometimes it isn't.* There are, however, ways of thinking and skills that can help us navigate more effectively through the various steps of the creative process. We can develop mindsets (Carson actually calls them brainsets) that build on our strengths. We can introduce and encourage some of these mindsets and skills in our children:

Keep an Open Mind

Creative people are more open to seeing possibilities beyond the tried and tested norms by which most of us live each day. They are more comfortable searching for the unexpected and are curious to discover how and why. The ability to take in information with this kind of openness and receptivity, when coupled with the ability to refrain from judging ideas too soon as "good" or "bad," is, for Carson, the "first and arguably the most important strategy for thinking and acting creatively" (2010, p. 74). This is particularly true during the preparation and incubation stages when the goal is to take in, absorb, and entertain ideas, not shut them out. The more receptive we are to putting aside our preconceived notions and turning off that critical inner voice ready to cast its verdict, the more likely we are to come up with novel ideas. This concept is similar to one we have discussed previously: maintaining an attitude of curiosity instead of certainty. When we approach a problem in an attempt to come up with a creative solution, we want to cast our net far and wide.

Keeping an Open Mind: Tips for Kids

Make an Idea Book. We want children to look at the world with the openness and inquisitiveness of a scientist or an inventor. Thomas Edison is credited with more than 1,000 patents and inventions, ranging from the phonograph to the electric light. During his life he compiled more than four million pages of ideas and observations in notebooks that he would refer back to for inspiration. Encourage your children to keep an idea book in which they jot down interesting facts or problems they encounter during the day. This is a book to stimulate their curiosity and ability to observe what is going on around them.

Don't worry about the solutions. (We'll get back to that soon.)

Ask Open-Ended Questions. Open-ended questions can be gateways to new frontiers for exploration, especially if we let our child's imagination substitute for Google. Runco (2010) recalled driving with his son, who asked him why Sacramento, and not San Francisco or Los Angles, was the capital of California. Runco could have easily turned the question into a history lesson. Instead, he simply asked, "Why do you think so?" He responded to a question with a question and encouraged his son to come up with as many ideas as possible. (See Questioning and Posing Problems for more tips.)

Gather Data through all your Senses. Most of the time, our brains turn down the volume on the stimuli from all the smells, sights, sounds, tastes, and touches that constantly bombard us. Although this automatic pilot is usually good for efficiency, says Carson, it can close off a whole world of sensory delights that we need to enrich our creative instincts. *(See Chapter 14 on Gathering Data through our Senses and Chapter 15, Responding with Wonderment and Awe, for tips .)*

Balance Routine with Novelty. We want to make sure our school age children are exposed to experiences in which answers or solutions are not so neatly defined. *(See Chapter 13, Thinking Flexibly, for tips.)*

Imagine and Think Hypothetically

Costa and Kallick (2000) write about the importance of examining alternative possibilities from many angles. Creative people, they say, might start with a vision of a finished product and then work backward to finding a route to make that vision a reality. They might also imagine themselves in the place of another person or even an animal. Temple Grandin (2005), an animal scientist and author, writes about how her perceptions and experiences as a person with autism contribute to her heightened understanding of what animals experience. Grandin literally put herself in the place of cattle as they moved through chutes at the feedlot. By crawling on the ground, using all her senses, especially sight, she attempted to experience the feedlot as they did. She was able to identify what frightened the animals and made them balk or rear up dangerously. She was able to make simple recommendations such as painting a ladder gray instead of yellow, or removing a shirt flapping in the breeze, or illuminating the entrance to a tunnel, because she recognized these visual triggers to their fear. Because of these insights, she was much sought after by the industry to put in place equipment and procedures that would dramatically improve the treatment of animals. Many of the feedlot operators believed she had some sort of mystical connection with the animals, but Grandin knew that she was just "seeing" what was really there, without any preconceptions.

Imagining & Thinking Hypothetically: Tips for Kids

- Sitting around the kitchen table at dinner or cuddled in a big armchair on a rainy day, let your child's imagination take you on a safari in Kenya, a trip to Mars, or an expedition to the center of the earth. Your child gets to choose his identity. Let imagination turn your child into a tour guide, astronaut, geologist, or the zebra you encounter on the safari.

- Jump from one period of history to another and explore how situations changed: going to school or playing in the early 19th and 21st centuries, or living in Iceland and Hawaii, for example.

Make Connections

Many researchers recognize two different categories of thinking that contribute to any creative endeavor. *Divergent* thinking is what generates lots of ideas and solutions and *convergent* thinking is where ideas converge as we narrow our choice and choose one idea.

When we maintain an attitude of receptivity and openness we stimulate divergent thinking. So does asking questions such as "What did you notice?" or "What do you think could explain that?" Most tests that measure creativity in children emphasize divergent thinking. These tests ask questions like, "How would you improve this toy?" "How is a carrot like a potato?" or "Name all the things you can think of to do with a paper clip or a shoe." Results are based on the ability of children to come up with a lot of ideas, the uniqueness of their ideas,

Making Connections: Tips for Kids

Word Games. Word games are no longer viewed as just a pleasant way to pass time. Neuroscientists now tell us that word and object association games activate different parts of the brain associated with creative thinking (Carson, 2010). They are also a great way to get kids used to coming up with lots of ideas and discovering unusual connections. In word associations, players start with a random noun and then connect as many related words as they can think of. With time and practice, the goal is to think less literally, to include words that sound the same or reflect more original connections. For example, *sail* might trigger words connected to boats or water, but it can also connect to sales, stores and all the related words they trigger. The same principle can be applied to functions of objects; for example, coming up with different uses for a lunch box.

Twenty Answers. Make up a game in which you describe a hypothetical problem and have your child come up with an many solutions as possible. What would happen if a pipe broke and you had no running water in the kitchen? Alternatively you could describe a solution such as putting a big bucket outside in the rain and have children describe possible problems it could solve. Aim for 20 ideas to encourage your child to think beyond the obvious.

and their flexibility to see things outside the more common frames of reference. Runco (2006) found that telling kids to be creative before taking these tests did not improve their performance. Far more effective was advising them to simply take their time, not to worry about spelling or grammar, and to come up with ideas that *only you can think of.*

Practice Getting to the Finish Line

In any creative endeavor, there is lots of toggling back and forth between divergent and convergent thinking. Generally, however, the need to bring something to closure, as we do in the Verification stage, calls for using the analytical and critical thinking skills of convergent thinking. At some point, it is necessary to focus one's thinking on one or a few possibilities. Through *convergent thinking*, we compare, evaluate and decide what fits and what doesn't.

Projects for display or presentation to an audience offer kids an opportunity to test their creative wings, whether as part of an assignment or an extracurricular activity or hobby. Children go through all the phases of the creative process, from thinking of ideas to turning those ideas into a viable, finished product, to experiencing the honest responses of peers or adults. The product might be a birdhouse to be hung in your backyard, a fundraiser for a local pet shelter, or an invention for science night at school. The measure of success for each of these projects will not necessarily be a final grade but how well these projects fare in real life: Do they work? Did the audience get it?

Practicing Getting to the Finish Line: Tips for Kids

Remember that Idea Book? Now is a good time to pull it out and inspire your child to see which ideas just might work. Using the problem-solving steps outlined in Let's Make a Plan in Chapter 9, have them test some of their hypotheses.

Be "unobtrusively" supportive of all those school and extracurricular projects that depend on your child's creative ideas. Encourage your child to keep an open mind, imagine and think hypothetically, make connections and create and innovate.

As your child gains more skill and expertise in any area of interest, stay aware of what kinds of supports (books, DVDs, classes, family field trips) might help her move along in her development without your pushing. If you can maintain that "unobtrusive presence" of warm support, yet giving her autonomy, chances are good that the habit of Creating, Imagining, and Innovating will find fertile ground in which to grow.

The senses, being explorers of the world, open the way to knowledge.

— Maria Montessori

Chapter 14

Open Up:
Gathering Data Through All Senses

Our senses ground us firmly to this planet. The upset we see in the face of a hurt child and hear in his voice, the aroma of a sauce simmering on the kitchen stove, the taste of watermelon vs. lemons—this is all oxygen streaming through the blood of our humanity, connecting us to the world in which we live and transforming our experiences from two-dimensional to three-dimensional encounters.

In a common writing exercise, students are asked to describe their favorite room. "Use all your senses in your description," the teacher will advise, "including the smells, colors, and sounds that fill this room, even the taste of foods you remember eating there." This teacher knows that our senses are the conduits to memories that store all those reasons why one child will choose this particular room above all others. It was the detail of the scent of roses in a vase on her kitchen table, for example, that triggered for one 7th grader the memory of the roses that her grandfather grew in the garden where she played growing up. His quiet and caring

Gather data through all senses

Use your natural pathways!

Pay attention to the world around you. Gather data through all the senses. taste, touch, smell, hearing and sight.

demeanor and the long afternoons spent with both her grandparents came rushing back to her.

To encourage children's awareness of what they are seeing, hearing, feeling, smelling and tasting, we need only sustain a little longer what parents intuitively do when their children are toddlers or in preschool. They fill as much of their children's time as possible with hands-on, multi-sensory experiences. They scoop up a handful of snow, shiver, and exclaim, "Cold. The snow is cold." They spread their arms open wide to show how much love they have. They touch fingers and toes as they count and sing songs about the number of sheep and bags of wool. They not only watch a setting sun but might mix yellow and red paints to replicate the big orange ball in the sky on paper. All day long they connect language to objects and experiences. Every day is show and tell and touch and learn.

This kind of "reinforcement" does not have to stop when children enter elementary school or even middle school. Seven- or ten-year-olds whose auditory skills are still developing need more than verbal or textbook descriptions. They need lots of experiences to construct meaning out of what they are learning. The more attuned they are to all the cues their senses take in, the richer these experiences and more accurate their observations will be. A key premise of the Habits of Mind approach is that children can be coached to become increasingly self-directed. What better place to start than how they experience their own five senses.

As you try the tips in this chapter,

- Build a vocabulary list with your child that captures the *sensations* of each sense; for example, slimy, silky, abrasive, or bitter. Use images if that helps: short like a Dachshunds' legs and soft like a rabbit's furry coat.

- Wonder aloud about the reasons for different sensations. Why do hot radiators and ice cubes both burn? Why do we have two ears and two eyes but one mouth?

- Explore how different sensations make you feel. How do you feel in the yellow dining room? How about the one painted a deep, rich red? How do the textures of your corduroy pants or fleece jacket make you feel? What kinds of touches make you feel warm and loved? Some of us prefer just a light touch, others a hearty hug, and some a tight squeeze. The sense of smell is said to be our most primal, and one that holds our earliest memories. How do you react to the scent of freshly cut flowers, evergreens, or something delicious baking in the oven? How does listening to Mozart on the commute home make you feel? What about listening to Lady Gaga?

- Find out the preferences and dislikes of your family members. Each of us has different sensory preferences, and a different threshold for what is pleasant and what is not. Some kids are very sensitive to different sensations. They may find bright lights, loud noises, or certain textures and tastes uncomfortable and even repellent. If you don't share those sensitivities, you might find it puzzling and hard to relate to. It can be quite a challenge to anticipate and provide for a child's sensory sensitivities, but think about it. A child who is overwhelmed by sensory input will often feel uncomfortable in his own skin and have more difficulty interacting freely with his environment. With care and patience, parents can introduce their child to new sensations (or those of increased intensity) at a level and rate their child is able to handle.

- Focus on the sensation of each sense as long as possible. In a family activity developed by Susan Kaiser Greenland (2010), cofounder of Inner Kids Foundation, each person takes a turn, describing a bodily sensation or sensory impression at that particular moment. For example, *My feet feel cold. I smell the cookies in the oven.* While this activity may appear simplistic, Greenland says before too long opinions slip into observations. *I see a pretty flower. I smell the stinky soap you clean with.* Comments like these are "opportunities to point out how opinions that we may not even realize we have sneak into what we say and do", says Greenland (p. 146). Use this activity to help your children become aware of their sensory impressions and as "training" for distinguishing between opinions and objective observations.

Giving Each Sense a Chance

Sound

Sharpen your sense of hearing. Think in terms of not just hearing but listening to sounds with as much attention as you give a dear friend.

- Close your eyes and listen to the background sounds that occur without us taking notice. Get to know the nighttime sounds in your home—the hum of a refrigerator, the clicking of an old thermostat, the shushing of the heat—versus the early morning sounds–the whistling tea kettle, car doors closing, cackling crows, the news on the radio, or honking geese flying overhead. Make a list of both.
- At the beach or lake, listen to the water and pick out changes based on tide or wind.
- Find a wide-open space surrounded by nature. Sit quietly and listen to the sounds around you. How many different kinds of birds do you hear? Can you tell where they are? Do you hear crickets or cicadas or other insects? Can you distinguish one cricket or cicada from another? What do you surmise about the weather from the ruffling of the leaves and grasses around you?
- When listening to music, which instruments can you identify?
- Make an instrument or use one available to express different emotions. Describe the sounds of these emotions and how their rhythm and pitch differ.
- What images do different types of music conjure in your mind's eye?
- Listen to a recording or the spoken words of stories and poetry. Close your eyes and "see" what you are hearing.

Enhance Learning
- Hearing a recording of information often helps struggling learners. Sing or recite a multiplication table or spelling words or historical facts as a "back up" for your child.

- Play music indigenous to a country to help your child appreciate the culture he is studying.
- When watching movies, help your child to *listen* to how emotions are conveyed, not just by the choice of words but in the pitch of voice, the pace, etc.
- Experiment. Have your child listen to different music as inspiration while writing.
- Dramatize a story or poem or a speech by a president. Encourage your child to join you.
- Listen to and recite poetry, often.

Sight

Practice remembering what you see.

- Close your eyes and call out all the things in the room where you are. How much can you recall? Do you remember the big picture or the details: colors of the room, the patterns of the material on the chairs, how the light streams through the window, the landscape outside the window?
- Close your eyes and think about the people in your family. How clearly do you see them: the color of their eyes and hair and other details of their face, as well as their favorite clothes their gestures and expressions?
- Keep track of all the different shades of green you see on a walk through a park. Do you know the names of these different colors?
- Turn off the sound of a movie and try to read the story from the images you see.
- The next time you go to a museum, have your child choose one painting and describe it in great detail. Then ask your child to tell you the story in the painting. On another trip, view the artwork from a particular period or by a particular artist. What story does this group of paintings tell?

- Look at objects through a magnifying glass or telescope to appreciate the details. Look at the same objects through a kaleidoscope to see an entirely different perspective.
- Take pictures with a digital camera. Compare the picture with the image you hold in your mind's eye. What details stand out in your mind's image compared to the picture?
- Draw or sketch a favorite room, object, person, or scene.

Enhance Learning

Our ability to imagine what we are learning as well as to observe thoughtfully are important in all subjects, from language arts to math and science.

- When problem solving, have your child answer these questions first, "What do I observe about this situation?" "Are there clues in what I observe?"
- When reading from a textbook, encourage your child to visualize what they are reading.
- Take advantage of videos or simulations available on the Internet that are related to your child's curriculum: a demonstration of gravity, an image of a cell, a short clip on a rain forest, or a holiday celebration in another culture.
- Have your child cut out pictures from a magazine or make drawings to enhance her notes or journals for subjects that are more difficult.
- Have fun exploring maps or Google Earth.

Touch

Helen Keller became deaf and blind as a toddler as a result of meningitis. Her behavior became increasingly difficult, as her parents could use neither language nor visual cues to reach her. Finally, they hired Anne Sullivan, a young woman who was herself visually impaired, as a tutor for their daughter. After many discouraging, exhausting, and unsuccessful efforts to teach Helen, Anne held the child's hand under a stream of cold running water, while spelling the word "water" over and over with her fingers onto Helen's hand. Then, finally, Helen understood. Her mind snapped open to the understanding that experiences have words, and that she could learn those words from the way they felt on her hand. It was the

feeling of the cold water along with the feeling of the word being tapped into her hand that opened Helen's mind to learning.

Many of us over-rely on our senses of sight and hearing and give short shrift to the sense of touch. We can enrich the way we take in information from our environment, by reclaiming the sense of touch.

- Our most sensitive body parts are our hands, lips, face, neck, tongue, fingertips, and feet. The least sensitive is the middle of our back. What happens if you touch these parts of your child's body with different objects (an ice cube, a feather) or different textured materials, etc? (Source: Oracle Think Quest library.thinkquest.org/3750/touch/touch.html.)
- The sense of touch covers our entire body and contains nerve endings that send important messages to our brain about what they are encountering. An object can be hot, cold, soft, smooth, rough, or sharp. Without this sense, how would we know when the sand is too hot or the water is freezing cold? What else would we miss?
- Finger paint!
- Give your school age children opportunities to get a little messy, making mud pies outside, or working with clay or homemade play dough in the kitchen. These activities have the added bonus of strengthening hand muscles, which helps in writing.
- Equip kids with a net, a sieve, or colander and an old pot or two and turn them loose by the banks of a stream or at the lake or ocean shore. (Supervision may be needed.) The ever-changing feel of water is endlessly fascinating to children and stimulates all kinds of exploration, experimentation, and fun.
- Make a nature collage of different textures and identify their sensations.
- Go barefoot. Touch with your feet as well as your hands.

Enhance Learning

- Research with your child which animals have a highly developed sense of touch and why (catfish and cats will be on the list).

205

- Make models or manipulate objects with your child to better understand difficult problems; for example, make a mobile model of the solar system using Styrofoam balls and a wire coat hanger. Have your child demonstrate his understanding of a math problem by representing the process and the solution with paper clips.
- Enlist your older child to read *Pat the Bunny* or other toddler books featuring textures to a younger sibling or cousin. Ask her how the baby reacted to the textures. What does she remember about these books from when she was that age?

Smell

The best way to appreciate the sense of smell is to think about what it would be like not to smell. Smoke alerts us to fires. The smell of rotten food tells us "do not eat." Dogs have a million smell cells in each nostril that are hundreds of times larger than a human's. Smell is one of the primary ways dogs get to know and trust a person. Our nose and mouth share the same airway, which means our taste of food depends heavily on the sense of smell. If you cannot smell dinner, you are not as likely to have an appetite for it.

- Have family members describe their most and least favorite scents.
- List the scents associated with holidays, vacations, favorite meals, and daily rituals like brushing teeth, shaving, and washing dishes and clothes.
- Breathe in the air on a clear night at the ocean or in the woods after a storm. Can you describe each experience?

Enhance Learning

- List as many substances as you can with strong smells and then try to categorize the different smells.
- Investigate: Close your nose and find out how the smell of your most

favorite and least favorite foods affect their taste.

- Find out which animals have the best sense of smell? (Bears, sharks and moths.)
- Research the sense of smell of your family pet.

Taste

Thich Nhat Hanh (1975) describes two ways of eating a tangerine: quickly popping sections in your mouth or taking each section, one at a time, slowly chewing it, and savoring the taste. Buddhist teacher Jack Kornfield (2004) has a similar exercise for eating raisins one at time: observing their rich brown color and reflecting on the fertile earth from which they grew as well as the sunlight and rain that nurtured them before harvest. Cupping his hands, he holds one raisin and then brings it up to his ear to listen for the sound of the raisin. Then, taking the raisin between his thumb and forefinger, he brings it to his mouth, letting his tongue roll over the irregular texture of this one single raisin before biting and tasting its natural sweetness.

Encourage your children to slow down and savor the taste of food.

Enhance Learning

- We have thousands of tiny taste buds on our tongues that recognize four basic tastes: bitter, sour, salty, and sweet. Have your child close his eyes and test his tongue's sensitivity. Can he identify different foods by taste? Can he identify where on his tongue he tastes sweet (tip of tongue) or bitter (back of tongue) foods?
- Research what negatively affects our taste buds. (Smoking and lack of good nutrients are two.)

One way to open your eyes is to ask yourself, "What if I had never seen this before? What if I knew I would never see it again?"
— *Rachel Carson*

Chapter 15

Love Affair with the World:
Responding with Wonderment and Awe

Very early on, an infant begins to notice interesting things going on just beyond the perimeter of a parent's arms. From that first glimmer of curiosity a baby shows in the colorful toy twirling overhead or the silly faces big sister is making emerges an abiding passion to see, hear, feel, and understand all that the world has to offer. Wonder and Awe come easily to a young child for whom everything is new and amazing. It needs be nourished and protected, however, if this "love affair with life" is to take root and grow with the child into adulthood. One of our most important roles as a parent is to "sponsor" our children in the world, to encourage an appreciation for the magnificent diversity and beauty of this planet we inhabit as well as for the rich potential of the human mind, body, and spirit.

Responding with wonderment and awe

Have fun figuring it out!

Finding the world awesome, mysterious and being intrigued with phenomena and beauty.

Pursuing the Possibility of Passion

Scientist/writer Rachel Carson, credited with first promoting the need for environmental awareness in the 1950s, used to take her young nephew Roger down to the ocean on stormy nights. In her classic book,

The Sense of Wonder (1965), she recounts how, in between squeals of laughter from pure joy, was their "spine-tingling" recognition of the grandeur of this moment where "great and elemental things prevailed." This excursion was one of many adventures Carson shared with Roger, starting from the time he was just a toddler. On calmer evenings, with a flashlight in hand, they would search for nocturnal crabs along the shore. The woods after a rainstorm was also a favorite destination. Sometimes they would look for tiny spruce saplings to decorate with berries for an imagined holiday celebration for small woodland animals. Even watching the moon migrate across the sky held their attention as they looked out the living room picture window.

> **A sense of wonder is a prerequisite for the inquiring, curious mind as well as for the creative spirit.**

Carson was nourishing Roger's budding love affair with the world. She knew that this would be achieved not so much by her identifying the names of trees or plants or long scientific explanations but by the range of feelings Roger experienced during their explorations. These moments were a chance for him to become engrossed and connected with a world of nature that was magical and mysterious, dynamic and animated, and almost always unpredictable. Once *feelings* for all of these myriad experiences were aroused, Carson said, the desire to *know* eventually followed and, with that much more significance and meaning. A sense of wonder is a prerequisite for the inquiring, curious mind as well as for the creative spirit.

Carson identified only one requirement for a child to experience wonder: an adult companion willing to rediscover the joy, excitement, and mystery of the world we live in. This is the adult willing to slow down, even if only intermittently, to take in the moment, whether peering with the child at a colony of ants carrying bits of food back to their ant hill or going for a walk in the rain. This is the same adult who can stop on a city street and marvel at the construction of the towering skyscraper ahead or visit again and again the local fire station, railroad hub, planetarium, or the back door to watch the lightening bugs. To keep alive an adult's sense of wonder, Carson's advice was simple: Keep asking, "What if I had never seen this before? What if I knew I would never see it again?"

Moments of magic and wonder will have to expand to engage the older child. When an 8- or 9-year-old learns to surf the waves, we can help her attain a new sense of awe for the ocean, appreciating not only her own growing ability but also respecting the powerful force of this great body of water. Or instead of just watching fireflies, we can find out with our child exactly how these creatures create their nightly light show. Many school-age children enjoy building forts outdoors or camping, complete with learning to build a fire, cooking, pitching a tent, getting by with a flashlight, and sleeping under the stars. A guidebook (or Smartphone) for identifying and learning more about the constellations, plants, or animals you can encounter add content to the initial curious "noticing." So can a magnifying glass, telescope, flashlight, or pair of binoculars. And there is nothing quite like a pet to connect a child to the nonverbal but animated dynamism of nature, whether it is a chameleon or a dog, a fish or a cat. As children discover the many ways the sensory capacities of animals far exceed our own (think of the information a dog picks up through his nose, or the ability of a cat to hear tiny rustlings in the dried leaves), they develop an enhanced respect for them. A pet also generously gives its loyalty, affection and even protection, which it deserves to receive from us in turn. Caring for a pet is an important milestone in the development of a child's sense of responsibility. The animal's need for food, exercise, attention and a proper habitat, all introduce children to value of giving loving care to a being that totally depends on us, and foreshadows the responsibility of parenthood. The eventual, inevitable death of a pet is often a child's first experience with true grief. As sad as it is, this experience provides children with an opportunity to cope with and prepare for the inevitable losses we all must face later in life.

Early passions can spark a life-long interest. One mother recalls how her preschooler son's fascination for the large skeletal frames of dinosaurs triggered his curiosity about a time before humans roamed this planet. They searched out everything they could learn on the topic. She believes that the stories they read, the many visits to the museum, their pretend play, the countless drawings of *T. rex* taped up all over the house, the dinosaur-shaped cookies and decorated birthday cakes all supported his continuing curiosity about the transformations the planet Earth underwent many millions of years ago and continues to undergo today. Now in high school, this boy is passionate about the environment and involved in its preservation.

Sharing Passions

Sharing our own interests with our children is a powerful way to stimulate a sense of wonder and awe. Luke Geissbuhler (2010) included his 7-year -old son Max in an almost yearlong project to attach an HD video camera to a weather balloon and send it into the upper stratosphere "to film the blackness beyond earth." The idea was inspired by a film project Luke was working on. He presented the possibility to his son who immediately took him up on it. "Shared curiosity, persistence, and the joy of learning" kept them going, says Luke. "I would come up with problems, like how to release the parachute, and Max would throw out ideas. They weren't fully formed ideas but I would follow his thinking with him. If I saw real problems with his thinking, I would raise them."

"There were a lot of variables to overcome," Luke said about the project. The craft had to meet FAA regulations and safety was a consideration in determining where to launch the rocket. But, as each obstacle was dealt with, their enthusiasm remained undiminished. Nothing could compare with the joyful amazement Max experienced when he saw that rocket take off and monitored the incoming video stream of pictures of the earth from the rocket that he and his father launched.

Building a rocket may be beyond most parents' ability but not the lesson here—to continue to involve school age children in experiences that reaffirm their connection with the world around us. Does your child know your passions? Is it to be an expert skier crisscrossing down the slope? Does the beauty of an expansive bridge spanning a river take your breath away? Do you get a lump in your throat when you see horses galloping across a pasture? Do you dream of taking a space shuttle to the moon one day? Are you transported by the exquisite performance of a concerto or a medical breakthrough discovered by a Nobel Prize winner? In addition to sharing your skill and expertise with your children as Geissbuhler did, speak your amazement out loud. Tell your children what moves you, and what makes you wonder. "How does that delicate looking bridge support all that weight?" "Why does that piece of music always make me cry?" "What would it be like to look back and see the earth so far away?" If your child conveys that "bored to the bones" attitude, put the responsibility back on her. "Tell me what amazes *you.*"

Costa and Kallick (Boyes and Watts, 2009) say the person who has mastered Responding with Wonderment and Awe has a deep connection to his surroundings and is observant and intrigued by all sorts of phenomena in our physical world. This person wants to learn about our world and recognizes our role in protecting our environment, much the way Rachel Carson realized more than half a century ago.

The world can be a wondrous machine, an artist's palette, or a writer's thesaurus. Appreciating it requires a keen sense of observation, respect, and patience. You can't make a fox appear in the woods, but if you sit quietly and are in the right place at the right time, you just might see little fox kits newly out of the den, playing on a sun-drenched boulder. You can't make the sun shine, but the infinite variety of clouds making their way across the sky provides opportunities for speculation: What are they made of? What would it be like to be inside a cloud? What kind of weather do those enormous fluffy clouds bring? You can't make the daffodils bloom, but you could keep a spring journal: on what day do we observe those first tiny green shoots? How long till they bloom? What happens if it snows on them? Nature's formulae are tantalizingly out of reach, but their very mystery can fuel a life-long passion to learn more.

The habit of Responding with Wonderment and Awe is a wonderful companion on our life's journey. It keeps us intrigued and interested in our surroundings, and makes us thirsty to see and learn more. It contributes to our appreciation of the character and accomplishments of our fellow travelers. We become more open to recognizing acts of generosity, compassion, courage, discipline and self-sacrifice. Especially in times of strife and difficulty, the habit of Responding with Wonderment and Awe consoles and inspires us to look past the darkness to the beauty that is still there. It links us in real and profound ways to our spiritual heritage.

Music teacher Eric Katz (2010) at The Siwanoy Elementary School in Pelham New York developed this list of questions for wondering:

How does a snail move?

How is a mummy wrapped?

How much would it cost to buy a space shuttle?

How many days would it take to swim to Africa?

How do sharks hatch from their eggs?

What keeps a boat from sinking?

How do birds know which way is south?

How many eggs does a bakery use in one day?

How many bricks were used to build our school?

Why does it snow some days and hail other days?

Why do rubber balloons stretch?

Why do sunsets create many different colors?

Tips for Encouraging Wonder and Awe

- Start small. Designate some time on a weekend for the family to "stop and smell the roses" with no electronic devices or predetermined goals, just everyone's full and undivided attention outdoors. Push out of your mind day-to-day responsibilities, and breathe in. Take a walk and take in the world. What do you notice?

- Let your senses take over and your thinking subside. With your undivided attention, focus on each sense, separately. Listen, look, breath in, taste, smell, and touch. Be curious. Be fully present to our earth and all its inhabitants.

- Imagine you are living thousands of years ago without the comforts, knowledge, and achievements that we take for granted.

- Be receptive but don't expect surges of feelings. Be patient and open to surprise.

- Complete this statement every day with your child: "I wonder..."

Chapter 16

Look at It Another Way:
Thinking Flexibly

Thinking Flexibly is essential to both our creative thinking and problem solving. It is no surprise that this Habit of Mind weaves its way into virtually all life situations, at school and at work, in our parenting, and in the roles we assume in our families and communities. The ability to think flexibly is a key component of adaptability and how effectively and nimbly we can respond to unexpected challenges and difficulties. It can be the deciding factor in our choice to pilot an entirely new kind of product in our firm, in how we react when our spouse is offered a new job in another part of the country, or in how we mobilize when we discover that our child has a learning disability. It will influence how well we can work on a school committee with people we may not like but with whom we have to get along because the cause is important. Our flexibility will be an asset in any one of these situations, making us more effective, productive, and bringing us more satisfaction and fulfillment.

Thinking flexibly

Look at it another way!

Being able to change perspectives,
generate alternatives,
consider options.

While change defines every period in history, the current pace of transforming ideas has never been greater. It is safe to say that change will be a constant in our children's lives, as will the demand for them to think flexibly. Our own flexibility will no doubt affect our children's readiness to activate this Habit of Mind. Recognizing our own strengths as well as limitations is a good place to start. Parents need to consider the example they are setting. Would your children describe you as open to new ideas? Do you seek input before making plans for the family? Can you let little things go? Is effort as important as results? If, for example, your child or spouse is sincerely trying to help, can you accept that the end product may look a little different than what you wanted?

Encourage your child to pursue experiences that require "mental exploration."

Thinking Flexibly is part *attitude*—our openness to new ideas—and part *action* knowing how and when to expand our horizons and use new ideas and information. The latter can be taught. Attitudes can be modified but will require awareness and effort. Some people are more easy-going. They take changes in stride. In a give-and-take situation, they don't mind giving. Others are more set in their ways. They find it difficult to tolerate deviations from what they think or how they think things ought to be. This is evident in their opinions and in a host of little things: how the bed is made, how the dishwasher is stacked or the car parked, or how clothes are arranged in the closet. The trouble occurs when individuals are unable to adapt to other people not doing things their way. If you are thinking, "Impossible. It's too late for me to change," take heart. We believe firmly that raising children is a continual life lesson for parents. Encouraging any Habit of Mind in our children raises our own awareness and can boost our own practice of the habits as well.

Children, like adults, will either have a head start or an extra hurdle in learning this Habit of Mind. A lot will depend on their temperament and that of their parents. Some children who are more cautious in Taking Responsible Risks may also be less flexible. Parents will want to move more carefully with these children, showing extra empathy and understanding while providing smaller steppingstones toward trying out new experiences and ideas. *(See strategies suggested in Chapter 12.)*

A Balance: Routines and Novelty

Like a high-rise building constructed to resist the tremors of an earthquake, this Habit of Mind requires a foundation that provides safety and structure. Children benefit from routine and predictability. Particularly in the primary grades, they are most focused on developing their competencies and learning how to do things "right." They are learning to follow new rules at school. They are hard at work mastering many skills: how to read, write, and spell, add and subtract, do a pirouette, or play defense in soccer. They may not be quite ready to try another way or hear different opinions from what they learning. They very well may challenge you if you contradict what their teacher or coach has to say.

Howard Gardner (2006) offers some alternatives to offset the purposeful living and thinking of this developmental period. He recommends making sure school age children are exposed to experiences in which answers or solutions are not so neatly defined. In addition to just allowing children time for free play, he suggests having children meet (or read about or watch a DVD about) creative individuals—artists, scientists, inventors, musicians, or authors—who push the envelope of the "norm." Hearing those experts talk about their interest in exploring the planet Mars or how they compose a song or describe practicing for a game or a performance gives children insight into the messy and bumpy journey involved in any achievement and the curiosity driving this commitment. Such encounters can provide a bridge between real life and textbook learning. To further increase your child's own comfort level with flexible thinking, encourage your child to pursue experiences that require "mental exploration." In programs like Odyssey of the Mind, children have to rely on their creativity to solve problems in a range of areas. In one challenge, teams of children must build a vehicle that travels as well as displays emotions. In another, students create an original musical based on the character of Hamlet.

Thinking Flexibly is part attitude— our openness to new ideas—and part action.

Gardner also suggests hobbies or activities such as playing chess, reading and writing poetry, or joining a school play. No single right answer or solution works in any of these situations. Children have to tap into their own resources— their imagination, previous training, and the mental library we discussed in Chapter 13.

How Else?

Right answers to predictable problems are no longer the mainstay of the drill in many schools today. Educators recognize the value of children working to find several ways to solve a problem. Students in elementary school are often required to talk about their strategies and reasons for their answer to a math problem and to describe different ways to reach a solution. They write about topics in math and science that focus on process as much as answers. Peter Johnston (2004) describes how teachers use the phrase "How else?" to encourage students to think flexibly. After a child has solved a problem, a teacher will frequently ask "how else" she might have come to the same answer. By helping the student see the possibility of other choices and ways, Johnston says, the teacher is encouraging the child to become a flexible thinker with a repertoire of problem-solving strategies.

Parents can use a similar approach at home by encouraging their children to think about different ways of accomplishing a task or resolving a conflict. Sometimes individuals become fixed on their own one solution to a problem without realizing there are many possible alternatives. Simply by asking *how else* can we solve this problem, parents encourage flexible thinking. For example, Tyrone's late soccer practice means he can't do his chore to feed and walk the dog. While he assumes his mother will do it, she politely declines because she is busy cooking dinner at that time. She asks him *how else* he can resolve this matter. Tyrone eventually negotiates with his brother to trade chores with him until soccer season is over.

This Habit of Mind can also be used when children "catastrophize" minor setbacks and become discouraged and unwilling to try again. They see only what went wrong. One aspect of Metacognition is to assess how things went in order to be better prepared for next time. If an experience, say, a Little League game, did not turn out as well as hoped and your child is ready to quit, you can, in your supportive way, offer to sit down and analyze with her what happened and ways to make it turn out better next time. When the time is right, you could start the conversation by asking her to try to identify some of the things that she thinks went well. If she has difficulty thinking of anything positive about the experience, talk about a couple of positives you noticed. You could also describe a similar experience you once had. Be sure to relate how badly you felt at the time with how your child is feeling now. Then you might share how you were eventually able to see the situation differently and think about *how else* you could have responded.

You want to convey a sense of hopefulness to your child, that there is something valuable to learn in any setback. This may be all your child is ready for at the time. In either case, says Johnston, "Doing so sustains the possibility of choice while maintaining a sense of flexibility–there is always another way" (2004, p. 45).

Stretching Your Perspective

People who can think flexibly are not just willing to *change* their minds. They also do their homework before making up their minds. Flexible thinkers want to take into account all possible factors, so they typically approach a problem from several angles. At the outset, they want to expand their understanding of the situation. They try to survey the whole situation, getting a bird's eye view of

the all the factors they will need to consider. Here is where they will "zoom-out," getting just a general outline of some key issues, the starting and end points, and any factors that are clear enough at this early stage to decipher. A typical example would be Raoul, a 5th grader who comes home announcing he has a major social studies project to complete. Zooming out, Raoul and his parents establish the basic parameters of the assignment: When is it due? He has a month to complete all the aspects of it and be ready to make a presentation to his class. What will be required? He has to read at least two books on a revolutionary war figure or on a particular aspect of the war, write a detailed report, create either a diorama or some other visual representation of what he has learned, and then present what he has learned to his classmates. It would be understandable if a 10-year-old felt a little overwhelmed by the seeming enormity of this challenging assignment; but as his parents help him to break it down into more manageable pieces, he will be able to develop a plan for proceeding.

Once there is a general outline of the problem, you may then zoom-in to get a "worm's eye view" so you can examine the details more closely. In this example, it seems evident that Raoul's next step might be to choose a topic. But wait; that's much easier said than done. How does a child make a decision that he will have to live with for the next month? What *criteria* does he use to *identify* the subject of his research? A child might be tempted to grab at the first thing that comes to mind to lessen his anxiety about getting it done. He may have heard that a friend of his is going to research Thomas Paine, and he thinks that might be a good idea but he doesn't want to "copy" his friend. How will he decide?

The challenge in problem solving and in creative thinking is how to train ourselves to intentionally see beyond our normal range of vision. Children, in particular, don't have the experience to know where to look or what to look for. They need some guideposts to help structure their thinking. You may find some of the strategies suggested in Chapter 13 on Creating, Imagining, and Innovating and Chapter 9 on Metacognition to be useful in a situation like this. Here are a few additional suggestions for developing the ability to think flexibly.

Steps in Developing the Ability to Think Flexibly

In 1985 Edward De Bono (2011) devised a method used in business and taught in some schools in which six different-colored hats represent six different ways of looking at a situation. Each colored hat represents a different perspective to take into account. You "switch hats" as you switch your perspective. We particularly like De Bono's definition for the white hat and the red hat because they can help children figure out what they *know or need to know* about the problem or situation (white hat) and what they are *feeling* about the situation (red hat).

Start with what you know

As Raoul's parents are trying to help him decide on a topic for his report, they might stimulate his thinking by asking some general questions: How much of this time period in history have they already covered in class? What aspects of the Revolutionary War are especially interesting to him (or not)? What would he like to know more about? What questions might he come up with that have not been addressed in the texts or class discussions? In this instance, it just happened that the family lives in the Hudson Valley— an area that had many Revolutionary War skirmishes. Raoul had been intrigued by glimpses of West Point across the Hudson River, as they traveled north to see his grandparents, and had always wanted to see that historic place. He remembered seeing a sign along the road that commemorated "the first chain" that was strung across the river to keep British ships from advancing, and decided that he wanted to know more about it. He also would like to know more about the battles that took place in this region.

Now think about how you feel

Time to put on the "red hat." Raoul feels excited and relieved to have identified an area that he wants to research and is especially motivated by the idea that such important events in history took place right in his own neighborhood more than 200 years before. But he also feels some nagging doubts: What if he can't find enough information? What if his teacher didn't think it was a good idea? Was he up to doing this research in just a month? Wouldn't it be easier to do something on George Washington? His parents help him to sort through his positive and negative feelings. He decides that he would like to go ahead with the topic, but will run it by his teacher tomorrow, just to reassure himself that it would meet the requirements of the assignment.

> The challenge in problem solving and in creative thinking is how to train ourselves to intentionally see beyond our normal range of vision.

Visualize the end product

When we think flexibly, we may visualize a successful outcome and work our way back to the beginning. Having a successful outcome in mind is motivating, and can help us through that early period of uncertainty and doubt. Raoul imagined his diorama, which would depict the beautiful Hudson River with the craggy highlands rising above, and the fort at West Point nestled below. He also imagined presenting his research to his classmates and pictured himself standing in front of the class holding a length of chain to demonstrate what an enormous undertaking chaining the river must have been. Visualizing these aspects of his project was not only motivating; it also helped him to clarify the details of what he really wanted to do.

Consider the pros and cons

If we were trying on DeBono's hats, the pros and cons would be the yellow hat and the black hat, respectively. We have already covered the advantages of doing a cost-benefit analysis (*see Chapter 12*). This is part of the careful planning process that helps you know in advance what you are getting into. For Raoul, the benefits include doing a project that is likely to be original and interesting. The fact that he will be learning about important events that took place close to home makes it more compelling. He already has a clear vision of what he wants his diorama to look like, and he is hoping to visit West Point to get a firsthand look at where it all took place.

As he systematically goes through the negatives, he still has concerns about whether there will be reading material and resources at his level. He wonders if his parents will have the time to drive him to West Point or be willing to help him get the research materials that he needs.

Getting back to the worm's eye view

This perspective enables us to tackle all the little details that bring a project to fruition. Raoul, with his parents' help, will develop a timetable for completing different tasks. He will have to identify and locate the resources that will cover his topic. Then it will be necessary to schedule time for reading and note taking. He will need to assemble supplies for making his diorama and plan enough time to make sure that it looks the way he has visualized it.

Think about how other people will be affected

It is a rare decision or undertaking that does not have some impact on others! In some of the organization development literature we mention in Thinking Interdependently, it is clear that innovative change is doomed unless the feelings, beliefs, and reactions of those affected by the change are taken into consideration. An important perspective in flexible thinking is *how do other people feel about what I am saying, or proposing, or doing?*

As adults, we see the importance of this in every arena of life. We know how disconcerting it feels to have someone make a decision that affects us, without seeking our input. As parents, we realize that children are sometimes not developmentally ready to assume the perspective of another person. (This is something that usually begins to emerge in a more mature way starting around age 10 or 11.) We can nudge our children along in this direction by simply asking them to *reflect* on how their words or actions might make a person feel. We are not suggesting that everyone necessarily has veto power, or that there might not be good reasons to go ahead anyway, even in the face of reluctance or concern from others. But it is always better to know what you are dealing with. You could talk it out with the other person and find a reasonable compromise; they might be persuaded that there is no reason for anxiety; or you might take their concern as a cue that you may in fact be on the wrong track. Just imagine how much better things would be if each of us routinely took into account the feelings of others before moving ahead with a decision.

In the case of Raoul, he is concerned that his parents might be inconvenienced by having to help him locate research materials and by having to drive him over to West Point. His parents, of course, reassure him on both counts. They are pleased that, by systematically considering so many different perspectives, their child is well on his way to an excellent learning experience.

Simply raising your child's awareness that he *can* think more flexibly puts him on the path to doing so. Deliberately invoking different perspectives, however he chooses to visualize them (using the zoom in/out button; DeBono's different colored hats; or your own formulation) should pay off for him in better planning and greater complexity of thinking. As you share this habit of Thinking Flexibly with your children, be comforted in knowing that you are giving them a powerful tool for the 21st century.

Chapter 17

Lighten Up! Finding Humor

Imagine this: You are in a windowless conference room at a meeting that has been going on for the better part of the afternoon. Everyone is tired, out of sorts, and out of ideas. It feels like the gears have frozen in the mental engine that makes up this group. Suddenly, the new employee, just out of college and very quiet so far, pretends to chomp on a cigar and does a dead-on impersonation of Groucho Marx, muttering out of the side of his mouth, "We've got to stop meeting like this." The room breaks into relieved laughter. Moods lighten. A few people get up to stretch and then everyone gets back to work, a little more refreshed and invigorated as ideas start to flow again.

Finding Humor is a very handy Habit to have in your back pocket.

People who can see the humor in difficult situations are generally optimistic, sunny, and resilient. They are not so likely to get flattened by adverse events, and when bad things do happen, they recover their equilibrium more quickly. When someone possesses a good-natured sense of humor, it is a social asset. We can assume that our young Groucho Marx

Finding humor

Laugh a little!

Finding the whimsical, incongruous and unexpected. Being able to laugh at one's self.

impersonator will not have trouble finding someone to sit next to in the company cafeteria.

While humor is not as all encompassing as creativity, the two habits do share many common characteristics. Both rely on an ability to view ordinary situations from an unusual vantage point. Generations of stand-up comedians have made a living by looking askew at the most everyday relationships and experiences. It is the very familiarity and identification with the comic's story, coupled with an unexpected twist, that makes us laugh. Creativity and humor both incorporate an element of surprise, whether it be the climax of a story, the clever solution to a stubborn marketing dilemma, or the punch line of a joke. Both also make frequent use of visual images and analogies.

Humor greases the wheels of our mental processes. Daniel Goleman (1995) asserts that laughing "seems to help people think more broadly and associate more freely" (p.85). The creative benefits of laughter have even been demonstrated in research. Goleman recounts one study in which people were asked to solve a problem on a test of creativity. (The problem was to find a way to attach a candle to a corkboard wall so that it would not drip wax. They had to do this using only a candle, matches, and a box of tacks.) Prior to solving the problem, one group was shown a funny film, one group watched a film about math, and one group did physical exercises. By now, you won't be surprised that those watching the funny film were more successful than the others in solving the problem. Humor nudged them out of the rut most people fall into on these tests called "functional fixedness." That is, the laughers were able to think of unconventional uses for the objects and thus solve the problem. (They used the box holding the tacks as a candleholder and tacked it to the wall.) Were the people who saw the humorous film benefiting from reduction of stress and the relaxation that laughter can trigger? Or was watching the film more akin to the stretching that trained runners do before a marathon, loosening them up and enabling the test takers to think more creatively?

People who can see the humor in difficult situations are generally optimistic, sunny, and resilient.

Humor for All Ages

Humor is often called the universal language because it transcends all cultures and every age. Even babies enjoy the playfulness of seeing parents sporting a towel over their heads or will anticipate with glee as an adult pops up from below the high chair to play peek-a-boo with them. Two-year-olds know you are teasing them when you ask with deadpan seriousness, "Are you my Uncle Jack?" Of course, both our ability to appreciate humor and to be humorous evolves over time as our capacity to understand nuances of language and life situations matures. Four- or five-year-olds may be laughing along with the rest of the family at a riddle or slapstick, but not really "getting the point." Not until around age six or seven can they begin to reason logically and find humor in word play and multiple meanings. A child has to know the "typical" and alternative meanings of words to enjoy riddles, says Doris Bergen (2000), a professor and co-director of Miami University's Center for Human Development, Learning, and Technology. For example: Q: Why are Saturday and Sunday strong days? A: Because the rest are week days.

Between ages seven and twelve, as children's knowledge of topics grows and deepens, so does the subject matter of their humor. Nine-years-olds can even identify that a particular joke is a play on words, Bergen says. Unfortunately, with maturity we may also begin to see the negative use of humor, such as ethnic or "insult jokes" that hurt or make fun of others. Kids will also tell jokes about subjects they are too embarrassed to discuss. Keeping in mind the old adage about there being truth in humor, you might use the occasion of overhearing your child tell such a joke, to check in with him about his understanding of the subject matter. It might be time for one of those important "talks."

Not until adolescence will your child likely enjoy the political satire that defines so much of late night comedy. The art of telling a joke—getting the timing and the sequence right—will come later, although many an adult still stumbles through a joke, never seeming to master this art. As one late night television host warned a guest who was obviously trying hard to get a joke in, "Comedy isn't easy."

Costa and Kallick (2000) say those proficient in Finding Humor have a positive or productive outlook no matter how difficult the situation. They are quick-witted yet sensitive to the difference between clowning around and using humor to raise people's spirits. This naturally makes them more well adapted socially, particularly if they can laugh at themselves and with, not at, others. They appreciate what goes into humor and are able to generate funny stories, metaphors, and puns. They are whimsical. They enjoy satires and irony and incongruities. They never seem to lose their playfulness and spontaneity.

Encourage Your Child to Find Humor in Everyday Doings

- Take a time out from adult worries to have some fun with your child. Enjoy good-natured teasing, making silly faces and gestures, and mixing up words. Have a joke book handy for those times when you need some props.

- Get to know your children's style of humor. If they are receptive, lighten up tense situations with a little humor, but be respectful of their responses just as you want them to be respectful of others.

- Introduce age-appropriate humor, such riddles for primary schoolers; jokes and cartoons for older elementary children; and, for everyone, timeless classics such as reruns of *I Love Lucy*, a pro who knew the art of making fun of herself.

- Enjoy a family joke night or a monthly comedy night with your family, an evening when the venue is strictly about laughing over a good movie or book.

- Talk about inappropriate humor on the playground or on television so your children have a clear understanding of your expectations. Help them understand the difference between good-hearted humor and mean teasing. If someone's feelings are hurt and your child says she was "just joking," remind her that if both people aren't laughing, it's not a joke.

• Enjoy your child's humor and don't forget to ask her, What did you enjoy today? Anything strike you as funny?

And the next time your six-year-old comes up with a new knock-knock joke or your ten-year-old impersonates you losing your car keys, take a moment to enjoy not only their humor but also their creative instincts.

Chapter 18

It's Not So Complicated:
Thinking and Communicating with Clarity and Precision

In Chapter 5, "Say What you Mean and Mean What you Say," we discuss this Habit of Mind in terms of communicating our thoughts and feelings clearly and precisely within the family. We talk about the benefits of developing an enriched "feelings vocabulary" and following through with "action messages" so that children understand that our words have meaning. This chapter builds on those ideas and strategies by looking at ways children can *practice* the critical thinking and communication skills they need to become successful problem solvers, both in and out of school. The explosion of information and ever-growing number of channels for sharing information make Thinking and Communicating with Clarity and Precision more important than ever. People who master this Habit of Mind display several common traits:

Building on ideas and strategies by looking at ways children can practice critical thinking and communication skills...

- They use and value correct terminology. If they don't know a word, they find out what it means.

- They know what they know and recognize that what they *don't* know *can* hurt them. They take the time to get the information they need.

231

- They understand the difference between fact and opinion. They do their own research to assess whether facts support popular opinion. They check their sources. They are not swayed by vague promises, overgeneralizations, or appeals to emotion. They back up their own views with data and facts.

- Their language is precise. They elaborate on ideas using concise and descriptive language in their written and spoken explanations.

You might assume that this habit is best taught in school but, once again, family life provides the original and perhaps best arena for encouraging clear thinking and communicating in children. At the dinner table with the whole family or during one-on-one conversations with parents, children can *hear, learn, and practice* language that will challenge them intellectually and help them to deepen and extend their thinking. It is at home, where children are not competing with a classroom full of other students and where they are doing what interests them (or at least what is familiar to them), that their language and thinking skills can be nourished by parents to become richer and more complex. Using the stuff of everyday life, parents can gently push the boundaries past vocabulary that is easy and comfortable.

You might assume that this habit is best taught in school but, once again, family life provides the original and best arena.

For example, if it is the season for local elections and the roadside is peppered with campaign signs, you have an excellent opportunity to explore some ideas about local government and the duties of the mayor or town board members. Discussions about voting, ballots, political parties, taxes and what they pay for, all contribute to your child's understanding of how the world works. In a similar way, many children understand the concepts of mathematics but they flounder on the *language* of it. They get confused about the meaning of specific terms. But think of the opportunities we have of using those terms in everyday life. When setting the table, the knife and spoon are *adjacent* to the plate, and they line up next to each other so they are *parallel*. Each of these ideas is brought to life by the specialized vocabulary that accompanies it. Obviously, you want to keep a light touch with these conversations; the most effective way to kill budding curiosity is a long, pedantic lecture. But if you adopt a tone suggesting, *Oh, isn't that interesting,* and you speculate together about whatever it is you are discussing, you may introduce some new words and concepts and also spark in your child an interest in a new subject.

Islands of Expertise

Kevin Crowley and Melanie Jacobs (2002) use the term "islands of expertise" to explain how parents and children together "co-construct" a body of knowledge in a specific topic. This happens naturally, and you probably can give many instances of it in your own family. Sometimes it starts with a bedtime story that piques a child's interest in some topic, such as wolves or trains or dinosaurs. The child is fascinated and asks for the story again and again. Let's take the typical example of dinosaurs. Parents begin to build on this interest by finding other books or DVDs or computer games that also cover dinosaurs. They buy a set of plastic dinosaurs for their child to play with. They start having conversations about the different types of dinosaurs, plant-eaters versus meat-eaters, how they protected themselves, where their fossils are found, how they became extinct, and so on. The child's spontaneous artwork reflects her new passion, page after page of mighty *T. rex* in different poses, or the  long-necked Apatosaurus. Lunchboxes, pajamas, and room décor all are sprinkled with the dinosaur theme, and family trips to museums or fossil sites are now planned around this shared interest.

Crowley and Jacobs point to the collaboration that takes place between parent and child in the development of islands of expertise through their *shared attention* to the topic of interest and parents' support of it through reading, choice of toys, searching out relevant websites, museum visits, and, of course, conversation. The word "collaboration" implies a balance of energy and initiative. At any given time, either the parent or the child may ask a question or start the conversation with a thought or observation. Mostly this happens during ordinary moments of family life, at dinner, riding in the car, or in the drowsy moments before falling asleep. As time goes on, the conversations become more complex. Parents and children relate the information from a newly acquired book to what they read before or what they learned at the museum last month. They look at the topic from different perspectives, talking about something from an historical or scientific perspective one day (*If the dinosaurs had not become extinct, would mammals have been able to evolve?*) and then in context of a movie or book on another day. All these conversations increase a child's ability to think about, understand, and communicate that understanding.

Crowley and Jacobs discuss how islands of expertise become "platforms" from which parents and children begin to have conversations about much bigger concepts and questions. A child's question of "Why aren't there any dinosaurs living today?" leads to a rudimentary exploration of more sophisticated concepts: how the earth has changed over different epochs of time; the forces that lead to gradual or sudden extinction of species; the theory of evolution and what different living things need to survive. The way parents use language to ask questions and "notice" information that might prove interesting to the child greatly affects his learning. In an ingenious study conducted at the Carnegie Museum of Natural History in Pittsburgh, parent visitors volunteered to allow the researchers to record the conversations they had with their children as they walked through the dinosaur hall (Palmquist & Crowley, 2007). During the visits, which averaged a mere eight minutes, parents successfully helped their children assimilate new vocabulary words and understanding about these prehistoric creatures. They did this by noticing details in the displays and paying careful attention to explanatory signs, which they shared with their children. They named the specific types of dinosaurs on display. When talking about what they saw, they would sometimes make comparisons to what they had seen previously, or they would speculate about the meaning of what they were looking at. One father compared the teeth of a plant-eating dinosaur to those enormous sharp teeth of the meat-eating tyrannosaurus. In another conversation, intrigued by a huge flying reptile, a mother traced different kinds of wings in a display, thinking out loud with her child about the long line of the pterosaur wing, the wing of a bat, and finally that of a modern bird. The researchers found that these kinds of conversations were very effective—in such a short time—in increasing the knowledge that children had about these creatures.

Crowley and Jacobs (2002) acknowledge that these typical kinds of collaborative parent-child conversations are not as complete or as structured as the formal instruction a child would experience in school. They use the term "explanatoids" to describe the brief "fragments of explanatory talk" (p. 8) that are characteristic of parent-child learning dialogues. But these explanatoids, offered in the spontaneous give and take of family interactions and casually returned to throughout the days and weeks, may be even more powerful and memorable than what is presented in school. This is because they are shared and repeated in many different ways, and because they center on an interesting experience that is happening right at that moment and will likely be part of their collective memories.

Over time, of course, children will put aside these early passions. Dinosaurs or trains may no longer fascinate as they once did, and children move on. The value of those experiences is far from lost, however. The pattern has been established of following through on an interest by talking, reading, and seeking knowledge. The vocabulary that was learned and the concepts and understandings that were constructed during those early years stay with the child, provide a foundation for what she will be learning in school, and become transformed again and again into ever more sophisticated and complex conceptualizations. All those experiences with naming and classifying those early objects of interest, with thinking and reading about them, and imagining them, serve as a template for future learning. They serve as a powerful introduction to Thinking and Communicating with Clarity and Precision.

As children grow older, they may be ready to move on to more formal instruction in a particular area of interest. At that point, parents may seek the expertise of an instructor or enroll their child in a program sponsored by a school or educational center to continue the child's learning. That might well be the next step, but parents should never doubt the value of their own role. When a child's first impulse to know more is met with the supportive interest of a loving parent, it is a powerful motivator to a child's intellectual curiosity.

New 21st Century Literacies

Finances, health, consumerism, and the media are among the new 21st century "literacies" that are now being taught in schools. Each possesses its own specialized vocabulary and represents topics that adults need to understand. These literacies are another opportunity for practicing this Habit of Mind and for ensuring that our children know not just what words mean but how things operate. You just need to reflect on the fate of consumers lured into interest-only, no-money-down, variable-rate mortgages to realize the importance of being knowledgeable about personal finances. In the Charles Schwab Foundation 2009 Young Adults & Money Survey, the majority of respondents said they had not been adequately prepared to manage their finances and thought the topic should be taught in school (CBS Money Watch.com, July 15, 2009).

> *Seven-year-old Kyle asked his parents for a new game system for his birthday so he could play the same games as his friend Robby. When his mother, Judy, explained how expensive new systems were, Kyle refused to take no for an answer. He was full of ideas about how they could purchase the system with a check or a credit card, oblivious, Judy realized, to how money was still necessary for either of those transactions. Nor did Kyle seem to respond to her explanations about budgeting and saving or her questions about whether it was necessary to purchase a separate game system. Judy became acutely aware of how little Kyle seemed to understand finances. In the convenience of online banking, he had never seen his parents go to a bank to make a deposit and was unaware of all the bills they paid online each month or how credit cards or checks worked. While his parents were careful to live within their means, Kyle had no real understanding of how they managed their household and kept up with the expenses for three children. After this incident, his parents decided they needed to demonstrate the reality of financial matters more explicitly. They started keeping a folder of the bills to be paid and talking to Kyle about what they were for. Kyle was already receiving a small allowance but had not yet managed to save any money. They purchased a piggy bank for him, offered him a couple of opportunities to earn extra money, and explained that he could start saving for special things like a new system.*

When a child clamors for something they've seen advertised, parents can seize the moment, perhaps offering an explanatoid, to counterbalance the gravitational pull of the commercial.

Other families may choose to be even more explicit in teaching children the relationship between income and expenses, but variations of this story happen every day. We tell our children not to eat a particular food because it is not healthy, but they may have no idea that it is the sugar, salt, or fat content or the cooking method that is of concern. We may not take into account the impact on our children's beliefs and attitudes from seeing thousands of advertisements in stores and on television, the Internet, and billboards, all with one intention: to create an emotional need for a product so that it will sell. Without bringing these concerns to our children's attention, how can we expect them to sort through the maze of information they hear every day and know how to receive and use (or not) different types of information? Based on an extensive review of research, the American Psychological Association concluded that until children are about eight years old, they are unable to understand the persuasive intent of advertisements (Wilcox et al., 2004).

When a child clamors for something they've seen advertised, parents can seize the moment, perhaps offering an explanatoid, to counterbalance the gravitational pull of the commercial. That would be the time to explain how commercials are designed to make you feel that you just have to have the item being advertised. Ask your child to take note of how many commercials for games show a kid joyously shouting, "I won!" as if, in reality, you could *always* win a game. Explain to them some of the tricks that photographers use to make the foods in commercials look impossibly delicious. Providing our children with factual information can help them make sense of the messages of advertisements. Let them see you reading labels and pointing out why this cereal is okay but not that other one. Let them hear you question a claim that sounds dubious. When we name things and demonstrate how they affect us, or point out discrepancies in how they may appear to be and what they really are, we give children the resources they will need to eventually make wise decisions and choices on their own. We are training them to think and communicate with clarity and precision.

Family Discussions

Describing how students like to learn, educator Mike Schmoker (2011) refers to a survey in which more than 80 percent of students said discussions and debate "excited" them the most (Azzam, 2008, p. 84). Are we surprised? Even school-age children have lots of opinions about topics ranging from the environment and world peace to hunger and local issues.

Discussions can be an opportunity for children to hone the skills of this Habit of Mind, provided its standards are applied to your conversations. This habit requires sound thinking as well as good communicating. Discussions with our children will be more effective when they reflect well thought out opinions and data. One way to begin is to have your children discuss something they learned in school. If you know your 2nd grader is learning about sea creatures, you can invite your child to take a teaching role within the family. *What have you been learning about in your research? What are some things that might have surprised you that you didn't know before? Help me understand the differences between a crustacean and a mollusk.*

You also might want to consider hosting some family discussions during dinner. Former Senator Ted Kennedy attributed the thorough research and preparation that defined his career in Congress to the disciplined conversations he had with his family while growing up. "I will not champion a bill or a cause, no matter how complex, until I have understood it well enough to satisfy the standards my father set for table talk," he wrote just before he died (Kennedy, 2009, p. 22). All children were expected to read up on a given topic before dinner and participate with insightful comments. Jennifer Finney Boylan (2011), author and a professor of English at Colby College, recalled that her father's passion for debate often meant having dinner guests with a range of opinions. To keep everyone open minded, it was not unusual for her father to ask his guests to reverse their earlier positions at some point in the evening for the sake of a good argument.

Families might choose to have a family debate night once a month. You could approach this with a kind of good-humored formality, as if you were hosting a book club meeting. Serving favorite foods may result in a receptive group of participants. The topic could be chosen the week before to give everyone a chance to prepare. For optimal discussions among students, Schmoker (2011) recommends careful selection of age-appropriate topics. He likes ones that reflect controversy: two different views. Who is right and why? Or make an argument for why you would prefer to live in one period over another; or discuss a character in a book the family has read or from a movie you have watched. In the story "Jack in the Beanstalk," is Jack heroic, or not? For current events and news items, publications such as *Time for Kids* include articles that can be read by children as young as seven. For older siblings, try weekly magazines or articles from newspapers. Once the topic is selected, Schmoker advises "close reading." In a classroom setting, this means taking notes, underlining, and discussing the text itself in some detail. Parents might want to model this process with primary grade children, checking in as you read together to make sure they are understanding the article.

A few basic ground rules should ensure a stimulating but civil conversation:

- Any arguments must be backed up with facts or evidence. When in doubt, go to the text or cite other sources.

- When disagreeing with someone else's conclusions or arguments, first restate what the person said to make sure you understood her correctly.

- Express disagreements courteously and respectfully.

- Stay on topic, but make room for humor.

Afterward, ask everyone what they liked about the discussion and how it could be improved.

As your children become more adept in these conversations and discussions, look for important aspects of Thinking and Communicating with Clarity and Precision, such as children's ability to describe their thoughts and feelings, analyze arguments, synthesize conflicting opinions, and infer opinions or meaning from the discussion.

Use Thinking Words

Often we select words that are vague generalizations. What exactly do we mean when we tell our children to "think" or ask in dismay, "what were you *thinking?*" There are many different ways of thinking, each suitable for different situations and problems and each with its own terminology. While words such as "analyze" or "conclude" may not be the first words that come to mind when deciding which movie to select or in making any one of the many decisions that we face each day, words like these can cause children to reflect in a more complex way. Try the following alternatives in suggesting a particular kind of thinking:

Instead of "talking about," try "exploring consequences."
"Let's explore the consequences of signing up for
the play and for basketball this winter."

Instead of "look at, "try "compare and contrast."
"Let's compare the quality and price of these two shirts
you like. What do you notice?"

Instead of "pick out," try "identify."
"Can you identify which fruit is ripe?"

Instead of "what do you think," try to "analyze the situation."
"Let's analyze this situation from the perspective of the baseball players, the neighbors, and the police and get our facts straight before we form an opinion. Let's start with what we know."

Instead of just "accepting" what you read or hear as true, try "examining evidence."
"Let's examine the past voting record of this candidate to see if what this advertisement claims is true."

Instead of "jumping" to conclusions, try "drawing" conclusions.
"Based on this evidence, I conclude that this advertisement is not accurate."

Instead of "wondering," try "speculating."
"What do you speculate will happen if it rains this afternoon during the game?"

Instead of "guessing," try "estimating."
"Can you estimate the total cost of taking five children to the movies and dinner vs. playing miniature golf and eating at home?"

Instead of "thinking," try "predicting."
"What do you predict our neighbors will do when you tell them that you broke their fence?"

Instead of "prejudging," try "examining assumptions."
"It sounds like you already made your mind up that you won't enjoy this book. What assumptions are you basing that opinion on?"

Instead of "figuring out" what happened, try "examining causes and effects."
"Let's examine what caused the circuit not to work in your experiment. How will this affect your results?"

Instead of "presuming" to know, try developing a "hypothesis."
"What are your hypotheses about why our tomato plants are not growing this summer?"

Label Habits of Mind When You See Examples of Them

Another way to improve the precision of your children's language is to recognize and label examples when family members demonstrate a particular Habit of Mind (Costa & Kallick, 2000, p. 27):

You really *persisted* in solving this problem.

You *listened* to your brother and *empathized* with his feelings.

I can see you are thinking about how you want to approach this problem. Take your time; I know you are *thinking about your thinking*.

That is an interesting *question*. You are posing a real *problem* that we should solve before going away.

I noticed that in *checking over* your work for *accuracy*, you found some errors. That shows that you really care about the quality of your work.

I see you learned from that mistake. You are *applying past knowledge to a new situation*.

This is a very innovative solution to this problem that no one else thought of.

I noticed you managed your impulsivity and decided not to reply to your friend's text while doing your homework. You didn't let yourself get distracted and now you're finished!

Provide Data, Not Solutions

You can encourage clarity of thinking by giving your children information, and then letting them process it and decide how to use it. Costa and Kallick (2000, p. 27) offer the following examples:

The noise you are making is disturbing us. Is there a way you can work so that we don't hear you?

Since it is your sister's turn to use the computer, what do you need to do?

I like it when it is not an emergency and you wait until I am finished speaking on the phone.

What must you remember for your field trip tomorrow?

This paragraph would be correct with two additions. Can you figure out what they are?

You said you need to review the chapter for your social studies test. This movie won't be over until 9:30. What do you need to do?

Thinking and Communicating With Clarity and Precision empowers our children to effectively navigate the oceans of print and spoken language they face in every arena of life. Using correct terminology and selecting the most precise language to convey meaning, not only extends learning but also prevents misunderstandings. Teaching them to back up their opinions with data, and to expect the same of others, will prepare them to better argue their own case when necessary, and to also evaluate the merits of sales pitches, political arguments, or other claims to their allegiances or finances.

Perfection is not attainable, but if we chase perfection we can catch excellence.

———*Vince Lombardi*

Chapter 19

Show Time:
Striving for Accuracy and Precision

The book and film, *Apollo 13*, tell the true, riveting story of how three astronauts and their counterparts at Mission Control were faced with a catastrophic systems failure of their spacecraft. With very little power left, their computer shut down and in miserably cold conditions, they had to figure out the *exact* angle at which to re-enter the earth's atmosphere, or risk being flung out into space with no hope of rescue. Hurtling through space in their cramped, darkened spacecraft, they got busy with pencils, paper, and a slide rule. Suffice it to say, there has probably never been a more suspenseful illustration of the importance of Striving for Accuracy and Precision.

This Habit of Mind emphasizes getting a task *right* over getting it *done*. We saw in the last chapter how children can learn to think and speak with more clarity and precision. Now it is time to put that same emphasis into practice with their homework, sports, music, or anything they do where quality counts. Instead of taking short cuts, users of this habit take time to focus on meeting the requirements, from start to finish. They read and follow the directions. Their measurements are exact. They verify facts and sources. They

> ## Striving for accuracy
> ### *Check it again!*
> Always doing your best.
> Setting high standards.
> Checking and finding
> ways to improve
> constantly.

are willing to edit to make changes and improvements. They check and recheck their work before signing off. Like a fine craftsman, they take pride in what they do. This is what we are striving for here.

Young children can be taught to appreciate the importance of Striving for Accuracy and Precision. Every day, we depend on people who must take this Habit of Mind seriously: from the air traffic controller and the bus driver to bank tellers, doctors, and construction workers. This Habit of Mind is essential for students. Many children who are quick with mental math are impatient when it comes to showing their work. They may copy the columns of numbers sloppily and make careless errors because of it. Homework assignments that are not copied down neatly or in the right place may not get done or be done poorly.

Before beginning a task is the time for careful preparation.

At home, we often have to pay careful attention to details and follow instructions—when setting up the fish tank, measuring out a dose of medicine for a sick child, balancing a checkbook, etc. Similarly, teams count on every player to strive for accuracy; everyone is expected to follow the playbook in football and has to get the ball just inside the foul line in tennis. Members of a violin quartet play by these same standards. In each of these examples, the finished product depends on how precisely every step is followed.

By pointing out everyday instances in which Striving for Accuracy and Precision contribute to our safety, our aesthetic enjoyment, or our sense of satisfaction for a job well done, children are more apt to grow and sustain that value within themselves.

With your support, they will also learn for themselves that cutting corners and carelessness has consequences. Alas, that math page may have to be redone, this time with the place values aligned. Did she forget to measure the exact dimensions of the project before cutting the poster board? Uh-oh, now she'll have to come up with a way to fix it. As long as we neither pile on more criticism nor overprotect our children when this happens, these moments can provide valuable learning experiences. Failing to work accurately and precisely carries its own unfortunate consequences, an invaluable learning experience for children.

Two Prerequisites

Often, the main impediment to developing this habit is our old nemesis, impulsivity. That urge to just get it done and over with, the impatience we feel when asked to read the directions carefully or check our efforts afterward, all work in direct opposition to our need for accuracy. Mastering some of the strategies already discussed for managing impulsivity, minimizing distractions, and increasing focus will increase the likelihood of improving the quality of one's work.

Metacognitive strategies also contribute to a higher quality outcome through their focus on planning and intentional work. Metacognition provides a timeline and framework for when to activate this Habit of Mind:

Before beginning a task is the time for careful preparation. This is when children need to read and make sure they understand the directions. For some, this may require the extra step of telling you the directions in their own words to be sure they get both the big picture and the specific details required. This is also a good time to review rubrics or scoring guides that show how their work will be evaluated. (We address rubrics in Chapter 9 on Metacognition.) Keep in mind that, while we want our children to eventually develop their own internal standards of excellence, scoring guides make explicit the level of accuracy and precision required for an assignment. The more a child knows specific criteria for achieving excellence at the outset, the more directed he can be in meeting expectations.

During the task, metacognition keeps a student asking, "Am I on track with this? How will I know if I am doing this correctly?" One teacher tells his students to check in after reading or writing every page or, if necessary, paragraph. Where am I? Do I know where I am going next?

After completion, the metacognitive strategy of evaluating their efforts enables children to make the necessary changes that move them ever closer to excellence. This step is what distinguishes one final product from another. Even when children do not make substantial revisions, there is still real value in reviewing the rubrics when they are finished. At the very least, they will know how their work could have been improved and what they can do to make it better next time.

Encouraging Accuracy and Precision in Children

Talk About It —When Is this Habit a Must?

Let your children know what this habit means to you and the different times when Striving for Accuracy and Precision is most important. For you, this might be accurately completing research your coworkers depend on, figuring out the weekly food budget, filling in forms for school, and getting your children safely to school. Both of you can list when this Habit of Mind is a 100% must-do. Talk about the consequences if you do not pay attention to the need for accuracy and precision.

Kids' lists will vary by age. A 1st grader may strive to be accurate with his math facts or spelling words, when crossing the street, or when following the sequence of steps for tying his shoes. Your 6th grader may include having good references in his history essay, monitoring her science experiment carefully, or practicing his scales or foul shots for the school band or basketball team. The conversations with our children about this Habit of Mind are akin to preparing the soil before planting the garden. The more that children understand the difference between getting a task done and doing it well, the more they understand the need to take steps to getting it right.

Observe Your Children

If you want to make Striving for Accuracy and Precision a priority, spend some time observing your child's capacity for this Habit of Mind. Is she naturally cautious and careful by temperament? Is he happy-go-lucky and oblivious to details? Or is he somewhere in between? Think about how she approaches her homework and tests. Does she lose points because of careless errors in her calculations, grammar, or spelling? Is he not paying enough attention to the question? Is her work sloppy because she's rushing? Is he impulsive?

Extend your observations to your child's commitment to extra curricular activities and favorite pastimes. Is this Habit of Mind a problem in whatever he does, or is he fastidious when it comes to building a LEGO rocket but rushes his schoolwork? Is she only willing to put in time to practice her dance routines? Is your child attentive enough some of the time and simply needs to move to the next level?

Think about your child's behavior and any patterns you can pick out or areas needing attention. Share your insights with your child's teachers and coaches or other instructors, who can also offer their perspectives on your child and their expectations for your child's age group. Educator Chip Wood (1997, p. 108) says not until they're about nine years old do most children "take care with the final product" in the classroom. This is when they have more mastery over basic skills and a more solid understanding of key concepts such as multiplication, spelling patterns, and the scientific process. They are more apt at this age to put in the necessary effort their schoolwork may require. Professionals, especially the seasoned ones, can help you define reasonable expectations at any age and may be able to offer further suggestions for helping your child.

Share with your child your observations and what the coach or teacher suggests. See if he agrees with your perceptions. Some insights may be very helpful. For example, you can point out to your child that the same attention to detail he shows in building his rocket ship is necessary in math. Have him tell you the steps he followed and see how they may apply to schoolwork. If there are specific areas your child needs to address, now is a good time to set some goals together. Consider what your child's teachers advised and your own observations.

Practice This Habit of Mind Together

Choose a project to do together that will demonstrate and reinforce the kind of accuracy and precision your child is striving to achieve in the goals you both set. Try that recipe for a checkered chocolate/vanilla cake or a soufflé and note how important it is to follow directions exactly. If you have a child who is careless about calculations and measurements, build a model airplane or build a jewelry box and aim for precision. For the child who needs some prodding in math, ask her to plan and budget lunch for the week. Go to the store together to purchase the food with a set dollar amount. Calculate costs and change. For the child who doesn't pay attention to punctuation, give him something to read with no punctuation and see if he understands it.

Think aloud about the process of completing the activity you choose, emphasizing all the different ways you have to pay attention to details. With your

Don't be afraid to acknowledge that accuracy and precision can be stern taskmasters.

child, write down all the steps she followed to get the task right.

If your child is resistant, tap into one of their passions to illuminate this Habit of Mind. For your budding saxophone or basketball player, try to get tickets to a concert or game or watch a DVD from home. Besides commenting on the masterful precision and accuracy of the superstars, do some research on how much time they actually spend practicing. Even seasoned professional musicians practice every day. Point out their mistakes too. This juxtaposition of wins and misses, or wins and practice time will make it vividly clear to your child the tremendous investment of effort that goes into achieving real excellence.

Revise!

The work of writers, artists, architects, lawyers—almost every profession—demands time for revisions before signing off. In school, children often participate in peer reviews in which they edit each other's work. Using a checklist, they look for grammatical mistakes and misspellings and check the quality of the writing. Does it make sense, achieve its purpose, etc.? At home, children should perform this task with their own work. Sometimes parents wonder how involved they should be in this process. It's one thing to help a child who requires a little help to understand a point he's not sure of. To proof, revise, and correct his homework is quite another. Doing the work for him deprives your child of the opportunity to learn skills. It also deprives your child's teacher of insights into what he is capable of doing on his own. Instead of doing the work for him, we recommend that you review the work and indicate to your child if you see any errors in grammar or addition, etc., but you let your child find and make the corrections himself. You can make a game of it. "I see three errors in the top row of math problems. Let's see how long it takes you to find and correct them." Electronic spell checks are also helpful if the child takes note of her errors and the corrections. For persistent problems, work with the teacher to clarify what you can do at home.

Take One Step at a Time

Depending on your child's propensity for this Habit of Mind, you may have to start small. For children in elementary school, "doing your best" may well lay the groundwork for this Habit of Mind. "Doing your best" is about *striving*. A process is implied. Excellence is a standard children need to strive to achieve. Reinforcing the goal of Applying Past Knowledge to New Situations, we want children to learn from their mistakes. Work with your child to make a checklist to guide his homework. Here are some possible steps you might want to include:

Before:
- Read directions several times to make sure you understand them.
- Check the standards set in the class rubric. Identify which ones to pay particular attention to.
- Make sure you have the right tools, books and worksheets.

During:
- Check in throughout the process: Am I on the right track?

After:
- Check: Is my work complete? Does it meet the criteria set in the rubric? Did I follow all the directions?
- Double check: is my work accurate in meaning, grammar, spelling, calculations, etc.?

Understand the Emotions That Get in the Way

Don't be afraid to acknowledge that accuracy and precision can be stern taskmasters. Very few of us are willing to put in our absolutely best effort all the time, for every single assignment we do. If we are stressed, burdened, or bored, it will be difficult to summon the focus and motivation necessary to do our most accurate work. Use your empathic listening skills to allow your child a chance to vent. If you recall from Motivation Factor (in Chapter 7) when children feel they have some autonomy and choice they are much more likely to be motivated to do their best work. As you review your child's assignments ahead of time, you might talk together about which ones will require more effort than others; which ones will she want to be a "wow" when she's finished and which might be an "okay." When your child is working hard at a tedious or exacting task, provide specific encouragement: "I know it can be grueling to keep checking your work like this, but you will be so proud afterward." "You're showing such patience in making it just right."

Finally, you want to be emotionally attuned to your child's own perceptions about how well he did. If your 4th grader is beaming because, for the first time, she pulled together a four-page research paper on Native Americans, that would not be the best moment for you to point out a glaring spelling error on page 1. There will be time before she turns it in to give it a final check. Her excitement now is about having done something so grown-up, something that would have seemed unimaginably difficult when she was in 3rd grade. What she needs at this moment is for her parent to share in her pride of accomplishment; someone to reflect on how long it took to do, the effort she expended, how careful she was to cover all the requirements, and how satisfying it will feel to see her good work up on the bulletin board. The sustenance she gets from your shared pride in her accomplishment will nourish her motivation to achieve.

Self-Criticism

Children are sometimes unduly critical of their own efforts. They often have a picture in their minds of how something *should* look (based on their own impressions from books or from the work they see done by older siblings), and their own developmentally appropriate efforts just don't measure up in their own minds. This is a situation where Listening with Understanding and Empathy can help. Here is a conversation that illustrates how a thoughtful father enabled his child to identify and work through his overly critical appraisal of a paper he had written:

Dad:	Jason, I think you did such a good job on this biography project. Look at all the information you collected. We never did this kind of good work when I was in 2nd grade.
Jason:	(sounding deflated) But it's really not that good.
Dad:	(a little surprised) You don't feel you did a good job?
Jason:	No. I don't.
Dad:	(gently) You just don't feel that good about it.
Jason:	I really liked the biography I read about Gandhi, but it was hard to describe all the things he did, and I'm not sure I did a good job. There were so many things he did.
Dad:	So, you really liked learning about Gandhi, but it sounds like maybe it wasn't so easy deciding what to put in and what to leave out.
Jason:	Yeah. And I don't think the other kids will like it. Most of them are doing American presidents or baseball players.

Dad: You think they might not be interested in someone kind of different?

Jason: Well, I didn't think I'd be interested either, but when I read about him, I thought he was so great.

Dad: Tell me what impressed you so much about Gandhi.

Jason: Did you know that when people went on those marches for Civil Rights, Martin Luther King said that there should be no fighting. They should be peaceful. He got that idea from Gandhi.

Dad: That is an amazing fact. You see, just by talking with you I learned something new. Now you've gotten me really interested in Gandhi. What else can you tell me?

In this conversation, the father supported his son's intrinsic interest in this historic figure who might have been a little different than those chosen by his classmates. In reality, Jason was having a little crisis of confidence that was resolved simply by his father's warm interest. Rather than critiquing the work or if, in fact, he could have done a better job following the parameters of the assignment, this father focused on helping his child to express his own reservations. Chances are better that, through this kind of supportive conversation, Jason was willing to think about some ways to improve his report.

How Good Is Good Enough?

As with all the Habits of Mind, our aim is for children to take ownership of the practice of Striving for Accuracy and Precision. We hope that they will develop that internalized compass that will tell them "this is just great" or "I need to work a little harder on this." Parents have a difficult balancing act between leaving it completely up to the child, setting appropriate standards and expectations, or completely taking over responsibility for quality control. We support the middle way, but acknowledge that it is a more challenging path for parents. To set *appropriate* standards and expectations, you must have a good understanding of what is developmentally possible and beneficial for children of different ages. This is where the teacher's expertise is so valuable. She will have a frame of reference for what children at her grade level typically can and cannot do, and will be able to help you in establishing a good understanding of where your child fits in and how to challenge and support her.

You also need to know your own child's strengths and limitations. The best gift parents can give a child is their loving acceptance and delight in exactly who their child is. We never know how far a child can go and would never put limits on our expectations for that child's success. But many parents focus on external manifestations of academic success by demanding straight A's, stellar achievement in all areas, or acceptance to an elite college, and they push relentlessly for their child to achieve this level of performance. This can be counterproductive and even damaging, for even if the child meets those goals, the accomplishment belongs more to the parent who pushed than to the child. It can be an empty victory if years later she may find herself stranded in a college, course of study, sport or career that just is not a good fit for her. Far better, we think, to nurture that intellectual curiosity and to provide the tools that Habits of Mind offer, so the child will not just be capable of high achievement, but will want to achieve *because she is interested.*

Becoming More Accurate and Precise

Beginner: The child does not see errors in work, and puts in minimum effort rather than investing time and attention. He does not revisit work to correct errors.

Apprentice: The child begins to check work for errors and corrects errors when prompted; she shows some improvement in handing in work that shows she has taken care to be more accurate and precise.

Practitioner: The child takes time and care to check over work to make sure that it is free of errors. He sets high standards for accurate work and maintains those standards.

Expert: The child consistently checks for accuracy and precision without being asked. She takes care with an assignment; her completed work is free of errors, and she sets a standard of excellence and strives to meet expectations in all areas possible. (Boyes and Watts, 2009)

Section III

The Self-Directed Child,
The-Self Directed Family

*Creating interdependence within
the family builds a positive structure
that gives family members a firm
foundation and a strong identity from
which to venture out into the world.*

Chapter 20

Teamwork: Thinking Interdependently

The Alpert family was facing a serious situation. Grant's elderly father had recently died, and his mother, Beatrice, was not doing well. Grant had gotten a call from his Aunt Ellie, Bea's younger sister, saying that she was very concerned. She told him that Bea wasn't taking care of herself: The house was a mess, neighbors said that the lights were left on all night, and when Ellie went to check, she found food left out for days, uneaten. Of even more concern to Ellie was that her usually meticulous sister appeared to be disheveled and unkempt. She also looked as if she had lost weight, and seemed vague and confused. Ellie apologized for not keeping better tabs on things, but she was herself overwhelmed with her job and with caring for her sick husband. Grant thanked Aunt Ellie and promised to get on top of the situation.

> ## Thinking Interdependently
> ### Work together!
> Being able to work with and learn from others in reciprocal situations. Team work.

After hanging up, Grant and his wife, Bethany, talked it over. He felt stricken to think of his mother so alone and vulnerable. Because they lived several hundred miles away and he was in a difficult period at work, he hadn't gotten back to see her since the funeral two months ago. He did *call her nearly every day to check in, and, although she sounded subdued, there was nothing in their conversations that would have clued him in to her condition. He was worried about her safety and ability to take care of herself. As he and Bethany talked it over, there were so many questions: Was this a normal part of grieving? Was it the beginning of Alzheimer's?*

That night at dinner, Grant and Bethany discussed the situation with their children, Lucy, seven, and T.J., ten. Grant opened the conversation by saying, "I talked with Aunt Ellie today. She's a little worried about Nana." Without giving details that might cause anxiety to the children, he added, "She thinks Nana's still having a hard time because she misses Grampa so much." Lucy looked down, "I miss him, too," she said quietly. Bethany reached over to squeeze Lucy's hand. "I know, honey. Grampa always used to say you were his best girl." T.J. looked very serious. "Dad, Nana's all alone in that big house. It must be so lonely for her without Grampa there." Grant felt his throat tighten. "I think you're right, T.J. I miss Grampa, too. We all do. But we're here together. We have each other. Imagine how Nana must feel." Lucy added softly, "Nana must miss cooking for him and watching 'American Idol' with him." The family sat quietly for a moment, each taking in their feelings and concern for this woman they all loved. Then Grant spoke.

"Mom and I have been thinking about what we could do to help Nana. We have some thoughts about it, but were wondering what ideas you both might have."

As the family talked about the situation, T.J. suggested they invite their Nana to come stay with them for awhile, until she felt better. Grant and Bethany initially had thought that one of them might fly out for a weekend to see her, but as they discussed the situation, they began to think that, if Bea agreed to come, they could get a better handle on what her needs might be. There would be a lot to work out that would not begin to be addressed in this first conversation. Bethany was concerned about her own work schedule and whether it could be flexible enough to accommodate doctors' visits and other appointments. They had a small house. If Bea came to stay with them for a longer period, how could they make that work? Grant was stressed by his own work demands and his feeling that he was just barely able to give his family the time they needed as it was. How would the addition of another person—however beloved—affect that? Grant and Bethany both wondered about the children's reactions:

Would they be able sustain their original enthusiasm if their grandmother stayed longer than the usual week or so? How would they handle it if she had significant medical or cognitive problems? The children were mostly excited about the thought of her coming to stay with them, but had some concerns as well about whether they would be able to continue with their normal schedule of activities and play dates. Finally, they understood that all of their discussion was theoretical until Nana herself was part of it; would she even want to leave her home to stay with them?

As they talked, Grant remembered something that had happened when he was in high school. His mother had taken in a friend of his, Lou, whose own mother had died suddenly that year. Bea had treated Lou as though he was her own son: She went to his basketball games, parent-teacher conferences, and wept at his graduation. Grant realized with a jolt, that his mother had never questioned the inconvenience or the expense; she just did what she thought was right. He told that story to his family and they sat there quietly for a moment. Bethany smiled at him and said, "I think we'll take our cue from Nana. There will always be room and time for someone we love."

The children were filled by a sense of mission to surround their Nana with their love and attention. As they all talked together that evening, they started to make plans for fixing up the small office as a room for her. The children had lots of ideas for making Nana feel loved and needed. Lucy thought she would ask Nana to teach her how to make real chocolate chip cookies. T.J. wanted to hear stories about when Grampa was in the war, and his early days on the farm. He wondered if it would make Nana too sad to talk about Grampa or if it might make her actually feel better. He also remembered how, when Nana visited last year, she played catch with him in the yard. Maybe she would like to come to some of his baseball games. Bethany realized that she had never finished updating that family photo album and wondered if Bea would find it comforting to work on it with her. As Grant got up from the table to call his mother, he gazed appreciatively at his family as they were still making plans and thought how good it felt to be all pulling together.

Thinking Interdependently is the Habit of Mind associated with great teamwork. The NASA team that put astronauts on the moon is one example that comes to mind. We also think of spectacular innovations in technology and medicine. Most of the Nobel Prizes given out in the sciences are awarded to *teams* of researchers and innovators rather than individuals. The characteristics and attributes of Interdependence have been researched for decades now, and the knowledge that has been gained informs the way businesses are structured, how diplomacy is conducted, and how schools implement important changes. Such collaboration and teamwork is increasingly recognized as critically important in almost every endeavor. Books have been written about the formation and functioning of corporate and research teams, and now, *virtual* teams, brought together by technology across great distances to work together. (See, for example, *Team Work: What Must Go Right/What Can Go Wrong* by Carl E. Larson and Frank M. J. La Fasto.)

An article in the *New York Times* (July 11, 2011) describes how medical schools are now considering an applicant's communication and relationship skills as equally important as grade point average. The article cites the large number of preventable deaths that occur in hospitals due to poor communication and lack of teamwork. In addition to strong math and science skills, these medical schools are looking for candidates who show curiosity, who can listen, and who show a willingness and ability to work well with others. In education, schools have been encouraging cooperative learning groups for students for many years now, and, on a district level, many school administrators are working to implement a more collaborative model of leadership. It is well understood that, when people share common goals and are able to work well together, the results, whatever the endeavor, are superior to either a top-down or competitive way of working.

Thinking Interdependently is what happens when we take each of the Habits of Mind and *put them to work in a group setting*. It is *collaborating with a sense of purpose and mission*. It is a way of thinking and communicating and working in which each person's strengths are valued and encouraged, while the talents of the group compensate for relative weaknesses of individuals. It is the ability to speak up, contribute to the discussion, and to advocate for a particular position or plan. It is also knowing when it is time to take your own plan off the table if it doesn't seem to fit where the group is going. When we think interdependently, our efforts and abilities are magnified synergistically. As we collaborate and cooperate—not just on finding a solution but on discovering many different ways to approach problems—the power of our thinking is increased exponentially by the dynamic interchanges between ourselves and others in the group. We become more than the sum of our individual contributions and talents.

Thinking Interdependently is what happens when we take each of the Habits of Mind and put them to work in a group setting.

With Interdependent Thinking, the process is as important as the product. A group learns from every experience with Interdependent Thinking how to do it better next time. Individuals become increasingly adept at reading each other's cues, listening, knowing when to advocate for an idea and when to throw their support behind other's idea, and how to put each member's abilities to most effective use.

Family life can also benefit from intentionally activating this Habit of Mind. Creating interdependence within the family builds a positive structure that gives family members a firm foundation and a strong identity from which to venture out into the world. For children, it provides the security of feeling good about where they come from and what their family stands for. It creates positive expectations and confidence that family members are valued for exactly who they are and that each one has important contributions to make. When a family develops the habit of thinking and working interdependently, parents and children listen to each other and learn how to communicate well. Interdependent thinking teaches them how to manage differences of opinion and how to get their own needs met, while still respecting the needs of others in the family. Children who are part of a family that thinks, works, and plays together interdependently are going to bring those skills of relating and working with others into the world with them, where they will be very much needed.

The Habit of Mind of Thinking Interdependently can improve one's ability to navigate within and contribute to any size group, from friendship to marriage to family, school, work, and beyond. In this chapter, we look at how some of the principles derived from research can be applied to the way we work together as a family *team*. And, because Thinking Interdependently spirals outward in an ever-encompassing way, we also look at some ways to encourage it in the home-school connection, in the community, and ultimately, in a global way.

Let us look at the major factors that contribute to thinking and working Interdependently.

A Vision for the Family

Research tells us that it is important for a group, team, or organization to have a clearly articulated vision or sense of identity—a vision that its members understand, think about, agree with, and try to live up to. Grant's memory of his mother taking in his bereaved friend served as a beacon for him, a model of the right way to treat others. By telling the story to his children, he made that generosity of spirit a *family trait* that belonged to them as well. Many schools and corporations now create "vision statements" for their organizations in an attempt to set out on paper the aspirations and values they hope to live up to. When treated as a living, working document, the vision statement can serve as a guide to behavior.

Why not think about creating a vision statement for your own life, for your marriage, for your family? It would be in keeping with the spirit of *intentionality* that the Habits of Mind encourage: to clarify our values, goals, hopes, and dreams for ourselves, then together as partners, and finally as a family. Having a vision in front of us of the kind of person we hope to be and the kind of life we want to live can help keep us focused on what is truly important

> **The most profound adjustment for couples is making the transition from "I" to "we."**

If we use Costa and Kallick's formula—What does it look like, sound like, feel like?—you can begin this process. Consider when you are happiest and most at peace. What kind of work do you love doing? In what settings do you feel healthy and safe? Do you love being in the mountains, suburbs, city? What kinds of social situations make you shine? Who are the people you most enjoy being with? Where do you picture yourself in five, 10 or 20 years, and what do you hope to be doing? What hopes and dreams did you have when you were younger? Do you still have them? If not, why not? What dreams do you have now? Imagine writing your own obituary. How would you want to be remembered? What, in the long run, are the most important values you hold? What do you need to do to actually live by those values in your own life? Write down the thoughts you have as you ask yourself these questions. Think about crafting those thoughts into your own personal vision statement, and tinker with it until it is your best approximation of a statement about the life you hope and plan to have.

The most profound adjustment for couples is making the transition from "I" to "we". If there is no common, agreed upon vision for the marriage, conflict is bound to arise, often repeatedly, over the same issues. Even if you did spend lots of time before marriage in deep conversations, chances are the realities of life have intruded with challenges and obstacles and opportunities you may never have imagined. In addition (as discussed in Chapter 1), long-buried scripts from our parents' marriages can find their way into our own. Just as Adrienne found herself re-enacting with her daughter her own mother's anxiety about inconveniencing others, we also have been imprinted with patterns of communications, ways of resolving or not resolving conflict, and roles and expectations that we experienced from our parents' marriage when we were children. These ghosts of marriages past can intrude on our own best intentions and create difficulties unless they are brought to the light of day and discussed and understood jointly.

John M. Gottman, in his books, *Seven Principles for Making Marriage Work* (1999) and *The Relationship Cure* (2001), emphasizes the importance of each partner affirming and honoring the hopes and dreams of the other. In the latter book, he proposes guided questions for couples to consider together, not all at once but one or two at a time in recurring conversations (p. 239). The questions cover broad topics such as how couples view their individual roles in the marriage; how they want their home to be; the importance they place on extended family, religion, education, money; how they believe children should be disciplined; how they would prioritize spending leisure time, and so on. For each question, partners are encouraged to think about the current situation, the situation as it was when they were growing up, and finally, what they would hope the situation could be. If an adequate amount of time is given to these conversations, and they are conducted with all the good communication skills Habits of Mind encourage, you can see the opportunities for increased understanding and intimacy. These conversations can help you create shared goals in the marriage. With greater clarity of goals, hopes, and expectations between partners, you could expect to see an increased ability and willingness to pull together on behalf of each other.

If you are a single parent, you may want to carry out this exercise on your own, or in conversations with other supportive people in your life, such as a friend, cousin or parent. Or you may reach a point where you are able to think and speak deeply with an ex-spouse about your reconfigured roles and how you will fulfill them cooperatively on behalf of your children.

In his book *The 7 Habits of Highly Effective Families* (1997), Steven Covey devotes a great deal of attention to the concept of developing a family *mission* statement. His chapter, "Begin with the End in Mind" (p. 70), asks us to consider our hoped-for outcomes in raising children. What important character traits, values, and skills do we hope our children will carry with them into adulthood? Like Gottman, Covey suggests a list of questions couples can discuss prior to opening up the conversation to the entire family. His discussion of the process his family used to develop their own mission statement, —their "family compass"—is a striking description of interdependence at work:

> As we interacted, self-awareness became *family awareness*—- our ability to see ourselves as a family. *Conscience* became *family conscience*—the unity of the shared moral nature of everyone in the family and the clarity that came from discussing these things together. *Imagination* became *creative synergy* as we hammered out the issues and came to something everyone could agree on. And *independent will* became *interdependent will* or *social will* as we all worked together to make it happen (Covey, 1997, p. 78).

Covey's book provides a step-by-step process for developing a family mission statement and is replete with examples. Clearly, making the time and effort for partners and the family as a whole to have these important conversations can be a profound contribution to developing a clear, strong, and protective sense of family identity.

Enhancing a Sense of Family Identity

Talk, Talk, Talk!

There are so many toxic influences competing for our children's time and attention. We cannot assume that children will absorb our values unless we put in the time to make it so. Whether or not you choose to go ahead and develop a family mission statement, you can still take the time to have in-depth conversations about how "we want our family to be." As you talk together about what a happy family looks like, sounds like, feels like, take notes so that you can all build on what is said. You can ask, "*What feels best about being in our family? What makes you feel glad to come home? What are some things that maybe don't feel so good, or that you wish you could change?"*

Keep in mind how important it is to carry out these conversations in a respectful and affirmative way. This is a time for everyone in the family to think and speak freely. If older siblings are used to interrupting or crowding out the youngest, make sure you create conditions where everyone's contribution is encouraged and valued. This is a perfect time to Listen with Understanding and Empathy and to continue teaching that habit to your children. If anyone in the family uses this time to bring up a complaint or concern—great! Use those empathic listening skills to paraphrase, come to a good understanding of the concern, and take the opportunity for everyone to figure out some ways to make

it better. These conversations do not have to be somber or heavy. You can weave them into the conversation at dinner, while you play board games together, or on family car trips. They invite everyone in the family to think about ways they can actively create the family they want to be.

Seize every opportunity you can to talk together. In Chapter 3, "Fully Present: Managing Distractions" we suggest turning off cell phones and other devices that keep family members plugged in and unavailable to one another. Tell stories about significant events that happened during your childhood or during that of an older relative. One woman recalls sitting in her grandmother's kitchen, enthralled as she listened to her great-grandmother talk

of being caught in the great blizzard of 1888. When the little girl grew up, she would re-tell the story to her own children whenever school was cancelled because of heavy snow. Do you remember when the Berlin Wall fell? When the under-rated U.S. Olympic hockey team beat the (then) Soviet Union team? Do you remember a time before you had cell phones? Tell those stories! If the events of the day don't seem to give enough material for conversation, or people are in the mood for more light-hearted fare, there are lots of resources out there for other conversation starters. A company called Family Time Fun (www.drugstore.com/family-time-fun-dinner-games-and-activities-ages-5/qxp204029) puts out a variety of game-show style devices (flashing lights, a cute little tune) that ask fun, silly, or at times introspective questions. There are several books available that provide intriguing and thought-provoking questions to help jump-start conversations at the dinner table or in the car. If you can develop a habit of having enjoyable and stimulating conversations together, chances are your children will come to prefer them, at least sometimes, over the more solitary pleasures of video games.

Take the Time To Be Together

Taking the time to be together conveys more emphatically than words ever can that you want and choose to be with your child. Children move out and away from the family orbit before you know it. While they are still young, establish in no uncertain terms that doing things together is your best idea of a good time. Attend their practices and games, go to school talent shows, and seek them out when you are doing everyday chores to keep you company. (Not all the time, of course—everyone needs some alone time and time with friends—but enough to leave no doubt that you value and enjoy their company.)

> **We need to frequently recalibrate the way we interact with our children to keep ourselves in tune with their growing maturity.**

As children grow toward adolescence, they may begin to behave as though they don't ever want you to be around, or are embarrassed by you. Don't believe them. The ways in which we interact change over time. We need to frequently recalibrate the way we interact with our children to keep ourselves in tune with their growing maturity. Look for ways that you can tap into your kids' increasing competencies. Many of us who are not "digital natives" have relied on our offspring to help us navigate the mysteries of newer technology. If you need directions to get somewhere, you can ask your children to program the GPS for you. Even better, learn something new together. One family decided to start a garden, and everybody got involved in researching the hardiest plants for their climate, making compost to create good soil, and dealing with garden pests. Their eight-year-old girl, a gifted artist, was given a notebook to draw the different plants and insects that intrigued her and to sketch out different possible designs for the garden. Each one in the family had a slightly different relationship and commitment to the garden, but it was clearly a family project.

Family Rituals Instill a Sense of "We-ness"

Most families have their own rituals around holiday celebrations, but other opportunities to create loving rituals abound: How we greet each other in the morning and upon our reunion after school and work; the way we say goodnight; the way we celebrate the first day of school and the first day of summer vacation. Some families have a pasta and movie night at home on Friday to unwind from the week; others take the whole family to their favorite local restaurant; others share the tradition of Shabbat dinner. We can have rituals for going places: One four-year-old made up a simple song for the family to sing as they headed for their weekend cabin on Saturday mornings: "We're going to the country, ho, ho, ho" (repeat chorus a thousand times.) Now years later, the children grown, the mother still smiles as she hears that happy song in her memory whenever she heads north. Family rituals impart a sense of delicious anticipation in their familiarity and comfort. They make everyone feel just so lucky to be part of their own particular family.

Promote Positive Family Traits

Many years ago, Dr. Anne Frost, while speaking at a PTA meeting, made a deep impression on Lauren when she advised parents to nurture resilience in their children by treating it as a family trait. She would tell her children, "We're the Frost family! We can solve this problem!" Frost knew she was on the right track when she was about to leave the house to take a statistics exam. Her son, seeing her worried face, told her, "Mom, you'll do just fine. We're the Frost family. We can solve any problem!" She left the house feeling heartened by his confidence in her. Lauren loved that story, and not only repeated it at parent meetings over the years, but took it to heart in her own family. Some years later, she was engaged in an apparently futile search with her three-year-old to find a pair of winter gloves small enough for her little hands. After going through the many gloves on the rack, she was about to give up when her daughter's voice came around from the other side of the rack, "Don't worry Mom, we'll find some. Our family never gives up!" They kept looking and, sure enough, the little girl managed to find the last pair of extra small gloves on the rack. Lauren remembers sending a silent thought of thanks to Dr. Frost. She was glad her daughter found the gloves, but even happier that her daughter had already absorbed a sense of herself as belonging to a family that does not give up, and was able to show it with her persistence. If you start building that positive family identity early on, just think of the protective function it can provide later, when the challenges are so much greater than finding a pair of gloves.

Think about your own family history. What stories of courage, of overcoming adversity, of persistence against the odds, of strength and ingenuity can you tell your own children? When children hear such tales from your earlier days, or from long ago, they hold within them the conviction, "That is the stuff I am made of. I can do this, too."

We're not talking about instilling a belief that one family is *better* than another. Rather, we encourage the idea of making certain family values and dispositions explicit. Family traits such as optimism, kindness, persistence, generosity, ingenuity, courage or the willingness to work hard, are sources of pride and reasons to celebrate. By doing this, we are taking the steps of turning who we *want* to be into who we *are*.

Communication Is Critical

Another key element of Interdependent Thinking is the use of good communication skills. A generation or two back, it was the norm for parents not to share information or decision making with their children. Big issues, such as money or sexual responsibility were rarely talked about. It was considered impolite to talk about politics and religion because the assumption was that an argument would inevitably ensue. Children rarely had the opportunity to witness or participate in a problem-solving kind of discussion. When conflicts arose, a typical response would be to shut down thinking and discussion, either by leaving the room or by having loud arguments. With such few models and opportunities to practice good communication skills, it is no wonder that the ability to listen carefully, to find common ground, and to come up with good solutions seems so daunting now.

We have already considered how all the Habits of Mind related to good communication can improve understanding as well as our connectedness to one another. When we paraphrase to clarify what a family member has said, we're not just making sure we get it right; we are showing that we *care* enough to get it right. When we use our metacognitive skills to monitor our own tone of voice and body language, we make sure that we are in sync with each other. As we question and pose problems, we encourage children to think more deeply and to come up with possibilities on their own. The positive presuppositions with which we enter into a conversation convey our confidence in children's ability to work this problem through. The family is the perfect place within which to nurture these all-important abilities.

Usually, when we engage in Interdependent Thinking, we are working together on some sort of problem to solve. (The exception might be planning a vacation, or just having fun together, where one idea or joke builds on another and another in a cascade of creative energy.) For the Alpert family, the problem was the apparent deterioration of Grant's mother after the death of her husband and the difficulties posed by the substantial distance between them. In a family, it is obvious that parents would normally take a leadership role in a discussion such as the one the Alperts had. Parents have greater knowledge, wisdom, financial resources, and responsibility for decisions that are made. Nevertheless, including children in a collaborative way to deal with a family concern not only teaches them the process of problem-solving, but increases the likelihood of a good solution, since they were brought in on its crafting.

Eight Norms of Collaboration

In his book, *The School as a Home for the Mind*, Costa (2007) identified eight "norms of collaboration." These norms specify different communication skills that create harmony and lead to better outcomes within groups. Many of these skills are already familiar to you from earlier chapters, but look at them now in the context of working together as a family. These norms can be labeled as you spontaneously use them, so that everyone in the family has a chance to learn them.

1. Pausing

Costa emphasizes the importance of creating space for each person to contribute. He explains that such "silent time" allows for more complex thinking and leads to better decisions (Costa, 2007, p. 146). Pausing, which we have already discussed as "wait time," also promotes more respectful listening.

TIP: Here, you might say something like, "That's such an interesting question, Erin. Let's just give that a few moments to sink in before we respond." If you are the one asking a question, preface it with something to this effect: "Now I want everyone to really think about this question first, please, before responding."

2. Paraphrasing

(See Chapter 4, Listening with Understanding and Empathy.) Costa identifies several different types of paraphrasing, some of which convey empathy and others that summarize what has been said. In the context of this chapter, his concept of the "group paraphrase" is especially useful. The group paraphrase is an effort to sum up where the *group's* thinking might be at any given moment. At some point in the Alpert family discussion, for example, Grant might have said, "So, it sounds as though everyone is on board for inviting Nana to come and stay with us for awhile. Do I have that right?"

> **TIP:** In a family discussion, "take the temperature" every once in awhile by asking something like, "So how are we all doing with this? How do you feel about where we're going so far?" When you do this, be sure to encourage everyone at the table to express their opinion.

3. Probing and Clarifying

This includes the Habits of Mind of Thinking and Communicating with Clarity and Precision, and Questioning and Posing Problems. Here our goal is to continuously clarify our mutual understanding. We want to be sure that we all have the same understanding of what we are talking about. In the example above, Bethany Alpert might have responded to Grant's group paraphrase with a question of her own: "I think we would all feel better to have Nana here with us. But what do you mean by 'awhile'? Are we thinking of a couple of weeks, a month, or are we thinking of asking her to come live with us forever?" There would be no way to answer that question just yet. So many different factors would go into that decision, not the least of them being Nana's wishes. But it is important to put the question out there and to consider all the ramifications.

> **TIP:** If your child expresses an opinion, ponder it for a few moments, perhaps paraphrase, and *then* ask, "Can you tell us more about your thinking?" Whenever thoughts seem vague, incomplete, or too general, ask questions in an *inviting* way that will encourage deeper thinking and clearer communication.

4. Putting Your Ideas On and Pulling Them Off the Table

When we Think Interdependently, we seek input from everyone in the group. The process is meant to produce solutions that are the best combination of each group member's thinking. Few things are more frustrating than dealing with someone who keeps forcibly arguing his own position long after it is clear that it does not have the group's backing. It can be so hard to let go of a cherished idea, but knowing when to "fold 'em," is a key skill in collaboration. We have all been in groups where one dynamo seemed to suck all the oxygen out of the room by dominating the discussion. It is especially important that the younger or less verbal family members are accorded time to organize their thoughts, and that they not be interrupted or over-ridden when it is their turn to share.

> **TIP:** If some family members are not participating, you can encourage them. Comments such as: "We need to hear from everybody around the table. Kelly, I can see the wheels turning in your mind. Share those thoughts with us." This can encourage participation. Good paraphrasing will also encourage reluctant participants to elaborate on their thoughts and to feel that they are making valued contributions.

5. Paying Attention to Self and Others

In the chapter on Metacognition, we discuss the importance of increasing your awareness of your own thoughts and feelings, and of the impact your behaviors might have on others. In a group conversation, self-awareness continues to be important even as we encourage an increased awareness of the others in the group. In the Alperts' conversation, there was a moment where such awareness really opened up the discussion. When T.J. pointed out that Nana must feel so alone in that big house, and Lucy followed up with her comment that Nana must really miss cooking for and watching television with Grampa, Grant heard them on an emotional level and was struck—perhaps for the first time—by the immensity of her loss. Children are often amazingly observant and perceptive. By paying close attention to the content of what they say and to the emotions that lie beneath, we can come to an understanding we might not otherwise have reached.

> **TIP:** Use your metacognitive strategies to monitor your own reactions and how you are conveying them. It's not at all unusual for things to get frustrating when a group is having difficulty coming to consensus. Are you feeling yourself getting a little annoyed or impatient? Consider what is more important—to "win" a particular point, or to come to a group agreement

that *everyone* can feel good about? Remember, the larger purpose is not just to deal with the immediate situation at hand, but also to increase your family's ability to think and work interdependently.

6. Presuming Positive Intentionality/Positive Presuppositions

Activating our best hopes and beliefs about one another makes collaborating satisfying and productive. Sometimes, however, family members inadvertently get assigned certain roles such as "the quiet one," "the clown," or "Mr. Excitement." Children, even if they get a negative reaction, may test us by performing according to role expectations. Often when children assume such a role, it is because they are not confident of getting attention in a more positive way. An antidote to this is to make sure you sincerely acknowledge even your child's tiniest efforts toward appropriate engagement.

> **TIP:** If for example, older siblings are tempted to ridicule the apparently silly comment of the youngest, make sure you stop the action and review your expectation that everyone's comments be respectful. Then turn back to the youngest, and see if you can help him re-phrase his comment in a more appropriate way. You can make a comment to the effect that, "Sometimes what might seem silly or far-fetched at first ends up being a really creative solution."

7. Providing Data and Nonjudgmental Feedback

Every decision has to be made on the basis of good data. If you are working on a family budget, you need to know how much is coming in and what your current and anticipated expenses are. You have to have some numbers to work with. If you are thinking about buying a car, you'll need to have in mind how it will be used (for long distances, a family car, off-road vehicle, etc.), and the factors that have to be considered: price, mileage, resale value, and safety, to name just a few. When having a family discussion, try to encourage more specificity and ask people to back up their assertions with data.

Nonjudgmental feedback is a way to use data to continuously improve the quality of how the group works together. This means collecting "data" about how the conversation went. It is especially helpful to provide feedback to children when they have done something well. When a child listens thoughtfully without interrupting, or when she builds on something her sister has said, you can acknowledge it afterward. That way she will know, *Oh, that's what they are looking for us to do.*

> **TIP:**   You might take a couple of notes during a planning conversation and refer back to them afterward. What we are looking for here is a quick, "How did we do?" It can be especially powerful to offer a couple of simple statistics such as, "Everyone contributed in our conversation. I counted three comments from Mom, four from T.J. and four from Lucy. Everyone pitched in. How do you guys think it went?"

8. Pursuing a Balance Between Advocacy and Inquiry

This is the value of looking deeper into one's own and others' positions. We need to be able to state the reasons for our views and how we came to them, as well as asking others to do the same about their own positions. It is especially important to ask questions in a way that sincerely invites deeper thinking, and not in order to demolish the other person's position. Such discussions can make people anxious if they are not used to them. If someone asks you to back up your opinion with data, it can feel threatening, particularly if done in a challenging tone of voice. If an adult approaches a family meeting with the same level of intensity and advocacy that she would bring to a meeting of law firm partners, or a marketing group, it could cause everyone at the table to shut down and run away from any further meetings. The key to getting interdependent thinking rolling is to remember that it is not a forum in which one person "wins," but an opportunity for each one to contribute to shaping solutions. If we explain to our children that we can get to much better solutions if we "dig a little deeper," *and* if we are careful to do this in a respectful, patient way, they will learn to be unafraid of really considering different points of view. With the Alperts, Grant could have gotten defensive about Bethany's asking for more specificity about how long Nana might be staying, but hopefully he would understand that the quality of their planning would be enhanced with the increased clarity her question prompted.

> **TIP:**   You can model tolerance for having your position questioned by asking family members to point out any inconsistencies or flaws they may see in *your* reasoning. Of course, if they give you feedback, you have to try to consider it in an open-minded way and ask for further clarification to help you understand their point of view. This modeling can serve as a template for when you need more information from someone else. You could

acknowledge that it isn't always easy to be asked to back up your opinion—that it wasn't so easy for you, either—but that it really helps in the long run for everyone to get a clearer idea about each other's thinking.

Don't feel you have to memorize these eight norms of collaboration or systematically implement them. It does help, however, to have them rolling around in the back of your mind, to pull out as needed. The more you use them, the more likely you are to have them available to you, because you will see for yourself how much better communication flows as a result.

Managing Conflict

> **When we resolve conflicts, there should be no "losers."**

We have mentioned the importance of vision and strong communication skills in Thinking Interdependently. A third key element of high-functioning groups is their ability to resolve conflicts peacefully in a way that makes each person feel good enough about the outcome.

We tend to think of conflict as a bad thing. Whenever people care deeply about something, there are bound to be differences in values or opinions, which can easily escalate into harsh words, hurt feelings, and inability to move forward. We often feel badly when this happens and may then question whether the team, community group, PTA, or church committee is really "right" for us. We would like to say at the outset that conflict, with all its unpleasantness, is an absolutely normal phenomenon of people working in groups. It is normal, predictable, and, when *managed effectively,* can even result in *beneficial* outcomes. Conflict feels so bad because most of us haven't been taught how to get past the "fight, flight, or freeze" response that pops up automatically when we feel threatened. When conflict arises, we may be tempted to argue, to walk away, or we may feel paralyzed—unable to say or do anything effective. Using metacognitive strategies can help us through those initial moments when we feel flooded by feelings.

When we are Thinking Interdependently, we give up the idea of prevailing or winning. Instead, our fervent hope is to work out a solution that meets the needs of everyone in the family. Adopting an attitude of curiosity instead of certainty can lead to a deeper understanding of what others are thinking and feeling. Instead of reacting by pushing back or withdrawing, you can open up, unafraid, to find out more about what the other person really needs.

When high-functioning groups have Vision and Good Communication Skills, the likelihood of conflict is diminished. If a family is developing a sense of itself as a cohesive unit, people who care deeply about the happiness of each other, who see themselves as being united in working together toward common goals, that strong sense of family identify will motivate them to work hard to find win-win solutions. When good communication skills become habitual, it is difficult for intransigent conflicts to persist. If you deal with a conflict by nothing more than approaching it with your positive presuppositions on your sleeve and by Listening with Understanding and Empathy, chances are good the conflict will dissolve. When you add to those skills what you already know about the problem-solving process (identifying the problem, brainstorming solutions, considering the pros and cons of each possibility, and deciding on a course of action), it is clear that you already have effective tools for resolving conflicts.

Within the family, we can handle conflicts by using some of the techniques described in Chapter 4 under the heading, *When Siblings Squabble*. Look for common ground; for example, "It sounds like everyone is really disappointed that we had to cancel our beach vacation. I am, too. But we all can agree that we want to do *something* special this summer. We might not figure it out right away, but I bet if we really put our heads together we can come up with a great Plan B."

In personal relationships, grievances and hurt feelings often are not addressed at the time they happen.

When working through a conflict on a family level, it is important for each person to feel that they have been heard and understood. Someone in the family, an adult or older child, may have to assume the role of mediator to ensure that each person gets to speak without being interrupted. Then some sort of group paraphrase might get the discussion moving in a positive direction: "Sounds like none of us is happy with the messy way the house is looking, but we have different ideas about what to do about it. Can we begin to find agreement on some of those ideas?" When we resolve conflicts, there should be no "losers." Unless everyone feels a stake in the solutions that have been generated, there is likely to be sabotage or lack of effort. If you come to resolution, make sure you congratulate everyone for their respectful listening and their willingness to work hard on the problem.

In personal relationships, grievances and hurt feelings often are not addressed at the time they happen. Unfortunately, by not dealing with the situation, the animosity can get worse or the relationship eventually just withers on the vine. When we develop the habit of speaking up respectfully and clearly with a grievance (and keeping an attitude of curiosity rather than certainty), we have a better chance of tackling problems when they are small and manageable. If someone approaches *you* with a concern, use your metacognitive strategies and your ability to paraphrase in order to stay open to what the person is saying. Keep in mind that, despite the anxiety we may feel when faced with conflict, we are really being given an opportunity to make things better.

Thinking Interdependently: Home-School Connection

The home-school connection is another important realm in which our habit of Interdependent Thinking is useful. Most schools routinely employ cooperative learning groups at different times throughout the school day for a variety of subject areas. Most often, they are comprised of children with a range of abilities, but cooperative learning groups may also be set up for children who are ahead

in one area or who may need additional support. These groups are meant to extend the instruction the teacher has already given, whether to the entire group, a smaller group of students, or even to an individual student. Although it is beyond the scope of this chapter to elaborate on the merits of cooperative learning, a comprehensive body of research demonstrates its effectiveness. (For a pithy overview of cooperative learning, go to http://college.cengage.com/education/pbl/tc/coop.html) Depending on the actual techniques used, students who learn in cooperative groups have shown increased achievement, improved problem-solving ability, increased motivation for learning, and improved ability to get along with students of different ability levels or ethnic backgrounds.

These benefits do not just happen as a result of putting children in groups, however. Students need to be *taught* to contribute in a group, to give others a chance to contribute, and to treat each other with respect. At times when all the students in a group are challenged by new content, they may help each other by asking questions and working hard to make connections together. Other times, an individual may be ahead of the group and temporarily assume a "teaching" role with the others. That can benefit everyone. The student "teacher" consolidates and expands his understanding because he has to organize it so as to explain to the others. Students often are able to grasp something that is explained by a peer, because that peer intuitively knows how to put it into language that is accessible to the others. In most classes, cooperative learning groups are constantly shifting and reconfiguring so that children have opportunities to work this way at one time or another with everyone in the class.

For parents who recall a more competitive model of classroom organization when they were growing up, this may look quite different from what they experienced in their own classrooms, and it may create some concern. Parents may wonder how teachers can track each student's individual progress based on work that is done in a group. As children get older, and as a class grade may depend heavily on group projects, concerns may increase about certain students not pulling their weight, or that a student's grade may be lowered because of a less capable or less motivated student. In a well-run classroom, the teacher is expected to anticipate and address these issues. Of course, as with any situation, if parents have concerns, they need to speak with the teacher. But parents should be assured that schools are not sacrificing individual excellence by teaching Interdependent Thinking. On the contrary, more and more varied opportunities for excellence arise when students, and adults, think and work interdependently.

But let's look in on a particular group in a 3rd grade classroom. Here, the teacher is working with four advanced math students. Each one of them has scored above grade level expectations in math, and the teacher puts a lot of time into providing them with enriching and challenging materials that will stimulate ever deeper levels of understanding. Today they are grappling with word problems that require several steps of multiplication and division to arrive at an answer. The teacher is more interested in helping the students develop their math reasoning skills than their calculation skills, which are already excellent. She encourages them to read through each problem and then discuss their thoughts before putting a pencil to paper.

You see the children thinking, pencils poised. Then one child asks a question: "But what are we looking for here? What is the problem you're asking us to figure out?" The children pore over the problem again. A child says quietly, "I think…," and three other heads swivel toward the speaker. As she hesitantly explains her thinking, another student sits back in admiration: "I didn't see that!" he exclaims. Another student looks puzzled. "I don't get it. Could you explain again how you figured that out?" This time more confidently, the girl goes through a step-by-step explanation of her thinking. They talk some more and ask more questions, and then the group begins to work out the complex problem on paper. Each student in the math group is challenged by the others to push her thinking a little farther, to dig a little deeper in order to increase her mastery of the subject.

You can see how so many of the Habits of Mind support this process: Each Habit has something valuable to contribute to Interdependent Thinking. Just for starters, here are some thoughts those 3rd graders might be having as they activate several different Habits of Mind:

Metacognition: *What information will I need to have before even starting this problem? How will I know if I am on the right track?*

Managing Impulsivity: *I'm not going to rush to be first with an answer. Let me slow down and read through the directions carefully.*

Thinking and Communicating with Clarity and Precision: *Wait a minute. The problem says how many will be left over. They're talking about a remainder. I need to find the remainder.*

Thinking Flexibly: *I'm not getting this! Is there another way for me to be looking at this problem? Maybe I'll start at the end and see if I can work my way back.*

Persistence: *I thought this would be a snap, but it's just not coming to me. Well, challenging problems are often frustrating at first. I know I'll feel great when I finally get it.*

Listening with Understanding and Empathy: *I want to hear what Rajiv has to say. I like the way he figures things out.*

278

For these young math students, the teacher will need to monitor the group to keep them thinking interdependently. Are they staying on topic? Does each student have a voice in the discussion? Is everyone contributing? How are they handling it when they get stuck? She will jump in as needed to ask a good question, to offer encouragement or to make a suggestion, but her expectation is that these students will begin to monitor their own and the group's functioning with more independence as time goes on.

The interdependent thinking that goes on in cooperative learning groups is great practice for the teamwork that will be expected in most endeavors as children go on to higher education and the world of work. There is a bit of a paradigm shift here, however, for parents. We suggest that, when chatting with your child about school, you begin to frame some of your questions and comments to support the habit of Interdependent Thinking. The older, competitive model would have us expressing most interest in how our child performs vis a vis the other students in the class, and some of our questions might reflect that: "How did the other kids do?" "Was that the highest grade?" It is so natural and understandable that parents want to know how their child compares with others in the class. The problem is that questions and comments that evoke comparisons with others do not really help the child build on his intrinsic interest and motivation for learning. They are really extraneous to learning. Rather, questions that focus on what is inherently interesting in the material he is learning, on the challenges and triumphs your child experiences in mastering those skills and content, and on the problems and satisfactions of working with others are more conducive to encouraging the self-directed learning we so value. If you keep in mind some of the ideas covered earlier in this chapter regarding vision, communication skills, and conflict resolution, your questions and comments should come more easily. You might ask your child what group-work she is engaged in and how she likes working that way. Ask her to explain how the kids make sure everyone gets a chance to participate and what happens if there are disagreements. Ask your child what she has learned from others in the group and what they may have learned from her. You may find that your child is so used to working this way that it is almost second nature. Or, you may discover that there are indeed some problems that crop up, and your child might appreciate support or suggestions you can offer.

Thinking back to the three main factors that contribute to successful group functioning, here are a few thoughts for supporting your child's ability to think and work interdependently at school.

Vision

Encourage and motivate your child in his group experiences. Certain questions can stimulate thinking about the "we-ness" of the cooperative learning group, such as, "How would you describe your group? What are some of the things you like about your group? Are there things you can think of that would make it work even better?" Recall that a sense of belonging and identity with the group enhances motivation. Questions such as, "How do you and your friends celebrate your successes?" or "How do you encourage each other when the going gets tough?" remind children that celebrations and support for each other through tough times are normal functions of groups. Respond to your child's comments in ways that foster appreciation for others. As your child describes how her group worked together that day, comments such as the following can reinforce the qualities that contribute to good collaboration:

- *It sounds like everyone is really motivated and working hard.*

- *From what you describe, each person is carrying his own weight. That must be such a good feeling—that together you can get this big job done.*

- *Isn't it interesting how each person has something valuable to offer? James brings a lot of energy to the group and Keisha, even though she is kind of quiet, had a really creative idea.*

If your child reports that she has done something that promoted interdependent thinking, for example, that she encouraged a quiet child to contribute, or that she asked questions in a way that helped the group clarify their thinking, try to be specific in your acknowledgment.

Communication

Continue to model and teach communication skills

You can use your own experiences at work or in other group settings to model a particular skill. For example, a parent could relate a story such as this to her child:

Last night at the book club, there was a new person named Marcia. I don't think she realized that our group listens respectfully to what everyone has to say. When Lilly made a comment about what she thought the main character's motives were, Marcia interrupted and said, "I disagree. It's not that at all!" Everyone was quiet for a moment, and then I said, "Lilly, I'm interested in what you said. Could you explain a little more about what you meant?" I wanted Lilly to feel good about participating, and it was a really good discussion after that. I think Marcia had to learn that we are not having arguments, and that everyone has something interesting to add to the discussion.

Teach paraphrasing

Older children, from about age 10 or 11, will find this easier than younger ones, but you could make a game out of it, first by paraphrasing what your child has said and then by having him paraphrase you. Explain how much better it feels when someone is actively trying to understand you by paraphrasing, instead of arguing with you. Whenever you have a chance to use paraphrasing in a somewhat charged situation, go back afterward and review how it defused the conflict. Explain how useful paraphrasing is in a group situation, in that it encourages people to fully express their thoughts and feelings.

Positive Presuppositions

It is so easy for children to misunderstand the motives and intentions of others. Teach your child the metacognitive strategy of questioning her own reactions and instant interpretations of others' behavior. Teach your child to "check it out" by asking a clarifying question or by paraphrasing. It works both ways. If your child reports that someone got angry with her for no apparent reason, suggest that she ask the other child if there might have been a misunderstanding and offer to work it out.

Conflict Resolution

Use examples from your own family's experiences with successful conflict resolution to encourage thinking about managing conflicts with peers. Teach your child that conflict is normal and a part of life, but it is how we handle it that makes all the difference.

Help your child develop a few strategies to deal with some of the strong emotions that come with conflict so he can stay calm and clear headed. Reflect on how tough it can be sometimes to get people to let go of their own need to "win," and encourage your child to ask the others in the group, "How can we figure this out so that everyone is happy?"

Speak with your child's teacher. To what extent does he structure the class for cooperative learning? How much instruction is provided in the skills of Thinking Interdependently? What kind of support does she give her students when they get stuck or encounter conflicts? What are your own child's strengths and weaknesses in working cooperatively? What else can you do at home to foster these important skills?

From Home to School and Beyond

An erupting volcano in Iceland grounds airline flights across Europe. An undersea oil well explosion and uncontrollable leak create havoc over an enormous swath of wetlands and shoreline. The effects on fisheries and on the oil-tainted environment will not be fully understood for years. An earthquake and powerful tsunami trigger an almost unimaginable nuclear crisis in Japan, and people thousands of miles away wonder about the impact of the incalculable number of gallons of radioactive water that went back into the sea. Wild and severe weather across the globe unleashes devastating floods, powerful tornadoes, and unyielding drought, which many scientists believe may be a harbinger of global climate change.

This litany is not to depress us but to underscore how very interdependent we are as a species. All of the situations above—some natural disasters, some created through human error, and some an unlucky combination of both—have in common the fact that they know no boundaries. Just as these worldwide disasters affect us all, so must the remedies involve and engage all of us. The Habit of Mind of Thinking Interdependently, from which we derive so much benefit at home and school, is essential for addressing the problems that give rise to such human suffering. But how can we even begin to have an impact on these problems that play out on such an enormous scale?

Again we ask you to consider the three major characteristics of high-functioning groups—Vision, Communication, and Conflict Resolution—and perhaps keep them in mind as tools for expanding your thinking about our world. Just as you may intentionally work on creating an achievable vision for yourself and your family, how might you imagine a more perfect world? What would have to happen for parts of that vision to actually become reality? We are not suggesting grandiose "if I were king of the world" fantasies, but simply, and maybe with the whole family, visualizing a more peaceful, harmonious, prosperous world. What would it look like, sound like, feel like? What would be possible in such a world that is not possible now?

In terms of communication, the internet and social media have made possible an amazingly expanded capacity to communicate and connect with others around the world in real time. It becomes more difficult to stay unaware of what is happening as Facebook and Twitter instantly send out scenes of famine, revolution, triumph, and heartbreak. We think of the "8 Ps" of communication, and especially, the one that starts, "Pay Attention." If we simply pay attention to what is going on around the world and keep open that attitude of curiosity instead of certainty, might we begin to wonder more about why these things are happening and what could possibly be done to make things better. Knowing what you do about resolving conflicts in your own family, you might begin to wonder if some of those same principles could be applied to the international conflicts we read about. Why not?

Children may be quite overwhelmed by violent and frightening images from the news, and we recommend that you shield younger children, especially, from graphic details. Even 10- or 11-year-olds are susceptible to great anxiety from what they see and overhear. Children need to feel safe and secure, and you will need to monitor their reactions to news and events of the day. (Stanley Greenspan's book *The Secure Child,* written after the events of 9/11, is especially helpful in its treatment of this issue.)

A powerful antidote to anxiety when events seem to spiral out of control is to focus on doing something that you *can* control. This could be something like writing a letter to the President, identifying ways to reduce your carbon footprint, growing some of your own food, or by supporting local farmers by buying their produce. Some families seek out do-able opportunities to put into action their sense of connectedness to the world beyond home and work. They may approach this in a formal way, by regularly volunteering for a community event, a food pantry, nursing home or animal shelter, or by practicing "random acts of kindness" such as dropping a coin in a nearly expired parking meter. When these activities are undertaken with a spirit of joy and generosity, and when children's contributions to these efforts are valued, it can bring home the idea that we have larger responsibilities outside our immediate sphere of interests.

Several years ago, a five-year-old boy in New Jersey saw television news reports about devastating floods that were wreaking havoc in the Midwest. He asked his mother if there wasn't something they could do to help the people who had lost their homes and possessions. The little boy's concern led to a community-wide effort, "Help for the Heartland," that sent out several tractor-trailer loads of supplies to the Midwest. Through her involvement with community groups and the schools, his mother enlisted dozens of others to volunteer their time and material goods to the effort. In press coverage of that undertaking, the boy's mother always gave him credit for setting things in motion with his compassionate question.

We know other children who have been inspired to contribute in some way. One boy used his musical abilities to put on a concert and asked the audience to contribute to tsunami victims. Others help make sandwiches and collect articles of clothing to distribute to homeless people for a Midnight Run. In whatever ways these efforts are manifested, they contribute in a real way to making the world a better place. They also benefit our children, who begin to realize the satisfaction of extending themselves beyond their personal boundaries into an interdependent world—a world that very much needs people like them.

…the dynamics within ourselves and within the family slowly can change for the better. We have discovered that the Habits of Mind are also very much Habits of the Heart.

Chapter 21

Putting It All Together:
Remaining Open to Continuous Learning

If there has been a constant theme throughout this book, it is that Habits of Mind are best instilled in children by parents' own example. By practicing your own Persistence, or Flexible Thinking, or Listening with Understanding and Empathy, and then making explicit what you are doing by labeling and explaining each habit, you teach more powerfully than any professor or text ever could. Perhaps this is most true of Remaining Open to Continuous Learning. This is the habit that keeps us intellectually and emotionally alive throughout our lifespan, and the one that beckons to our children, "*Come, look, listen, there is so much to explore and to find out.*" We do this best by living this habit and sharing it with our children. When you reflect on your own intellectual or creative passions, which of them started in childhood? Can you identify an adult who may have sparked your curiosity? Often such beginnings are rooted in a loving relationship: The father who built his own telescope and revealed the rings of Saturn to his son and daughter late on a summer night; the great-uncle who led an expedition of cousins and grandchildren through the woods in the early spring, identifying animal

Remaining open to continuous learning

Learn from Experience!

Having humility and pride when admitting we don't know; resisting complacency.

tracks and the first green shoots of the season; the grandmother who started piano lessons in her mid-80s and who practiced religiously; the beloved teacher who introduced us to the unexpected satisfactions of poetry. If we ourselves find the world to be an irresistibly interesting place, however stressful and difficult it may be at times, our children will be much more likely to absorb that same conviction and passion for learning.

...it is that intrinsic joy in learning something new or following an arc of inquiry that motivates us and drives us forward.

We have said before that it is that intrinsic joy in learning something new or following an arc of inquiry that motivates us and drives us forward. No external rewards, no matter how enticing, can match the satisfaction of pursuing that which gives us the most intellectual and emotional satisfaction. Costa and Kallick (2004) write, "We want to see students develop a love of learning and not depend solely on the judgment of others to determine the value of what they are learning" (p. 68). We call this "self-directed learning," and in self-directed learners we see people who are intrigued by challenges and confident in their ability to take on difficult problems. Beyond the motivational aspects, however, self-directed learners also have the set of skills, exemplified in the various Habits of Mind, to tackle problems *effectively*. In addition, a crucial component of self-directed learning is to review the situation in hindsight, to assess what went well and what didn't, "constructing meaning" from those experiences, positive and negative, so that we may learn to do better the next time.

You may wonder how you will be able to identify the particular habit needed for any given situation: Will this situation call for Striving for Accuracy, Thinking and Communicating with Clarity and Precision, or Thinking Flexibly? Or all of the above? By starting small and with a little bit of practice, it will begin to fall into place. Bena Kallick (2009) compares the Habits of Mind to a colorful and vibrant collage in which different habits overlap and figure-ground is constantly shifting. One habit may come into focus at a particular moment and then recede as another glides into the foreground. You may indeed, be activating two or three habits at a time. What does happen is that, as you have some small success with, say, Managing Impulsivity or Listening with Understanding and Empathy, you are encouraged by the results to activate that habit again in a similar situation. With each activation of one habit or another, you are on your way to making that Habit of Mind your very own.

As you begin to think about the Habits of Mind and how they may be useful in various situations, you start to develop a sensitivity to context. You start to spontaneously notice those moments in which you think, *Ah, this is one of those times I'd better manage my impulsivity,* or, *It's going to be such a busy day. Maybe I should plan it out a little more clearly before I leave the house.* Or, *He seems upset. I want him to feel my support, so I'm going to listen empathically and try to understand what is going on.* You might decide to start with one habit at first, Metacognition, for example, and then simply be on the lookout for "metacognitive moments." As you begin to practice one and then another habit for yourself, you gradually involve your family in also beginning to practice them.

In addition to these spontaneous opportunities, there is a more structured way of identifying situations that call for specific Habits of Mind. Costa and Kallick (2004) identify three important characteristics of self-directed learners: They are *self-managing, self-monitoring,* and *self-modifying.* It can be helpful to look at these three characteristics in terms of discerning which habits for which purposes might be especially useful.

Self-Managing Learners

Individuals who are self-managing are effective in their very *approach* to a task or problem. They start out with an open mind. They are able to take in information and data even if it might contradict or differ from what they already think or believe. Imagine a situation in which your doctor is surprising you with some anxiety-provoking information about your cholesterol level, or your child's teacher may be informing you that your child is showing some difficulties with attention and concentration. It may take a conscious effort to *Manage Impulsivity* to keep from reacting defensively or emotionally, or from automatically rejecting the incoming information. Yet you ride out the emotional discomfort in order to fully understand what it is you have to deal with. Along the same lines, you would then expect the Habits of *Questioning and Posing Problems, Gathering Data with All Our Senses,* and *Thinking Flexibly* to also serve you well as you seek to learn all that you can. Recall the idea of taking different perspectives in the chapter on Thinking Flexibly: *How do I feel about this? What do I know and what do I need to know?* This awareness can help you get a handle on what you are facing. Of course, *Applying Past Knowledge to New Situations* is another way of gaining some mastery over a situation. *What does this remind me of? What other similar situations have I faced, and how did I handle them?*

We could also see how *Thinking Interdependently* can enhance our ability to approach a problem. If two heads are better than one, than surely the teamwork and collaboration skills we discussed in Chapter 20 will provide emotional and logistical support. In either of the above hypothetical situations, you would want to consult with others, quite literally creating a team for this particular problem.

Certainly, the Habit of *Creating, Imagining, and Innovating* encourages you to bring your own unique set of talents and perspectives to any situation you face. The decision making process that goes into *Taking Responsible Risks* is particularly helpful in your assessment of whether a particular course of action is one you feel comfortable taking or not.

And, actually, *Metacognition*, that all-purpose tool, is indispensable at every turn. Metacognition is what helps us start to make a plan. Whenever you are faced with any difficult situation, Metacognition helps you run a systems check on yourself, to assess how you are feeling, what your first steps need to be, and what the pros and cons might be from your current vantage point.

Self-Monitoring Learners

Self-directed learners independently monitor themselves in order to keep track of how they are doing. Metacognition performs here as our executive assistant: *Are you staying on task? Are you following the plan? How much have you done so far, and what remains? Are you on schedule?* We also monitor our efforts to determine whether we are getting the results we hoped for. A plan might seem fantastic on paper but fall flat in its execution. We need to be able to assess what is working and what isn't while we are immersed in a task or project, so that we can make modifications if necessary. If you are having difficulties, recycling back to *Flexible Thinking* and *Creating, Imagining, Innovating* may enable a breakthrough.

Persistence is key in any undertaking that requires effort, whether it is cleaning out the basement or finishing a dissertation. And, as we learned in Chapter 7, there are specific behaviors that can help us to persist, many more than simply saying to ourselves, *never give up!* Even so, merely increasing your awareness that Persistence is called for can help you remember to tap into some of those strategies.

We also see the habit of *Striving for Accuracy* as an important tool for monitoring our efforts. Are we measuring up to the standards we set for ourselves? Are we paying attention to the details? When performing artists rehearse, they may spend hours of painstaking effort getting a short passage *exactly right*. It is this attention to detail that elevates a casual recreational undertaking to one of great craftsmanship and artistry.

Listening with Understanding and Empathy is the habit we have discussed mostly in terms of creating attunement, a sense of being "in-sync" with the other. We also considered its role in *Thinking Interdependently*, how those good listening and communication skills can enhance collaborative efforts. Think how essential such listening is when we are trying to monitor and assess our efforts. When people don't listen, they may miss those small voices that could be the canary in the coal mine, quietly warning us of danger ahead. If someone gives us feedback, we are best advised to hear that person out, openly and fully, without becoming defensive or arguing back. That doesn't mean you would necessarily accept everything they are saying, but certainly you would want to know of any concerns or problems and use them as a platform to find out more.

Self-Modifying Learners

Successful people, quite simply, learn from their experiences. They modify their behavior based on what they have learned. Everything that happens to us— every interaction we have, every challenge we take on, each success or apparent failure—becomes an opportunity to *learn something new*. Of course, this can only happen with reflection: *What was my role in this? What did I do well? What could I have improved on? How did others perceive my contributions?* If this sounds like *Metacognition* to you, it is indeed, as it always does our bidding, showing up at all the right times and places. *Metacognition* conducts the debriefing afterward and summarizes the lessons learned, so we can move forward and make progress.

We also see *Thinking and Communicating With Clarity and Precision* as essential for delineating the specific aspects of what went well and what needs improving. Recall in Chapter 18 how we wrote of the benefits of using correct terminology and, especially, more varied "thinking words" such as "analyze", "hypothesize" and "evaluate." Instead of saying, "That went well," we can evaluate which of our criteria for success were met.

Speaking of "that went well," a line that always brings a laugh after a particularly humiliating experience, *Finding Humor* helps put things in perspective. A good laugh keeps us humble and restores optimism and the willingness to try again. And, while we're laughing, let's not leave out *Wonderment and Awe*. We have often considered this habit in conjunction with the grandeur and mysteries of the natural world, but it applies as well to the unexpected accomplishments and triumphs of human effort. Every actor has, at one time or another, participated in a dreary, flat, and uninspired dress rehearsal, only to have opening night turn into a soaring, transcendentally beautiful theatrical experience. The director and cast will certainly want to debrief afterward so they can increase the likelihood of great performances to follow, but a wise director will allow time to savor the moment. It is those feelings of wonder and awe that inspire us to keep going despite the odds. Think back to certain feedback you received when you were young: a teacher expressed delight in your writing "voice;" a coach showed his confidence by putting you in to pitch relief in the bottom of the ninth inning; you did really well on an algebra test and realized you were up to the challenge. These experiences caused us to stand back in wonder as we thought, *maybe I'm better at this than I thought, maybe I really have something here.* When you are lucky enough to see that realization dawn across your child's face, you truly experience wonder and awe.

Continuous Learning

"The best thing for being sad is to learn something. That is the only thing that never fails…Learn why the world wags and what wags it. That is the only thing that the mind can never exhaust, never alienate, never be tortured by, never fear or distrust, and never dream of regretting…Look at what a lot of things there are to learn."
— *The Once and Future King* by T. H. White

Self-directed learners keep on learning. The very process of managing, monitoring, and modifying their thinking and their efforts, leads to the kind of successes that motivate and inspire further learning. But if, as the wizard Merlyn says, *learning* is the "only thing that never fails," then what gets in the way as we grow older? What causes us to become so set in our ways, to fall into ruts in our thinking, so that we start to only talk with the people who think like us and get our news and information only from sources that confirm what we already believe? What happens that makes us tend to narrow our perspectives as we age, making us less likely to tackle new intellectual challenges, to Take Responsible Risks and, instead, to stay well within the comfort zone of established knowledge and competencies?

A good laugh keeps us humble and restores optimism and the willingness to try again.

We could look at some possible causes from childhood all the way up through middle age for explanations. Ellen Langer (1997) suggests that the initial way we learn something may unfortunately contribute to a "mindless" and automatic approach. She cites examples of teaching a skill such as holding a tennis racquet or playing the piano, in which beginning students are told to focus on the one right way of performing that skill. Children practice and practice till they are able to master that technique exactly as taught. Yet when you study those who have achieved mastery in their fields, their own techniques, almost without exception, are very different from what beginning students are taught. Langer hypothesizes that the rigid adherence to an authority's definition of the one right way, stunts creative growth, decreases motivation, and impedes higher level functioning. She describes a study she conducted in which two groups of novice piano students were presented with a very simple exercise to learn. They were all given the same basic instructions, but the group assigned to the "mindful instruction" condition were also explicitly told not to rely on rote memory, to try to change their style every few minutes, and to try to notice any thoughts or feelings they might have while practicing. The two groups were then taped while playing their simple piece, and the tapes were judged by musical experts. The group given the mindful instructions was judged to be more competent and creative. Those students also reported enjoying the activity more than their counterparts who received the traditional instruction.

Langer also describes how the *way* in which information is presented can profoundly influence the way the brain processes it. If information is given as a flat fact, as something that is true in every circumstance, learning seems to end with the memorization of that fact. If, however, information is presented in "conditional" terms—that is, by adding qualifying words like "may be" or "at times"—then more complex and creative learning takes place. Why? It seems that, when you introduce a little uncertainty, for example, by saying, "in most cases, but not always" the brain gets busy considering all possible contingencies. In thinking about all the exceptions to the rule, why and how they might occur, we are scaffolding, summoning past knowledge, anticipating future applications, and building a rich network of connections instead of the "case closed" of a flat fact.

In his fascinating book *The Brain that Changes Itself,* Norman Doidge (2007) writes extensively about "neuroplasticity," the ability of the brain to change its very structure and capability simply through the activities and thoughts of its owner. He interviewed Michael Merzenich who was an early pioneer in this field. Merzenich is now engaged in research developing strategies and techniques for helping people maintain their cognitive capacity as they age. One explanation Merzenich offered as to why learning slows down is that, after an intense period of learning new things in childhood and early adulthood, we tend to settle into decades of comfortable middle age. During middle and late adulthood we tend to rely on skills mastered long ago, and rarely need to mobilize the focus and attention we use when we are just starting out. Thus, by the time people reach senior citizenship, they may be out of practice with using those skills, which can lead to memory loss and fuzzy thinking. Merzenich believes that taking on an intellectual challenge such as learning a new language, will activate that attentional system and actually strengthen the neurological connections that support it.

Barbara Strauch (2009) in a *New York Times* article, "How to Train the Aging Brain," cites research suggesting that some beliefs about the inevitability of cognitive decline as we age are not necessarily true. She quotes Kathleen Taylor, professor at St. Mary's College in California, who has studied and written about effective strategies for teaching adults: "The brain is plastic and continues to change, not in getting bigger, but allowing for greater complexity and deeper understanding." Taylor suggests that the way for this to happen is for adults to challenge their own entrenched viewpoints, to "jiggle (their) synapses a little bit," and to "challenge your perception of the world."

Langer (p. 111) also proposes that if we intentionally "view a situation from several perspectives" and keep an open mind, we not only learn better but enjoy the process more. She emphasizes the importance of increasing our attention to what we are perceiving in the sense of being alert to what is new or different about it. If we approach new information with the attitude that we already know what there is to know about it (an attitude of certainty rather than the attitude of curiosity we discussed in Chapter 6), we will miss many important details and facets and be less likely to remember and later apply what we have learned.

So much of this sounds like Metacognition, about Thinking Flexibly, and Questioning and Posing Problems. Simply asking "What do you notice?" promotes a curious and attentive approach. Just as we want our children to have this open-minded curiosity, so too can we intentionally cultivate it in ourselves.

Parenting as an Opportunity for Life-long Learning

Just when you think you've mastered infancy, your darling baby morphs into a bipedal force of nature. Within each large developmental stage of childhood, there are a thousand subdivisions, little shifts of those tectonic plates that signal your child is constantly growing and changing. Adding to the complexity, are the temperamental differences that can perplex you and challenge your flexibility. In addition to the "curriculum" your child presents, you find that there is also the need for *you* to grow in ways that permit you to practice letting go, to eventually relinquish control over to your newly minted, self-directed young adult. These developmental requirements can be so difficult sometimes: mothers everywhere feel the pang when their little one slows down in his declarations of eternal devotion and starts finding much more fun in hanging out with the guys. Fathers feel it when their children suddenly start criticizing and quoting other experts, such as Joey's father, next door. We know it is necessary, but still, it stings a little. With every new stage of development, we have to learn new parenting competencies, adjust our attitudes, and recalibrate our responses. It's not easy, especially when we feel that we've just gotten the hang of the stage that is now being left behind. It feels a bit like surfing, as you try to keep your balance, sometimes succeeding in brief moments of great joy and other times crashing ingloriously into the ocean floor. If, however, we remember some of the principles we've discussed that can keep us open to continuous learning, maybe we can maintain our balance a little better. If we try to stay alert to moments when a particular Habit of Mind might be useful, if we remember to reflect on our experiences afterward so we can be sure to learn something from them, if we can stay curious and flexible in our thinking, and remember how many different perspectives there can be, if we remember to *notice* and to ask questions, and, especially to listen with understanding and empathy, chances are pretty good that everyone will get to where they need to be.

A much loved psychology professor told his class once that you can pretty much be guaranteed admission to the Baseball Hall of Fame with a 330 lifetime batting average. That means that two out of three times, you're going to fail to get that hit and help out the team. And yet, one out of three hits adds up, and the cumulative effect is one of power and success. That might be a useful rubric to keep in mind. We suggest that you go easy on yourself as you consciously try to practice and teach the Habits of Mind. You may find, as we did, that as you read and think about the habits, they begin to find their way into your home. They surprise you sometimes by making unexpected appearances when you most need them. You may find yourself invoking the habit of Thinking Interdependently to collaborate with your children on some issue, and realize you're doing a good job Managing your Impulsivity and Listening with Understanding and Empathy. As you experience your family resolving a problem in a productive and positive way, you feel more inclined to try those habits the next time a problem arises. Intentionally activating your positive presuppositions with loved ones before a difficult conversation yields markedly more open, less defensive outcomes. Yes, there will be strikeouts, but every time we experience the effectiveness of one habit or another, there is a small ripple effect. Little by little, we begin to feel that we are making progress; we are no longer stuck; and we experience those moments of attunement that feel so wonderful and for which we are so grateful. We believe that simply by approaching situations with greater intentionality, by stopping to think first, and reminding ourselves of our larger purpose, the dynamics within ourselves and within the family slowly can change for the better. We have discovered that the Habits of Mind are also very much Habits of the Heart.

About the Authors

Lauren A. Carner received her doctorate in psychology from New York University. She has worked as a psychologist in a suburban school district for over 30 years, and maintains a small private practice. Over the years she has led many parenting groups and has presented programs on a wide range of topics including childhood anxiety, ADHD, setting limits, bereavement and more. Recently she has focused on the Habits of Mind as a versatile and powerful approach to parenting. Lauren lives about 50 miles north of New York City where she delights in gardening and in raising dairy goats, sheep and chickens.

Angela Iadavaia-Cox has been involved in books and parenting issues throughout her professional career. She began at Anchor Press/Doubleday where she edited *The Parenting Advisor* and other books by the Princeton Center for Infancy and Creative Plaything founders, Frank and Theresa Caplan. She also edited supplements such as *All About Children* for the New York *Times* and was a contributor and a managing editor for *The Organized Parent.* For the last 20 years, she has worked in a school district 15 miles north of New York City, providing information to parents on school programs and other topics, including the Habits of Mind.

References

Chapter 1

Siegel, D., & Hartzell, M. (2003. *Parenting from the inside out.* New York: Jeremy P. Tarcher/Penguin.

Chapter 2

Lehrer, J. (2009, May 18). "DON'T: The secret of self-control." *The New Yorker,* 26-32.

Mischel, W., Ebbeson, E.B., & Zeiss, A.R. (1972). Cognitive and attentional mechanisms in delay of gratification. *Journal of Personality and Social Psychology,* 21, 204-218.

Mischel, W., Shoda, Y., & Peake, P.K. (1988). The nature of adolescent competencies predicted by preschool delay of gratification. *Journal of Personality and Social Psychology,* 54, 687-696.

Goleman, D. (1995). *Emotional intelligence.* New York: Random House.

Popkin, M.(1993). *Active Parenting Today Parent's Guide.* Atlanta, Ga.: Active Parenting Publishers.

Dawson, P., & Guare. R. (2009) *Smart but scattered.* New York: The Guilford Press.

Chapter 3

Carey, B. (2019, May 23). "Families' every fuss, archived and analyzed." *The New York Times,* A1.

Richtel, M. (2010, August 25). "Digital devices deprive brain of needed downtime." www.nytimes.com/2010/08/25/technology/25brain.html?ref=y.

Richtel, M. (2010, June 7). "Attached to technology and paying a price." www.nytimes.com/2010/06/07/technology/07brain.html?ref=y.

Greenspan, S. (2002). *The secure child: Helping children feel safe and confident in a changing world.* Cambridge, MA: Perseus Publishing.

Chapter 4

Tannen, D. (1990). *You just don't understand: Women and men in conversation.* New York: HarperCollins Publishers Inc.

Chapter 5

Costa, A., & Kallick, B. (2000). *Activating and engaging habits of mind.* Alexandria, VA: ASCD.

McKenzie, R. (1998). *Setting limits: How to raise responsible, independent children by providing clear boundaries.* Rosedale, CA: Prima Publishers.

Willingham, D. (2005/06). "Ask the cognitive scientist: How praise can motivate—or stifle." *American Educator,* www.aft.org/newspubs/periodicals/ae/winter0506/willingham.cf

Chapter 6

Stone, D., Patton, B., & Heen, S. (1999). *Difficult conversations: How to discuss what matters most.* New York: Penguin Group.

Costa, A., & Kallick, B., eds. (2000). *Activating and engaging habits of mind.* Alexandria, VA: ASCD.

Chapter 7

Radmacher, M.A. (2009) *Courage doesn't always roar.* Conari Press © 2009. www.maryanneradmacher.com/about.php.

Allington, R. (2002). The six Ts of effective elementary literacy instruction. Reading Rockets. Retrieved 2011 from www.readingrockets.org/article/96.

Brooks, R. (2011, March). *I think the cure is worse than the disease: The importance of realistic expectations and self-compassion.* Newsletter www.drrobertbrooks.com/writings/articles/1103.html.

Brooks, R. & Goldstein, S. (2001). *Raising resilient children.* New York: McGraw-Hill.

Costa, A., & Kallick, B. (2000). *Discovering and exploring habits of mind.* Alexandria VA: ASCD

Costa, A. (2007). *The school as a home for the mind.* Thousand Oaks, CA: Corwin Press.

Csikezentmihalyi, M. (2008). *Flow: The psychology of optimal experience.* New York: HarperCollins.

Dweck, C. (2006). *Mindset: The new psychology of success.* New York: Random House.

Gladwell, M. (2008). *Outliers: The story of success.* New York: Little, Brown, and Company.

Ericsson, K. Anders, Krampe, R. T. & Tesch-Romer, C., (1993). The role of deliberate practice in the acquisition of expert performance, *Psychological Review* 100(3)363-406.

Howe, M. J. A. (1999). *Genius Explained.* Cambridge: Cambridge University.

Pink, D. (2009). *Drive.* New York: Penguin Group.

Carlton, M. (2004). "Motivating learning in young children." Adapted from, *Early childhood motivation.* In A.S. Carter, L.Z. Paige, M.D. Roth, et al (Eds.), Helping children at home and school II: Handouts for Families and Educators. Bethesda, MD: National Association of School Psychologists.

Chapter 8

Richtel, M. (November 21, 2010). "Growing up digital, wired for distraction." www.nytimes.com/2010/11/21/technology/21brain.html?ref=y.

Rideout, V.J., Foer, U.G., & Roberts, D.F. (January, 2010). Generation M^2: Media in the lives of 8-to 18-year olds. A Kaiser Family Foundation Study. www.kff.org/entmedia/mh012010.

Rich, M. (10/02/2010). "Finding Huck Finn: Reclaiming childhood from a river of electronic screens." *American Academy of Pediatrics.* www.aapexperience.org/2010/downloads/plenary slides/100210b-Rich-ReclaimingChildhoodfromRiverofElectronics.pdf

Barkley, R. (2000). *Taking charge of ADHD.* New York: The Guilford Press.

Rock, D. (2009). *Your brain at work.* New York: HarperCollins Publishers

Greenland, S.K. (2010). *The mindful child.* New York: Free Press.

Renzulli, J.S. & Reis, S.M. (1997). *The school-wide enrichment model: A how-to guide for educational excellence, 2nd ed.* Mansfield Center, Ct.: Creative Learning Press

Dawson, P. & Guare, R. (2009). *Smart but scattered.* New York: The Guilford Press.

Chapter 9

Costa, A. (2007). *The school as home for the mind.* Thousand Oaks, CA: Corwin Press.

Chapter 10

Brooks, D. (2011). *The social animal.* New York: Random House.

Dweck, C. (2006). *Mindset: The new psychology of success.* New York: Random House.

Chapter 11

Bronson, P., & Merryman, A. (July 10, 2010). The creativity crisis. *Newsweek.*

Calkins, L. (1998). *Raising lifelong learners: A parent's guide.* Reading, MA: Perseus Books.

Costa, A. (2007). *The school as home for the mind.* Thousand Oaks, CA: Corwin Press.

Costa, A. & Kallick, B. (2000). *Discovering and exploring habits of mind.* Alexandria, VA: ASCD.

Duckworth, E. (1987). *The having of wonderful ideas and other essays on teaching and learning.* New York: Teachers College Press.

Duckworth, E. (2009). Helping students get to where ideas can find them. New York: *The New Educator,* 5, 185-188. The City College of New York

Johnston, P. (2004). *Choice words: How our language affects children's learning.* Portland, ME: Stenhouse Publishers.

Meek, A. (March, 1991). On thinking about teaching: A conversation with Eleanor Duckworth. *Educational Leadership,* 48(6), 30-34.

Bronson, M.(2000). *Self-regulation in early childhood.* New York: The Guilford Press

Barkley, R.(1997). *ADHD and the nature of self-control.* New York: The Guilford Press

Chapter 12

Costa, A. L., (2000). Describing the habits of mind. In A.L. Costa & B. Kallick (Eds)., *Activating and Engaging habits of mind*, Alexandria, Va., ASCD.

Chess, S. & Thomas, A. (1987). *Know your child: An authoritative guide for today's parents.* New York: Basic Books

Chapter 13

Root-Bernstein, M. & Root-Bernstein, R. (2006). Imaginary world-play in childhood and maturity and its impact on adult creativity. *Creativity Research Journal*, 18(4), 405-425.

Carson, S. (2010). *Your creative brain: seven steps to maximize imagination, productivity, and innovation in your life.* San Francisco: Jossey-Bass.

Amabile, T. (1989). *Growing up creative: Nurturing a lifetime of creativity.* Amherst, MA: Creative Education Foundation.

Bronson, P., & Merryman, A. (July 10, 2010). The creativity crisis. *Newsweek.*

Costa, A. & Kallick, B. (2000). *Activating and engaging habits of mind.* Alexandria VA: ASCD.

Crain, W. (2002). *Reclaiming childhood: Letting children be children in our achievement-oriented society.* New York: Henry Holt and Company.

Gardner, H. (1982), *Artful scribbles.* New York: Basic Books.

Gardner, H. (1982). *Art, mind and brain.* New York: Basic Books.

Gardner, H. (2006). *Five minds for the future.* Boston: Harvard Business School Press

Goleman, D., Kaufman, P., & Ray, M. (1993). *The creative spirit.* New York: Penguin Group.

Grandin, T. (2005). *Animals in translation: Using the mysteries of autism to decode animal behavior.* New York: Scribner.

Gute, G. et al. (2008). The early lives of highly creative persons: the influence of the complex family. *Creativity Research Journal*, 20, 343-351.

Runco, M. (2003). Education for creative potential. *Scandinavian Journal of Educational Research, 47*(3), 317-324.

Runco, M. (2006). Divergent thinking and creative potential, Torrance Lecture Series, University of Georgia podcaster.gcsu.edu/podcastdata/UGA/Channel_29350/podcast_21042/21042.m4v

Wallas, G (1926) *The art of thought.* New York: Harcourt Brace

Chapter 14

Greenland, S.K. (2010). *The mindful child.* New York: Free Press.

Nhat Hanh, T. (1975). *The miracle of mindfulness: An introduction to the practice of meditation.* Boston: Beacon Press.

Kornfield J. (2004). *Meditation for beginners.* Boulder: Sounds True, Inc.

Chapter 15

Carson, R. (1965). *The sense of wonder.* New York: Harper & Row Publishers.

Boyes, K. and Watts, G. (2009) Developing habits of mind in elementary schools Virginia: ASCD.

Geissbuhler, L. (2010), *Space Balloon and interview.* Brooklyn Space Program. www.brooklynspaceprogram.org/BSP/Home.html.

Katz, Eric, 2010, Siwanoy Elementary School Town Meeting, Pelham, New York.

Chapter 16

DeBono, E. (2011). *Six thinking hats,* The de Bono Group, LLC, retrieved www. debonogroup.com/six_thinking_hats.php.

Gardner, H. (2006). *Five minds for the future.* Boston: Harvard Business School Press

Johnston, P. (2004). *Choice words: How our language affects children's learning.* Portland, ME: Stenhouse Publishers.

Chapter 17

Bergen, D. (2000). *Enjoying humor with your child.* Olney, MD: Association for Childhood Education International. acei.org/knowledge/acei-bookstore/ brochures/ No. 0000).

Costa, A., & Kallick, B. (2000). *Assessing and reporting habits of mind.* Alexandria VA: ASCD.

Goleman, D. (1995). *Emotional intelligence.* New York: Bantam Books.

Chapter 18

Azzam, A. (March, 2008). Engaged and on track. *Educational Leadership*, 65 (6), 93-94.

Boylan, J. (August 17, 2011). My old haunts. [The Opinion Page]. *The New York Times*.

CBS Money Watch.com. (July 15, 2009). Online interview. *What kids don't know about money*. From moneywatch.bnet.com/saving-money/video/what-kids-dont-know-about-money/319176/?tag=content;col1.

Costa, A., & Kallick, B. (2000). *Activating and engaging habits of mind*. Alexandria VA: ASCD.

Crowley, K., & Jacobs, M. (2002). Building islands of expertise in everyday family activity in G. Leinhardt, K. Crowley, & K. Knutson (Eds.), *Learning Conversations in Museums*. Mahwah, New Jersey: Lawrence Erlbaum Associates, Inc.

Kennedy, T. (2009). *True compass: A memoir*. New York: Twelve Publishers.

Wilcox, B. et al (2004). *Report of the APA Task Force on Advertising and Children*, American Psychological Association, www.apa.org/pi/families/resources/advertising-children.pdf

Palmquist, S., & Crowley, K. (2007). *From teachers to testers: how parents talk to novice and expert children in a natural history museum*. Wiley InterScience www.interscience.wiley.com

Schmoker, M. (2011). *Focus: elevating the essentials to radically improve student learning*. Alexandria VA: ASCD.

Chapter 19

Boyes, K and Watts, G. (2009). Developing habits of mind in elementary schools . Virginia ASCD.

Wood, C. (1997). Yardsticks: Children in the classroom ages 4-14. Turner Falls, MA: Northeast Foundation for Children.

Chapter 20

Larson, C. & LaFasto, F.(1989).*TeamWork: What must go right/what can go wrong*. Newbury Park, Ca: Sage Publications.

Harris, G. (2011, July 11). "New for aspiring doctors, the people skills test." The New York Times. www.nytimes.com/2011/07/11/health/policy/11docs.html?pagewanted=all

Gottman, J., & Silver, N. (1999). *Seven principles for making marriage work.* New York: Crown Publishers.

Gottman, J., & DeClaire, J. (2001). *The relationship cure: A five-step guide to building better connections with family, friends, and lovers.* New York: Crown Publishers.

Covey, S. (1997). *The 7 habits of highly effective families.* New York: Golden Books.

Costa, A. (2007). *The school as home for the mind.* Thousand Oaks, CA: Corwin Press.

Greenspan, S. (2002). *The secure child: Helping our children feel safe and confident in a changing world.* New York: Perseus.

Chapter 21

Costa, A. & Kallick, B. (2004). *Assessment strategies for self-directed learning.* Thousand Oaks, Ca.: Corwin Press.

Kallick, B. (September, 2009). Personal communication

Langer, E.J. (1997) *The power of mindful learning.* Cambridge, MA: Perseus Books Group.

White, T. (1958). *The once and future king.* New York: Penguin Group (USA). Doidge, N. (2007). *The brain that changes itself: Stories of personal triumph from the frontiers of brain science.* New York: Viking.

Strauch, B. (January 3, 2010). "How to train the aging brain". *The New York Times,* www.nytimes.com/2010/01/03/

Further Reading

Learning and Leading with Habits of Mind
Art Costa and Bena Kallick

This book presents a compelling case for why it's more relevant than ever to align the missions of schools and classrooms to teaching students how to think and behave intelligently when they encounter problems and challenges in learning and in life. Drawing on their research and experience in applying the habits of mind in all kinds of schools, the authors guide you through every step of making intelligent behavior a practical outcome in any school:

Explore 16 habits of mind and the significance of developing these habits as part of everyday success and lifelong learning.

Discover classroom-tested strategies, units, lessons, and tasks that help students learn good habits of mind and apply them in learning academic content.

Help your school cultivate a more thoughtful culture that encourages students to reflect on their thinking and assess how well they're using the habits of mind.

Make the 16 habits of mind part of the everyday life in your school or district through your curriculum development, school leadership, and staff development.

More on next page

Habits of Mind Across the Curriculum
Art Costa and Bena Kallick

Teaching students the intelligent behaviors they need to succeed in school and later in life is much easier when you have this collection of stories and observations from teachers who have used the principles of Costa and Kallick's book Learning and Leading with Habits of Mind in their classrooms. Through these first-hand accounts, learn how the habits of mind help students at all grade levels successfully deal with the challenges they face in school and beyond. Explore how teachers make thinking skills a foundation of curriculum, not an add-on. And discover lots of model lessons and teaching strategies that weave the habits of mind into daily instruction in language arts, math, social studies, and other subjects.

Here's your chance to benefit from the many schools that have adopted the habits of mind and infused them into their curriculum, instruction, assessments, and school culture.

Developing Habits of Mind in Elementary Schools
Karen Boyes & Graham Watts

Take educational outcomes way beyond facts and information with this collection of tools for teaching students how to think and behave intelligently when they encounter problems and challenges. A series of 42 tools, helps elementary school teachers plan lessons and classroom activities that teach students 16 thoughtful behaviors that promote successful learning in the classroom and beyond. Each tool includes a brief explanation, step-by-step instructions, worksheets, samples, and resource pages.

Developing Habits of Mind in Secondary Schools
Karen Boyes & Graham Watts

This series of more than 50 Habits of Mind tools helps secondary school teachers plan lessons and classroom activities for successful lifelong learning. Teachers choose from the extensive list of tools to
- Establish positive behaviors.
- Teach communication skills.
- Promote problem solving and decision-making.
- Demonstrate good character traits.

Succeeding with Habits of Mind
James Anderson

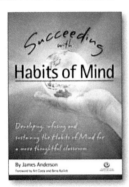

Beginning your learning journey with Habits of Mind is easy. Knowing where the next steps are can be elusive, and more challenging. In these pages you'll find practical guidance that takes you beyond introducing the Habits of Mind and helps you build deep understandings so you can succeed in developing, infusing, leading and sustaining the Habits of Mind in your school. You will learn how to:

Develop students Habits of Mind. Go beyond merely naming and requiring students to use the Habits of Mind. Understand what it means to grow and develop more mature Habits of Mind, so students actually get better at them.

Infuse the Habits of Mind into the curriculum. The Habits are not an extra or an add-on. Learn how to use the Backwards Design process to infuse the development of the Habits of Mind seamlessly into the day-to-day life of the classroom in a way that improves student learning outcomes.

Lead the change in your school. Understand the most effective ways to lead your school through the introduction of the Habits and beyond. Recognise the common challenges faced by school leaders and how to successfully get everybody onboard.

More on next page

Sustain the change. Ensure the Habits take root and become part of the norms of your school. Explore ways to instill the Habits of Mind into the culture of your school community.

Connect with others. Become a part of the Habits of Mind Teachers Network, access resources, join a learning community of teachers and leaders working with the Habits of Mind and extend your learning beyond the pages of this book.

Success is a journey. This book gives you the knowledge you'll need as you move beyond the basics and succeed in building an even more thoughtful learning community with Habits of Mind.

Mindful Garden of Verses
Marie Coita

Help introduce and explore the Habits of Mind with your students using this engaging collection of seventeen poems for children.

The hardbound book and accompanying learning resources helps brings the Habits of Mind to life in the early and middle years classroom. Features a poem that reinforces each habit, along with a delightful, colorful collage sure to capture the attention of students from the earliest years to year 8. Easy to use as a read aloud book.

Habits Center Stage: Using Drama to teach and enhance the Habits of Mind

Sandra Brace

Habits Center Stage is designed to support student understanding of the Habits of Mind, using Drama to make the learning come alive! Entertaining scenes and activities provide opportunities for numerous 'tried and true' teaching strategies: story telling, role playing, class team building...and more!